SELF-DESTRUCTIVE BEHAVIOR

SELF-DESTRUCTIVE BEHAVIOR

Compiled and Edited By

ALBERT R. ROBERTS

Research Director
State Law Enforcement Planning Agency
Trenton, New Jersey

*Mailing address: 1212 Whitehorse—Hamilton Square Road
Hamilton Square, New Jersey 08690

CHARLES C THOMAS • PUBLISHER
Springfield • Illinois • U.S.A.

616.85
R54
c.

Published and Distributed Throughout the World by
CHARLES C THOMAS • PUBLISHER
Bannerstone House
301-327 East Lawrence Avenue, Springfield, Illinois, U.S.A.

This book is protected by copyright. No part of it may be reproduced in any manner without written permission from the publisher.

©1975 by CHARLES C THOMAS • PUBLISHER
ISBN Q-398-03290-4
Library of Congress Catalog Card Number: 74-13111

With THOMAS BOOKS careful attention is given to all details of manufacturing and design. It is the Publisher's desire to present books that are satisfactory as to their physical qualities and artistic possibilities and appropriate for their particular use. THOMAS BOOKS will be true to those laws of quality that assure a good name and good will.

Printed in the United States of America
Q-2

Library of Congress Cataloging in Publication Data

Roberts, Albert R.
   Self-destructive behavior.
   Bibliography: p.

   1. Suicide. 2. Traffic accidents. 3. Narcotic habit. 4. Alcoholism. 5. Corpulence. I. Title. [DNLM: 1. Behavior. 2. Self mutilation—Prevention and control. 3. Suicide—Prevention and control. HV6545 R643s]
RC574.R6   616.8'5   74-13111
ISBN 0-398-03290-4

To Bev, Evie, Harry, Carole, and Bill

ACKNOWLEDGMENTS

Many individuals have helped in the development of this volume. Most important was the cooperation and thoroughness of my author team as reflected in their lucid, informative and relevant chapters. Special appreciation goes to my wife Beverly for her interest, understanding and supportiveness. I also thank her for her assistance with the necessary tasks of typing, proofreading, and preparation of the index. I am grateful to my brother Bill for his persistent and responsive encouragement on earlier drafts of this book and on my thesis on suicidology. The intellectual stimulation and constructive advice of Professors Joseph J. Grau and Ralph Ireland served as an impetus for this book.

ALBERT R. ROBERTS

No man is an island entire of itself; every man is a piece of the continent, a part of the main. If a clod be washed away by the sea, (America) is the less, as well as if a manor of thy friend's or thine own were. Any man's death diminishes me, because I am involved in mankind, and therefore never send to know for whom the bell tolls; it tolls for thee.

—John Donne, *Devotions*

CONTRIBUTORS

EMILE A. BENDIT—*Deputy Director, Division of Prevention, National Institute on Alcohol Abuse and Alcoholism, Washington, D.C.*

ALAN L. BERMAN—*Associate Professor, Department of Psychology; and Counselor, Counseling Center, The American University, Washington, D.C.*

WALTER R. CUSKEY—*Assistant Professor and Director, Health Manpower Project, Department of Community Medicine, School of Medicine, University of Pennsylvania, Philadelphia, Pa.*

THEODORE L. DORPAT—*Associate Professor of Psychiatry, School of Medicine, University of Washington; and Private Practice, Blakeley Psychiatric Group, Seattle, Washington.*

BONNIE M. EDINGTON—*Research Associate, Cuskey, Ipsen & McCall, Consultants, Havertown, Pa.*

ROBERTA G. FERRENCE—*Senior Research Assistant, Addiction Research Foundation, London, Canada.*

MARC HERTZMAN—*Executive Assistant to the Director, National Institute on Alcohol Abuse and Alcoholism, Washington, D.C.*

GEORGE K. JARVIS—*Assistant Professor of Sociology, University of Western Ontario, London, Canada.*

F. GORDON JOHNSON—*Assistant Professor of Psychiatry, University of Western Ontario, London, Canada.*

EDWARD S. LISKA—*Associate Clinical Professor of Psychiatry, San Francisco Medical Center, University of California, San Francisco, California.*

ALEX D. POKORNY—*Professor of Psychiatry, Baylor College of Medicine, Houston, Texas.*

ALBERT R. ROBERTS—*Research Director, New Jersey State Law Enforcement Planning Agency, Trenton, New Jersey.*

SAMUEL H. WAXLER—*Associate Clinical Professor of Medicine, San Francisco Medical Center, University of California; and Adjunct Associate Clinical Professor of Medicine, Stanford University School of Medicine.*

PAUL C. WHITEHEAD—*Associate Professor of Sociology, University of Western Ontario; and Research Consultant, Addiction Research Foundation, London, Canada.*

INTRODUCTION

This interdisciplinary volume focuses on the etiology, treatment, and prevention of self-destructive behavior. Each chapter will enhance the reader's knowledge and understanding of the various modes of self-destruction—including suicidal and subsuicidal behavior, such as one-car automobile fatalities, drug-related deaths, homicide followed by suicide, chronic alcoholism and cirrhosis of the liver, cardiovascular diseases and diabetis melittus exacerbated by compulsive overeating, and combinations of the above. Physicians, educators, psychologists, social workers and sociologists have been searching for a book which integrates the most up-to-date material on patterns of self-destruction. The material to be gleaned from within this book provides new insights concerning chronic risk-taking behavior, and concerning the heightening of coping mechanisms for both therapist and client. The social, psychological, medical, and psychiatric correlates of the most prevalent forms of self-destruction are all taken into account. Most of these behaviors are dealt with in individual chapters. In addition, each author has made reference to some of the acts which typically overlap.

Deaths resulting from suicide, drug overdoses, cirrhosis of the liver, and one-car automobile accidents are more prevalent than most people realize. This is, in part, due to the difficulty in obtaining accurate information surrounding and preceding the death, and establishing crucial links between variables. For example, with the exception of the opiates and alcohol, it is impossible to definitively assess the risks and dangers of certain mind altering drugs because in many instances the pharmacological properties and means of action of these drugs are poorly understood. It is also difficult to determine the dosages and effects of long-term ingestion; many times drug abusers do not have a family physician and come into contact with a hospital only after the effects of the drug have done serious damage.

What do we know about the prevalence of drug-related fatalities? Most addicts are aware that mainlining is a serious risk. Whether through the news media or word-of-mouth, most have heard about the dramatic increase in mainline deaths. Many others have seen friends suffering from viral hepatitus, tetanus, endocarditis, abscesses and other infections. A statistical study conducted by the Metropolitan Life Insurance Company indicated that the causes of death in 193 out of 203 (97%) drug fatalities were directly related to drug addiction, drug poisoning, and suicide by drugs.

More pronounced evidence of the self-destructive aspects of hard narcotic addiction is revealed by the following data: 1) The Office of the Chief Medical Examiner in New York City estimates that 4,271 individuals died from narcotic abuse in New York City during the decade of the 1960's. This is quadruple the rate from this cause during the 1950's when statistics showed 1,076 narcotic-related deaths. The number of drug-related deaths in New York City continues to climb each year; in 1969, the fatality rate reached the 1,000 mark, and one year later, it had climbed to 1,205 recorded deaths.[1] 2) Drug related mortality rates among the young are accelerating at an alarming rate. Abelson's New York City data indicated that between 1961 and 1969, drug-induced deaths for persons of all ages tripled, while deaths among younger addicts (below age 24) increased approximately five times.[2]

    3) In neighborhoods where impure drugs have taken lives, in territories where contaminated batches have been purveyed by one seller, in short, where two, three, or half a dozen and more deaths have occurred within days or weeks, one still finds addicts risking their lives with batches they know originated from the same pusher. Addiction alone does not explain this behavior, since other drugs or substitute sources often can be located with relative ease. The risk-taking and Russian roulette nature of the drug user leads him into consciously engaging in high risk, repetitive, self-destructive behavior.[3]

---

1. Metropolitan Life Insurance Company. "Drug-related Mortality," *Statistical Bulletin*, 53: 5-6 (1972).

2. P. B. Abelson, "Death from Heroin," *Science*, 68: 1289, (1970).

3. C. J. Frederick, H. L. P. Resnick, and B. Wittlin, "Self-Destructive Aspects of Hard Core Addiction," *Archives of General Psychiatry*, 28: 579, (1973).

Introduction

xiii

As of November, 1970, there were approximately 150,000 to 250,000 active heroin addicts in the United States. Other recent estimates are even higher, reporting "300,000 heroin addicts in New York City and 600,000 nationally."[4] Addicts are concentrated in the poorest areas of large urban ghettos, with almost half living in New York City. Almost 85 percent are male, and 60 to 70 percent are black, Puerto Rican, or Mexican American. The increased danger of death among drug addicts results from his life style, the type of drugs he takes and how he takes them. In a study of the causes of death among 9,276 opiate addicts during 1970 to 1971, the complexity of this high risk population is discussed.[5] Thus, the alarming incidence of drug-related deaths has been documented. Dr. Cuskey and Ms. Eddington's chapter, "Drug Abuse as Self-Destructive Behavior," provides a useful framework from which therapeutic and preventive models can be gleaned. Their continuum aptly distinguishes between life-enhancing and life-destroying polarities in drug-taking behavior—1) Acute Vs. Chronic Suicide, 2) Risk-taking, and 3) Accidental Effects.

Whether your interest is intensified in an overview chapter or a specific discussion of a self-destructive pattern, each chapter includes valuable original material. Chapter One, by Dr. Alan Berman is an excellent point of departure. The epidemiological difficulties in reporting and measuring self-destructive behavior are eloquently illustrated by his discussion of the concepts of intentionality, lethality, and differential reporting practices. For purposes of treatment and prevention of self-destructive behavior patterns, we need to develop models which identify ecological, psychological, and sociological correlates of the problem, and which facilitate the use of appropriate medical and social services—continuity of care to persons at risk. This volume, for the

---

4. The Drug Abuse Survey Project: *Dealing with Drug Abuse: A Report to the Ford Foundation.* (New York, Praeger Publishing), 1972, p. 4.

5. S. B. Sells, L. R. Chatham, and R. Retka, "A Study of Differential Death Rates and Causes of Death among 9,276 Opiate Addicts during 1970-1971," *Alcohol and Health,* Department of Health, Education and Welfare. (Washington, D.C.: U.S. Government Printing Office); and *Contemporary Drug Problems: A Law Quarterly,* 1: 665-706 (1972).

first time, provides the building blocks for developing such models.

Self-Destructive Behavior integrates eight specially written chapters by internationally known experts. It provides the first thorough analysis of the mounting number of life-threatening behaviors. This volume documents the etiology, prevalence, and treatment approaches. It is the editor's fervent hope that this book will serve as a catalyst, encouraging clinicians, researchers, administrators and planners to search for new preventive measures for combatting the destructive elements plaguing our society and personal life-styles.

CONTENTS

Page

Acknowledgments vii

Contributors ix

Introduction xi

Part I

PATTERNS OF SELF-DESTRUCTION

Chapter

1. SELF-DESTRUCTIVE BEHAVIOR AND SUICIDE: EPIDEMIOLOGY AND TAXONOMY

   Alan L. Berman 5

2. SELF-DESTRUCTION BY ONE'S OWN HAND: SUICIDE AND SUICIDE PREVENTION

   Albert R. Roberts 21

3. DYSCONTROL AND SUICIDAL BEHAVIORS

   Theodore L. Dorpat 78

4. THE SELF-INJURY PATIENT: SOCIOLOGICAL AND MEDICAL PROFILES AND IMPLICATIONS FOR PREVENTION

   Roberta G. Ferrence, George K. Jarvis, F. Gordon Johnson, and Paul C. Whitehead 97

Part II

AUTOMOBILE FATALITIES, DRUGS, ALCOHOL AND OBESITY

Chapter	Page
5. SELF-DESTRUCTION AND THE AUTOMOBILE	
Alex D. Pokorny	123
6. DRUG ABUSE AS SELF-DESTRUCTIVE BEHAVIOR	
Walter R. Cuskey and Bonnie Morel Edington	138
7. ALCOHOLISM AND DESTRUCTIVE BEHAVIOR	
Marc Hertzman and Emile A. Bendit	164
8. OBESITY AND SELF-DESTRUCTIVE BEHAVIOR	
Samuel H. Waxler and Edward S. Liska	188
Index	211

SELF-DESTRUCTIVE BEHAVIOR

PART I
PATTERNS OF SELF-DESTRUCTION

CHAPTER 1

SELF-DESTRUCTIVE BEHAVIOR AND SUICIDE: EPIDEMIOLOGY AND TAXONOMY

ALAN L. BERMAN

Marco P., a 22-year old Columbian, jobless for two months, had been selling his blood every week for a month at $5.00 a pint to feed his family. After turning himself into the hospital because of extreme weakness, he returned home to bed because he could not afford the medicines prescribed. He never left it again. Five days later he died of pernicious anemia.

Samuel T., 48, was killed when his car was struck by a freight train at a railroad crossing. Despite excellent road conditions, flashing red light, warning bell, and repeated whistle blasts, he drove at 10 m.p.h. into the path of the train. A post-mortem blood alcohol test showed no evidence of alcoholic intoxication.

Jason R., a 20-year black gangleader in Harlem, angered by the arrest of his friend, stormed into police headquarters, brandishing a pistol. He was shot through the heart by an on-duty officer.

W<small>HILE EACH OF THESE DEATHS</small> may be characterized by poor judgment, excessive risk taking, carelessness, and self-neglect, none have been categorized as suicide. Our current, and obviously inadequate classification of modes of death[1] essentially restricts the certification of death to four modes: natural, accidental, suicidal, and homicidal (N-A-S-H). Although each of these deaths involved a distinctly covert or unconscious role on the part of the decedent in facilitating his death, psychological factors become obscured when cause of death is recorded.

In suicidology, two basic questions confront the epidemiologist: (1) Is all self-destructive behavior suicidal? and (2) Is all suicidal behavior self-destructive? Regrettably, the answer to both appears to be a decisive no! However, available taxonomies so obfuscate data collection that scientific analysis and potential understanding of suicidal behavior remain mixed in a muck of confusion, contradiction, and gross generalization. The N-A-S-H classifications take no account of psychological intention, self-destructive life style, or degree of consciousness of the individual; Marco P. died a natural death, Samuel T. died of an accident, and Jason R.'s death was ruled justifiable homicide.

In spite of definitional inadequacies, suicide statistics are impressive. In 1972, there were 24,280 certified suicides in the United States, sufficient to rank suicide as the eleventh leading cause of death. As will be demonstrated later, even the most conservative estimate of the true number of suicides may be about twice this number. Furthermore, for every suicidal death there are six to eight survivor-victims who bear witness to that death through social stigma or personal pain for the remainder of their lives.[2] The social cost is high.

Epidemiologists concern themselves with statistics. Meaningful data collection and analyses obviously rest on meaningful definitions of the condition being investigated. The assessment of just how ubiquitous the suicidal act is remains a procrustean task.

DEFINITIONAL AND RESEARCH PROBLEMS

Suicide is the act of killing oneself. When an individual so acts, and his behavior results in death, this death is defined as completed suicide. Notwithstanding certain segments of society which continue to label a suicide death as a "victim" of suicide (as if some lethal "bacillus suicidus" were responsible), human beings distinguish themselves from other animal species in that they *choose* to commit the act of suicide. This aspect of choice also distinguishes a suicide death from the other three modes of death. It has been argued that one who consciously or unconsciously chooses a natural or accidental or homicidal death must, by definition, be considered as suicidal. These "hidden suicides" represent just one of several impediments to the study and measurement of suicidal phenomena. Additionally, problems are raised by the facts that (1) not all suicide deaths represent intentions to "die," (2) not all intentioned suicide deaths occur as a result of conscious acts, and (3) not all intentioned suicides result in death.

Differential Definitions

The noted and eminent suicidologist, Edwin S. Shneidman has pioneered the concept of subintentioned death, one that he believes "may be characteristic of a majority of deaths."[3] Subintentioned deaths or "hidden suicides"[4] are those in which the person plays some partial, covert, or unconscious role in facilitating or hastening his own death. The three brief vignettes at the beginning of this chapter all illustrate this concept, in part. Shneidman estimates that between 10 to 15 percent of all deaths are equivocal as to mode.[5] In most, the intent to die is difficult to discern—as it is either unconscious or, at least, uncommunicated—and the determination of intent must rest on inference and assumption, based on data gathered after the death has occurred. The evidence for this phenomenon is too extensive to be ignored. Consider the following examples and findings:

AUTOMOBILE "ACCIDENTS": Tabachnick, et al.[6] estimate that only 15 percent of traffic accident deaths are due to mechanical automobile defects, faulty road conditions, or signal devices. Meerloo[4] reported that 51 percent of drivers killed in New York in 1964 were intoxicated at the time of death. While evidence of skidmarks, use of safety belts, etc. may be used to differentiate accident from suicide, these are insufficient criteria. The individual who rams his car into a bridge abutment at high speed can no longer report to us his pre-terminal intention to live or die.

DEATH FROM PHYSICAL ILLNESS: The "uncooperative patient" who flaunts or continually disregards a prescribed medical regimen is well known to most who have worked in medical communities. Greene, et al.[7] studied individuals who died a sudden, "unexpected" death and found psychological and social factors associated with the time of death in 50 percent of the patients studied. The heart attack patient who refuses medical advice to attenuate or avoid certain behaviors/activities is certainly making a statement regarding his will to live.

DEATH BY MURDER: The case of Jason R. represents an example of a homicide in which the victim was a direct precipitator of his own death, i.e. where the victim victimizes himself. Wolfgang[8] appropriately coined this death: "victim-precipitated homicide." Wolfgang estimated that 62 percent of homicides may be victim-precipitated; three fourths of these occurring among black subcultures wherein it is seen as more courageous to die struggling to death.

DRUG DEPENDENCE AND ADDICTION: In 1938, Menninger proposed the thesis that alcoholism was a form of "chronic suicide."[9] Certainly all other addictions to known self-destructive agents could be subsumed under this rubric. Most drug-related deaths are unclassified as to cause of death by coroners and pathologists. An inestimable number of "suicides" do result from a state of drug automatism, a semi-comatose-like state wherein the drug abuser has lost all awareness of his behavior and may overdose himself without intent. Drugs may catalyze suicide. Addiction may be produced by, lead to, or accompany self-neglect and a breakdown in interpersonal relations; conditions which, in turn, facilitate suicidal thoughts.[10] Additionally, alcohol and drugs do tend to lessen controls, thus influencing the propensity to take risks under conditions of poor judgment and physical instability.

DEATH IN OLD AGE: The American society's general intolerance of both aging and the aged is well documented, making the "will to die" among elders perhaps more tolerable than the will to live. Those who manifest a will to die do, in fact, succumb sooner than would be expected from medical criteria alone. Self-injurious behavior among the elderly is extensive[11] and may effect a premature death.

THE UNIQUE AND THE BIZARRE DEATH: Cannon's 1942 classic study of "voodoo deaths"[12] documented and explained that people who believe themselves to be under the influence of a "hex" can and do actually die. Death in previously healthy individuals occurs through increased stimulation of the vagal and sympaticoadrenal systems, often within twenty-four hours despite all efforts to save these individuals.

Although accounting for only fifty or so deaths annually, "eroticized repetitive hangings" represent an even more bizarre form of self-destruction. Resnik[13] has recently reported on this form of self-bondage in the accompaniment of masturbatory behavior in males. In order to heighten sensations concurrent with autoerotic behavior, ropes, chains, belts, etc. are arranged about the body and neck in such a way that oxygenation is constricted and CO_2 is retained in the blood. The subsequent loss of voluntary control over the body may result in death.

The list of self-destructive behaviors which may be subsumed under the category of subintentioned suicide is long and varied. Other forms of addiction (e.g. to food, work, cigarettes), various forms of psychic suicide through mental illness (e.g. anorexia nervosa), and a variety of vocational and avocational pursuits (e.g. bridge painters, demolition experts, sky divers) all represent forms of behavior whereby the intentionality of ultimate death is equivocal. What is recorded and counted as suicide, therefore, may account for only a small part of actual "self-murders."

DIFFERENTIAL GOALS: Many goals—other than self-destruction—may play a determining role in suicidal deaths. The distinction between the man who seeks to end all experience by putting a bullet through his brain and the man whose goal is to transcend death, perhaps through similar means, in order to be reunited with his deceased wife is lost and probably unaccountable by current definitions of suicide. If suicide is the act of killing oneself, can he who believes in an afterlife and who terminates "life" be said to have ceased living? This surely is an issue for philosophical debate and perhaps should remain outside the realm of our current inquiry. However, fantasied goals of rebirth, reunion, vengeance, expiation, and altruism are often evident and of primary importance in suicidal deaths:

> A 78-year old man wrote the Medical Division of a federal agency volunteering himself for experimental purposes in tumor research work. His wife had died years earlier of cancer. He states that he has lived a full life and feels "there is nothing left for me—unless

it would be in some capacity for use of my body for experimentation."[14]

By current definition, this communication is suicidal. How similar are the "altruistic" self-immolations so prevalent during the Vietnam War? Or, consider the following report of death-defiance—is this not suicide?:

The Lord's Bidding

"He that believeth and is baptized shall be saved... if they drink any deadly thing, it shall not hurt them."
—Mark 16:16-18

> The literal interpretation of those words has spawned some of the more bizarre sects of Christendom. At the culmination of an evening service at the (Holiness Church of God in Jesus Name of Carson Spring, Tenn.) ... (assistant pastor Jimmy Ray) Williams poured a potent mixture of strychnine and water. 'A perfect love casteth out fear,' the preacher declared. So saying Williams and (Layman Buford) Pack drank the draught down, as the congregation chanted 'Praise God!'... Outside the church after the service the two men doubled up in an agony of convulsive twitching—and by morning both were dead.... At the weekend, the congregation was hoping to bring them back to life with yet another service—this time the worshippers planned to test their faith by turning blow-torches on their own faces and arms.[15]

DIFFERENTIAL REPORTING PRACTICES: Certification of the mode and circumstances of death is perhaps the primary function of the coroner or forensic pathologist. The medical examiner's office issues certificates of death in all cases of:

1. medically unattended deaths,
2. violent deaths,
3. deaths from unknown causes,
4. deaths occurring within 24 hours of hospitalization, and
5. deaths occurring in public space.

As such only about one third of all deaths may be referred for medical examination. Of those referred, the number of deaths examined, autopsied, etc. is governed by economic considerations (e.g. fixed budgets). Given the fact that in approximately 50 percent of the cases investigated by any medico-legal agency, the cause of death is proven incorrect when pre- and post-autopsy causes of death are compared,[16] it is apparent that reported "suicide" rates are, on the surface, grossly distorted. Additionally, differential practices among coroners and pathologists exist over time and over geography. For example, one California medical examiner's office refused to certify a death as suicide unless a verifiable suicide note was left by the decedent. In Los Angeles, notes are left in only about 20 percent of suicide deaths.[17]

These practices at the institutional level reflect the more *systematic* biases in our data. Other reporting factors additionally mitigate against the validity of suicide data. Just how many physicians certify suicide deaths as accidents or natural deaths for religious reasons, insurance benefits, or merely out of concern for the social stigma attached by suicide to the survivors is purely conjectural.

DIFFERENTIAL RESULTS: It could be argued—on philosophical grounds—that the act of birth itself is self-destructive, in that death is its natural and inevitable consequence. What distinguishes suicidal behavior from other necrotic modes is the intent of the act. A corollary to this variable of intentionality is that of lethality. The individual who jumps from a fifteenth story window is behaving differently from one who ingests ten aspirin. While both may want to die, the former appears to have a greater predisposition to actually die. Similarly, the context in which a "consciously" intentioned suicidal act occurs defines the seriousness of the act and the probability of the act resulting in death. Jumping off a high bridge at noon-time may be quite a different behavior than jumping at 3:00 A.M. The potential for rescue is clearly different. Even when the intent to die may be strong and the context lethal, the end result is unpredictable:

Suicide Attempt Becomes Revenge

UPI April 12, 1972. Vera Czermak jumped out of her third story window when she learned her husband had betrayed her. Mrs. Czermak is recovering in the hospital after landing on her husband, who was killed, the newspaper *Vecerny Pravda* reported.[18]

EPIDEMIOLOGICAL FINDINGS

The prevalence of death by suicide is obviously multiply determined, and, by itself, is an inadequate and misleading measure of the extent to which individuals engage in self-destructive behaviors. The number of false negatives (completed suicides which are deliberately camouflaged, mislabelled, or merely indeterminable as suicides) immeasurably exceeds the number of false positives. In the absence of reliable and valid statistics, the rates and estimates which follow must be viewed as highly conservative.

Suicidal behaviors can be conceived as falling along a 5-point continuum: (1) no ideation, (2) ideation, (3) threat, (4) gesture/attempt, and (5) completion. Only the poles, completion and lack of ideation, are absolutes; each of the three intermediary steps are internally dimensioned with regard to seriousness (e.g. lethality of attempt, degree of ideational preoccupation).

Degree of Suicidal Ideation

It is probable that everyone of us has contemplated our own or another's death at some point in our lifetime. In fact, Cameron, et al.[19] found that one in ten individuals may have at least a passing thought of death in any five minute period. With regard to suicide, however, from one fifth to one third of populations studied report *never* having had suicidal thoughts.[20, 21, 22] Leonard[23] found that 56 percent of a college age sample denied suicidal ideation entirely; 40 percent admitted to having had at least given minimum consideration to such thoughts.

In perhaps the largest sampling of its kind, Shneidman[24] surveyed over 30,000 individuals with regard to their death attitudes and behavior. Over one half of this group reported having seriously contemplated killing themselves; correspondingly, one third stated they were sure they would never commit suicide. While 80 percent of completed suicides have demonstrated previous suicidal ideation,[23] the relationship between the ideational mode of death and the mode of completed suicide is minimal. Shneidman's sample was given this hypothetical question: Suppose you were to commit suicide, what method would you most likely use?

Only 11 percent of Shneidman's sample chose a mode of high lethality (gunshot, hanging, jumping). In 1968,[25] 68 percent of all deaths by suicide were accounted for by these three methods. The implication, thus, is that the ideational wish for a suicidal death approximates more closely the characteristics of the suicidal attempt than completion.

Attempts/Gestures and Threats

A suicidal gesture is a suicide attempt of minimal lethality, or an act in which initiating moves of a potentially self-destructive nature are carried out but without the risk of significant physical injury. The goal of a suicidal gesture is not surcease but interpersonal manipulation, e.g. to coerce, seduce, frighten, or punish a significant other. A suicidal threat is merely the communication of the intent to gesture or attempt without the occurrence of actual behavior.

While no data exists with regard to the prevalence of suicidal threats, eight out of ten people who ultimately kill themselves have given definite warnings of their intentions to commit a suicidal act.[26] Similarly, there is a lack of prevalence data regarding suicide attempts/gestures among the general population. Those studies which have attempted to discern the extent of suicidal attempts are limited by their sources of data. Relying merely on hospital emergency admissions records seriously attenuates actual rates of attempt. The majority of attempted suicides are probably medically treated in physicians' offices and returned home undocumented. The number of less injurious attempts which never reach a physician or hospital is inestimable. Even when a wide range of reporting sources are contacted, underreporting still occurs. For example, Whitehead, et al.[27] found that nursing homes were highly resistant to reporting self-injurious behavior in their institutions, claiming that none occurred within a one year study period. This contrasts with Kastenbaum and Mishara's observation[11] that an average of 29 percent of an institutionalized geriatric population engaged in self-injurious behavior in only a one-week period of study.

Shneidman and Farberow[28] surveyed hospital and physician's records in Los Angeles County and found 5906 cases of attempted suicide (1957). On this basis they found a crude rate of attempted suicide of 120/100,000; this was approximately 8 times the number of completed suicides in that calendar year. Whitehead, et al.[27] identified all cases in London, Ontario of self-inflicted injury, overdose, or asphyxiation, whether or not there was evidence of suicidal intent. These researchers used the most extensive sources of reporting found in the literature, including records from hospitals, jails, family physicians, police, and social agencies. On this basis, they found a crude rate of self-injury of 730/100,000 per annum, and estimated that this figure was only about 50 percent of the true rate.

An alternative method of data collection involves going directly to the horse's mouth and asking the population at large about their suicidal behavior. Mintz[29] randomly distributed 3,085 questionnaires door-to-door in the City of Los Angeles. With a response rate of 67 percent, he found 3.9 percent of the surveyed population admitting to one or more suicide attempts in their lifetime. While the annual incidence of self-reported suicide attempts was not sought, the extrapolated prevalence of suicide attempts for this city's population approximated 75,000. Mintz thus estimated that there were approximately 5 million individuals living in the United States who had a history of one or more suicide attempts.

In a similar study, Berman[30] found that 2.6 percent of the population under 30 years of age admitted to having attempted suicide. This finding implies that there are currently 2½ million people in the United States who have attempted suicide *prior* to their 31st birthday.

These estimates, based on self-report data, do not take into account the degree of lethality involved in the reported attempt. In Shneidman's survey,[24] 13 percent of the respondents reported having actually attempted suicide. About two thirds of these were considered unlikely to result in death; 23 percent had a moderate probability of death, and 14 percent were of high lethality. Based on these results, there exist over 10 million people in the United States who have made at least one moderately to seriously lethal attempt at suicide. These figures are astounding!

Epidemiology and Taxonomy

In summary, the ratio of suicidal gestures to attempts appears to be about 2 or 3 to 1. The incidence of suicide attempts per annum is thought to be from between 120 to 730/100,000 population; and it appears that there are from 5 to over 10 million individuals currently living in the United States who admit to a history of suicide attempt.

The ratio of attempted to completed suicides is generally considered to be about 10:1, although this is probably a gross underestimate. In contrast to the suicide completer, the typical suicide attempter is more likely to be a single or married, white female, in her twenties or thirties, who ingests a non-lethal dosage of barbiturates.

Completions

Suicide attempts should not be viewed as "failed" completions. The person who completes suicide differs from one-time attemptors in both demographic and personality characteristics.[31] Some attemptors are persistent, making more than one attempt. Berman[30] found 13 percent of living, young, ex-suicide attemptors had made more than one attempt; Mintz[29] reports a figure of 17 percent. Maris[32] claims that only 10 to 15 percent of all attemptors ever complete suicide. However, probably as many as 35 to 40 percent of completed suicides have made at least one prior nonfatal attempt. This overlap is schematicized in Figure 1-1. What we do know of completed suicides is based on data tabulated by the National Center for Health Statistics for the entire United States.[33] Cause of death statistics for 1972 show an aver-

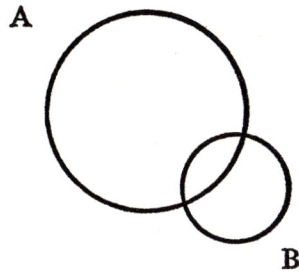

B (attempted suicides) = 10-15% of A

A (completed suicides) = 35-40% of B

Figure 1-I.

age of 66 suicides daily. The 24,280 completed suicides reported represent about 1 percent of all deaths, ranking suicide as the 11th leading cause of death during that year. The incidence of 11.7 suicides per 100,000 population in 1972 is not significantly different from the observed rates for the past 20 years; the rate not exceeding 12.0 per 100,000 since 1941.

Demographic Trends

Compared to other causes of death, suicide is most prominent during the adolescent and young adult years, ranking fourth for the age groups fifteen to twenty-four and twenty-five to forty-four years.

Suicide rates in general increase with age, although sexual and racial differences are apparent. Among whites, the modal rate for males occurs in the eighty-five years and over group, for females in the forty-five to fifty-four years group. For nonwhites suicide rates show less uniformity although rates peak for both males and females in the fifteen to twenty-four age bracket. The ratio of male to female completed suicide rates is almost 3:1. Since female attempt rates exceed those of males, it is apparent that males are more successful at completing or intention death more often than females. In 1964, the ratio between rates for white and nonwhite persons was 2.1.

Table 1-I shows suicide rates by age at three points in the last sixteen years. It is evident that completed suicide rates among the elderly have begun a slight downward trend while upward trends are appearing in the teenage to middle adult years.

TABLE 1-I
Suicide Rates[a] by Age Groups: 1956, 1964, and 1972

Year	All Ages	5[b]-14	15-24	25-34	35-44	45-54	55-64	65-74	75-84	85 years and over
1972	11.7	0.1	9.7	14.3	16.7	19.7	20.5	20.3	20.4	18.5
1964	10.8	0.2	6.0	11.9	15.6	20.5	22.7	22.1	23.9	25.3
1956	10.0	0.2	4.0	8.5	12.1	18.5	24.2	25.2	28.0	23.5

[a]Rates=/100,000 population
[b]deaths of children under 8 years of age are not tabulated as due to suicide

In general, marital status also differentiated observed rates with divorced persons showing the highest rates, except in the young adult years when the rate for the widowed peaks significantly above all other groups. The rate for divorced persons was from three to five times the rates for married persons under age sixty-five.

Geographic variations also appear. The suicide rates for the western states are highest, with the Pacific region averaging about twice the median rate for the Middle Atlantic States. While seasonal variations occur, they are not significant. Suicides are completed in greater frequency in the Spring months than in the Winter months.

Mode of Suicidal Death

Suicidal deaths by firearms and explosives account for about half of all suicides (see Table 1-II), occurring three times as often as nongaseous poisoning, hanging, strangulation, and suffocation. One reason why males complete suicide more often than females is the reliance of females on analgesic and soporific substances as suicidal agents. Of all means of injury, only poisoning by solid or liquid substances occurs more frequently among females than males. The potential for lethal effects here is highly variable and unpredictable, depending on factors such as individual tolerance levels, etc. One half of all these poisonings involved the use of barbituric acid and its derivatives. Eight of ten "poisoning by other gases" involved motor vehicle exhaust gas. Table 1-II also

TABLE 1-II
Percent of Suicidal Deaths by Specific Causes: 1950, 1960, 1968

CAUSE	1950	1960	1968
Poisoning by solid and liquid substances	10.5%	12.4%	15.3%*
Poisoning by gas in domestic use	6.5	1.0	0.2
Poisoning by other gas	6.2	9.4	11.0
By hanging, strangulation, suffocation	21.0	17.7	14.5
By submersion or drowning	3.9	3.2	2.2
By firearms and explosives	43.0	47.4	51.1
By cutting and piercing instrument	3.1	2.6	1.8
By jumping	3.7	3.7	2.2

*Only cause in which female rate exceeds that of males (almost a 2:1 ratio).

indicates that the means of completing suicide is gradually shifting away from methods such as domestic gas, hanging, drowning, cutting, and jumping to an increased reliance on firearms and poisoning by solid and liquid substances.

In summary, the modal suicidal completer is a white, divorced male over fifty-five years of age, living alone in the Western region of the United States. He dies by means of a gun during the Spring months.

Above all, the modal suicider is much more than a statistic. His self-destruction is only more affirmative and well-defined than either the thousands of other deaths which remain unclassified as to suicidal intent or the perhaps millions of others who through a variety of self-destructive life styles are never counted among the suicidal rolls. The cost of his death to his significant others and to society as a whole is immeasurable.

REFERENCES

1. Shneidman, E. S.: Suggestions for the revision of the death certificate. In Shneidman, E. S., Farberow, N. L., and Litman, R. E. (Eds.): *The Psychology of Suicide*, N.Y., Science House, 1970, 551-561.
2. Shneidman, E. S.: Suicide in the aged. In Davis, R. H. (Ed.): *Dealing with Death*, U. S. C., Ethel Percy Anders Gerontology Center, 1973, 25-32.
3. Schneidman, E. S.: The enemy. *Psychology Today*, August, 1970.
4. Meerloo, J.: Hidden suicide. In Resnik, H. L. P. (Ed.): *Suicidal Behaviors*. Boston, Little-Brown, 1968, 82-90.
5. Shneidman, E. S.: *Deaths of Man*. N.Y., Quadrangle, 1973.
6. Tabachnick, N., Litman, R. E., Osman, M., Jones, W. L., Cohn, J., Kasper, A., and Moffat, J.: Comparative psychiatric study of accidental and suicidal death. *14*: 60-68, 1966.
7. Greene, W. A., Goldstein, S., and Moss, A. J.: Psychosocial aspects of sudden death. *Arch Intern Med, 129*: 725-731, 1972.
8. Wolfgang, M.E.: Suicide by means of victim-precipitated-homicide. *J Clin Psychol, 20*: 335-349, 1959.
9. Menninger, K. A.: *Man Against Himself*. N.Y., Harcourt-Brace, 1938.
10. Whitehead, P. C.: Notes on the association between alcoholism and suicide. *Int J Addict, 7*: 525-532, 1972.
11. Kastenbaum, R., and Mishara, B. L.: Premature death and self-injurious behavior in old age. *Geriatrics*, (July), 71-81, 1971.
12. Cannon, W. B.: Voodoo death. *Psychosom Med, 19*: 182-190, 1957.

13. Resnik, H. L. P.: Eroticized repetitive hangings: A form of self-destruction. *Am J Psychother, 26:* 1, 4-21, 1973.
14. Butler, R. N.: The personal sense and social structure of legacy: An ethic to the future. In Group for the Advancement of Psychiatry (Ed.): *The Right to Die: Decision and Decision Makers.* V. 8, Symp. No. 12, New York: GAP, p. 704, 1973.
15. ―――――. "Americana," *Newsweek*, April 19, 1972.
16. Office of the Chief Medical Examiner. *Annual Report 1972.* Washington, District of Columbia, Department of Human Resources, 1972.
17. Litman, R. E., Curphey, T., Shneidman, E. S., Farberow, N. L., and Tabachnick, N.: The psychological autopsy of equivocal deaths. In Shneidman, E. S., Farberow, N. L., & Litman, R. E. (Eds.): *The Psychology of Suicide.* N.Y., Science House, 486-496, 1970.
18. *Washington Post*, April 13, 1972.
19. Cameron, P., Stewart, L., Craig, L., and Eppelman, L.: Frequency of death thoughts across the life span. Presented to the Annual Meeting of the American Association of Suicidology, Detroit, Mich., March 31, 1972.
20. Cavan, R. S.: *Suicide*, N.Y., Russell & Russell, 1965.
21. Oliven, J. F.: The suicidal risk: Its diagnosis and evaluation. *N Engl J Med, 245:* 488-494, 1951.
22. Lester, D.: Punishment experiences and suicidal preoccupations. *J Genet Psychol, 113:* 89-94, 1968.
23. Leonard, C. V., and Flinn, D. E.: Suicidal ideation and behavior in youthful nonpsychiatric populations. *J Consult Clin Psychol, 38:* 366-371, 1972.
24. Shneidman, E. S.: You and death. *Psychology Today*, June, 1971.
25. National Center for Health Statistics. *Vital Statistics for the United States,* 1968, Public Health Service, Washington, D.C.: U. S. Government Printing Office.
26. Lester, G., and Lester, D.: *Suicide: The gamble with death.* Englewood, Prentice-Hall, 1971.
27. Whitehead, P. C., Johnson, F. G., and Terrence, R.: Measuring the incidence of self-injury: Some methodological and design considerations. *Am J Orthpsychiatry, 43:* 142-148, 1973.
28. Shneidman, E. S., and Farberow, N. L.: Attempted and completed suicides. In Shneidman, E. S., Farberow, N. L., and Litman, R. E. (Eds.): *The Psychology of Suicide*, N.Y., Science House, 199-225, 1970.
29. Mintz, R. S.: Prevalence of persons in the City of Los Angeles who have attempted suicide. *Bulletin of Suicidology* (Fall), 7, 9-16, 1970.
30. Berman, A. L.: The epidemiology of life-threatening events. Presented to the Annual Meeting of the American Association of Suicidology, Jacksonville, Fla., April, 1974.

31. Maxmen, J. S., and Tucker, G. J.: No exit: The persistently suicidal patient. *Compr Psychiatry, 14:* 71-79, 1973.
32. Maris, R.: Current problems in suicide research. *Crisis Intervention,* 4: (3), 84-89, 1972.
33. Vital and Health Statistics: *Suicide in the United States:* 1950-1964, and *Annual Summary for the United States,* 1972. U. S. Department of Health, Education, and Welfare, National Center for Health Statistics: Washington, D.C.: U. S. Government Printing Office.

CHAPTER 2

SELF DESTRUCTION BY ONE'S OWN HAND: SUICIDE AND SUICIDE PREVENTION

ALBERT R. ROBERTS

FOR THOSE WHO VALUE HUMAN LIFE, the scientific study of self-destructive behavior and suicide prevention is both challenging and urgently needed. This overview chapter illustrates the fact that suicide is more prevalent than many people realize. The magnitude of this social and public health problem is revealed by suicide statistics on the steadily rising suicide toll, especially in industrialized countries.

The sociological theories of Durkheim, Gibbs, Douglas, Henry, and Short, as well as the psychological theories of Freud, Zilboorg, Menninger, and Hendin are critically analyzed for understanding suicidal and sub-suicidal behavior. This in-depth study also analyzes the statistical relationship of suicide rates to the method of committing suicide, age, race, sex, and marital status.

Appropriate diagnostic clues are discussed with the goal of identifying profiles and danger signs of individuals with high suicide potential. This chapter is additionally concerned with the nature, characteristics, and treatment of high suicide risk groups

---

Part I of this original chapter is adapted from Albert R. Roberts, "Suicide and Suicide Pevention: An Overview," *Public Health Reviews,* Vol. II, No. 1, (February, 1973), pp. 4-24, with the permission of *Public Health Reviews,* Tel Aviv, Israel.

such as prisoners, survivors who have recently lost a loved one from suicide, and chronically depressed hospital patients.

Finally, specific types of suicide prevention activities are thoroughly reviewed—with particular emphasis on survey research of suicide prevention agencies.

In recent years, suicide has been recognized by authorities as one of the major social and public health problems of our times, and this recognition is increasing year by year as the death toll continues to climb. While many people suffering from organic diseases are now cured through modern medical discoveries, no cure has yet been "discovered" to prevent suicide.

Suicide is much more prevalent than many people realize. Suicide rates in industrialized countries have been steadily rising in proportion to other causes of death. The number of recorded suicides in each of five countries in one year helps to illustrate the magnitude of this problem.

In the United States alone, in 1969, an estimated 22,200 persons committed suicide. Since 1961, there have not been less than 20,000 reported suicide deaths a year.[1] Several prominent authorities who have worked in this field, such as Louis Dublin, Robert Litman, Norman Farberow, and Edwin Shneidman, believe that a more accurate figure lies between two and three times this number.[2] Shneidman has pointed out some of the reasons for this gross under-reporting.

> Physicians and other certifying officials are loathe to label a death a suicide. The onus, anathema, stigma and taboo surrounding the

TABLE 2-I
Number of Suicides in Selected Countries

Country	Year	Number of Suicides
United States	1968	21,372
Japan	1968	14,601
West Germany	1967	12,743
France	1969	7,828
United Kingdom	1969	4,780

Source: *Demographic Yearbook, 1970* (New York: United Nations), 1971, Table 19; and *World Health Statistics Report*, Vol. 23, No. 11, 1970, (World Health Organization, pp. 1003, 1010-1011). For further information on suicide statistics see pp. 6, 15-16, and 98-99, in this book.

topic of suicide are not to be underestimated. Another reason for under reporting is that many deaths—perhaps 10 to 15 percent of them—are, in fact, equivocal or unclear as to the proper mode of death. In very few places in the world are these equivocal deaths systematically investigated and scientifically treated.[3]

Suicide is listed among the ten leading causes of death in the United States. The importance of suicide as a major cause of death in the United States and in other countries is further revealed by Table 2-II, which lists the rank of suicide among causes of death in four countries.

In addition to those who die, there is an extremely large group of persons who have made unsuccessful attempts to commit suicide. Several studies have indicated "that one in three suicide attempters eventually kills himself, and that one in three completers has a history of prior attempts."[4] If we take into account these attempted suicides, a more accurate picture is revealed—in other words, somewhere between 200,000 and 350,000 Americans attempt suicide each year, with about 30,000 to 40,000 succeeding.

The suicide rate is rising among the young, and particularly among women living in urban areas. For example, in Los Angeles, the suicide rate for women under 20 years of age jumped from 0.4 to 8 per 100,000 from 1960 to 1970; for women 20 to 29 years years of age, it climbed from 6 to 26. Among men under 20 years old the suicide statistics went from 3 to 10 per 100,000 in the past

TABLE 2-II
Rank of Suicide as a Cause of Death, Selected Countries

Country and Year	Rank of Suicide as One of 50 Major Causes of Death	Suicides as a Percentage of all Deaths
Finland, 1966	9	2.0
Hungary, 1966	6	3.0
Austria, 1966	11	1.8
United States, 1968	10	1.1

Source: *Demographic Yearbook, 1967* (New York: United Nations), 1968, Table 24; *Demographic Yearbook, 1970* (New York; United Nations), 1971, Table 19.

decade; for men in the 20 to 29 age group, the suicide rate went from 18 to 41 per 100,000.[5]

At the same time, the history of proportionately higher suicide rates for white males and females over the age of sixty-five seems to be declining in the United States, England, Norway, and Denmark. However, it is important to note that rates are still relatively high for the aged as indicated by the fact that the over-65 age group constitutes 9 percent of the population; yet, they account for 25 percent of the suicides in the United States. Farber[6] has suggested that one important reason for the reported decline has been the growth of social security plans which have the effect of easing the financial burden for the aged and thus reducing their suicide potential.

Suicide at any age is an irrevocably tragic event for the family and close friends of the victim. Intense human suffering, mental anguish, and guilt are often experienced by the survivors who lament the needless loss of a loved one.

The cost of death from suicide is difficult to estimate. It can be shown that each suicidal death might well cost the victims' respective country over a quarter of a million dollars. As an illustration, the modal suicidal person (in the United States) is a middle class, white, married, tax-paying male in his mid-forties. His premature death is disrupting and disorienting to his family, and deprives the family and society of about twenty-five years of emotional and financial support. The cumulative effect of suicide on society demands that it be studied as a major social and public health problem.

Suicide is a euphemism for self-destruction by one's own hand. From ancient times to the relatively civilized conditions of the present-day, the act of suicide (in the Western world) has remained socially taboo. One of the most penetrating and complex questions is whether a rational individual is able to intentionally destroy himself, or whether the suicidal act is caused by a mental disorder. Farrar[7] has clearly suggested that even in contemporary society, the family or friends of an individual who has committed suicide may prefer to think of him as "insane," or as contemptible rather than attempting the painful task of probing the puzzling question of how someone could kill himself in his "right" mind. Robert H. Felix has pointed out that on a cultural level:

> We cannot accept the fact of the inevitability of our own death, so that death generally is to us something of a personal affront. The greatest affront of all is for someone to demonstrate man's vulnerability not merely by dying but by determining the time and place and thus demonstrate by terminating his own existence, not only his mortality but ours also, for what man has done, man can do.[8]

Thus, accurate data collection is impeded by the negative feelings aroused in most people toward suicide and the stigma cast upon the deceased and his family. Because there is such a stigma placed on the act of suicide, evidence of willful intent—such as a note left by the victim—is often concealed by family or friends who feel that if the death were thought to be "an accident" then they would not be the target of disdain. Additional reasons for the difficulty in obtaining accurate research data on suicide include the following: a certification of death from natural causes may be made to spare the mourning family from public embarrassment; researchers may be reluctant to intrude upon the grieving family by asking questions that would reveal the precipitating events which occurred prior to the death; it is often difficult to determine definitively if the death was the result of an accident, or a voluntary act of suicide (i.e. did the man intentionally drive his car off the cliff or did it go out of control? did the woman drown purposely or because she inadvertently swam out too far and suffered a leg cramp?) All too often the victim may have had an alcohol, drug, or reckless driving problem which may appear to have *un*intentionally led to his death; insurance policies which stipulate that they pay premiums to the family of the deceased may be declared invalid if the cause of death is determined to have been suicide.

Self-injurious behaviors such as chronic alcoholism, drug abuse, self-mutilations, obesity, and "accident proneness" have been viewed as a sub-intentional wish to die.[9] Since many individuals who committed suicide had histories of self-injurious behavior, the following statement should be noted:

The greater the number and period of time for suicidal attempts in the history of the victim, the greater the likelihood of his death during the course of a self-injurious act or its consequences.[10]

Thus, it has been suggested that some accidental deaths such as those resulting from an overdose of narcotics or an automobile collision, may have been a *subintentioned* suicide. However, due to a lack of clear evidence of suicidal intention in such cases, it cannot be conclusively stated that such deaths were suicides rather than accidents.

Increased research is necessary to uncover the factors which lead some people to react to their problems with suicidal impulses while others in similar situations do not contemplate suicide. Investigations should study the environmental, personality, and medical indicators that would be helpful in identifying persons with high risks of suicide.

THEORETICAL AND TAXONOMIC VIEWPOINTS

We shall now briefly review the major theoretical and taxonomic explanations of suicide. This review of the rather limited theoretical perspectives will acquaint the readers with studies of suicidal phenomena.

The sociological and psychological explanations of suicide and suicide attempts have been incorporated into the frames of reference of many clinical psychologists, physicians, psychiatrists, social workers, and sociologists.

SOCIOLOGICAL THEORIES OF SUICIDE

In the profesional literature (particularly in the United States) the most frequently quoted study of suicide is the classic work (*Le Suicide*, 1897, published in English in 1951) of the famous French sociologist Emile Durkheim.[11]

Durkheim's classic study emphasized that acts which might seem to reflect individuality are to be understood, to a large extent, in terms of the influence of a social pattern. Individuals commit suicide as members of their society, and their self-destructive act is determined by their degree of integration into social groups. Thus, Durkheim classified suicide into three different types which he termed *egoistic, altruistic,* and *anomic. Egoistic suicide* occurs when an individual experiences a weakening of his commitments to group goals and norms; he no longer cares about religious, domestic, or political aspects of life (insufficient social integration). High suicide rates for Protestants, the unmarried and married couples without children were suggestive of this type of suicide to Durkheim. *Altruistic suicide* results from the individual's deep commitment to a particular group's norms and goals (excessive social integration). This type of suicide—for a group cause—was common in primitive societies, among elite types of military units such as the Samurai warriors or the kamikazi pilots of World War II, and among Hindu widows who committed suicide (called suttee) at their husbands' funeral as an indication of devotion to their husbands. *Anomic suicide* arises from rapid and extreme social change or crisis threatening the group norms of society, i.e. economic depression, divorces and separations. The individual becomes uncertain of the appropriate behavior expected of him and experiences a state of anomic-normlessness, an unbridgeable gap between aspirations and achievements, individual passions are out of control.

Durkheim's distinction between the causes of the three types of suicide is not clear, and it is doubtful whether an adequate distinction can be presented even on a conceptual level, much less in strictly empirical terms.[12]

Since we do not have any definitive empirical data on the causes of anomic and egoistic suicide, we can only present the least ambiguous general statement of Durkheim's theory: "So we reach the general conclusion: suicide varies inversely with the degree of integration of the social groups of which the individual forms a part."[13]

Jack Gibbs, in a discussion on social integration and suicide, critically assesses Durkheim's general theory as follows:

> The support for the theory lies not in its demonstrated predictive power but rather in Durkheim's forceful argument. As long as no universal measure of integration was involved, he could argue from knowledge of suicide rates and ascribe degrees of integration to each population accordingly. Perhaps we can sense that Catholics, Jews, and married persons with children are highly integrated

(i.e. enveloped in binding social relations), but sensing that something is true and demonstrating it are two different things. Moreover, what is the appropriate conclusion when the usual differences in suicide rates no longer prevail? One can say that the usual degree of integration has also changed, but this is merely arguing backward from knowledge of suicide rates. Interpretation and *ex post facto* explanations are a poor substitute for predictions. Durkheim provided no basis for predictions, and consequently his theory *cannot be subjected to any rigorous test*. Nonetheless, his achievement was not a small one, for his basic ideas have guided numerous subsequent investigations.[14]

Most sociological investigations have adhered to Durkheim's thesis by considering the variation in suicide rates as the major problem. These investigations base their findings on the assumption that correlations which are found between official rates and specific social conditions are valid. They neglect to focus on searching out the behavior of suicidal persons. All too often such investigations have not taken into account the unreliability of official suicide statistics.

Douglas enumerates five of the major problems Durkheim and his followers encountered in using official suicide rates as a basis of analysis.

1) Unreliability resulting from the choice of the official statistics to be used in making the tests of the sociological theories; 2) unreliability resulting from subcultural differences in the attempts to hide suicide; 3) unreliability resulting from the effects of different degrees of social integration on the official statistics keeping; 4) unreliability resulting from significant variations in the social imputation of motives; 5) unreliability resulting from better collection of statistics among certain populations.[15]

The sociological works of Peter Sainsbury, and Erwin Stengel in England, and of Louis Dublin in the United States are based on theoretical frameworks which are not derived exclusively from the Durkheimian approach.[16] These studies do not dwell, as Durkheim did, upon the nature and diversity of man's moral commitments to his society, but they do provide a voluminous and most useful amount of statistical and ecological data on suicide. Although these authorities have compiled suicide statistics from official records, they expanded on the Durkheimian tradition by carefully explaining the fluctuations as well as the weaknesses and spurious factors in their correlations and profiles.

Andrew Henry and James Short, in their contemporary work which fits the neo-durkheimian tradition, have correlated variations in suicide rates with the strength of the relational system in which the person is enmeshed. Individuals who are deeply and intimately involved with others should be low suicide risks, while those isolated from meaningful and sustained interpersonal relationships should be high suicide risks.[17]

Henry and Short point out several categories by which they measured the relation between suicide and strength of the relational system: 1) The suicide rate is high in the central, disorganized sectors of cities. It is here that anonymity, loneliness, and isolation from meaningful relationships reach their extremes. 2) Suicide rates are higher in urban areas than in rural areas because of the relative isolation from social relationships and anonymity of the city compared to the tightly knit relationships of the rural small-town dweller. 3) Suicide is higher for the single, widowed, and divorced individuals than it is for the married people who, by definition, are involved in at least one or more meaningful relationships than the nonmarried.[18]

PSYCHOLOGICAL THEORIES OF SUICIDE

Many authorities have studied about, and written psychological and psychiatric explanations of suicide. Most of these authorities have focused on possible motives for the self-destructive act as well as on setting up psychological and psychiatric taxonomies of suicidal phenomena. These types of studies have generally been limited because of the arbitrary nature of identifying motives and reasons, and insufficient direct observation of victims and suicide attemptors; even when strong evidence suggests specific motives or psychological characteristics among suicide cases, the prevalence of these characteristics in the total population is generally unknown.

Although no one has conclusively isolated a single formula or pattern to explain all suicides, a number of psychological motives which prevail in certain degrees of combination have been revealed. These motives and reasons for suicide are recognized to be the following: hate, revenge, overdependency, shame, guilt, fear, hopelessness or despair, loyalty or cultural ethos, traumatic experience in childhood, loss of a loved one, fealty to self-image, chronic illness or pain, and anomie.

It has been generally acknowledged that psychological approaches stem from Sigmund Freud's psychoanalytic theory of depression, and conceptualization of a death instinct, (thanatos) to accompany the individual's life instinct (eros).[19] As such, suicide is viewed as the result of a process wherein one's original feelings of love toward a love object, turned to love and hate as a result of feelings of frustration, rejection, and hostility which the victim internalized and directed toward himself. Since the love object had become internalized and part of the self, the ambivalent feelings which the victim failed to express outwardly were turned inward, against himself. The act of suicide is thus the victim's way of recovering the lost love object and, at the same time, a way of escaping from the severely threatening hostility of his environment and his own aggressive impulses.

Gregory Zilboorg considered the suicide act as a means of thwarting outside forces that are making living impossible. In his investigations, he reported that every potential suicide victim displays a strong unconscious hostility combined with an unusual inability to love others.[20]

Children who committed suicide have been viewed in psychoanalytic terms as attempting to free themselves from an unbearable situation, usually consisting of severe deprivation of love and lack of warm affectionate responses. It has been found that deprivation of love in childhood led to aggressive spiteful tendencies and resultant guilt feelings which were directed against the self.[21] Arrested psychosexual development due to loss of, or unavailability of, parents at crucial stages in a child's development has been correlated with suicide attempts.[22]

Karl Menninger, one of the most prominent protagonists of Freud's conceptualization of a death instinct, viewed suicide as the winning out of the destructive tendencies over the constructive tendencies. He distinguished three sources of suicidal impulses: the wish to kill, the wish to be killed, and the wish to die. Menninger also developed the following taxonomy of subsuicidal phenomena: 1) chronic suicide—ascetism, martyrdom, addiction, invalidism, psychosis; 2) focal suicide—self-mutilation, malingering, polysurgery, multiple accidents, impotence and frigidity; and 3) organic suicide—involving the psychological factors in organic disease.[23]

Other important extensions of the Freudian psychoanalytic tradition are presented in Hendin,[24] Jackson,[25] Meerloo,[26] and Zilboorg's[27] classificatory schemas of suicide. The components of these classifications can be succinctly outlined: suicide as communication, suicide as revenge, suicide as fantasy crime, suicide as unconscious flight, suicide as magical revival or reunion, and suicide as rebirth and restitution.

In future studies, an integration of the psychological and the sociological approaches to suicide would serve to improve our understanding of the precipitating events which lead some individuals to kill themselves. Edwin Shneidman summarized this vital need for integration of the clinical approaches of psychology with the group approaches of sociology in this way:

> A synthesis of these two lies in the area of the "self," especially in the ways in which social forces are incorporated within the totality of the individual. In understanding suicide, one needs to know the thoughts and feelings and ego functionings and unconscious conflicts of an individual, as well as how he integrates with his fellow man and participates morally as a member of the groups within which he lives.[28]

STATISTICAL AND DEMOGRAPHIC DATA

Statistical and demographic data on suicide account for the variation in rates among different types of populations. Evidence of differences in suicide rates between particular groups will be reviewed. Method, age, sex, race, and marital status are important characteristics in any analysis of suicide and attempted suicide. The frequency differs by each age group, racial group and sex. The difference between the sexes and races applies not only to frequency of suicide but also to the method employed.

Before proceeding to analyze particular social characteristics of suicide, let us review its causes. The following will give the reader a review of the diverse methods employed by suicide victims.

The detailed international list of the causes of death groups suicide according to these causes:

> suicide by firearms, by hanging, by gases (asphyxia), by drowning, by cutting instruments, by jumping from high places, by crushing [e.g. throwing oneself under a speeding train], and by poisons—arsenic, carbolic acid, corrosive sublimate, hyrocyonic acid, opium, strychnin, cyanide of potassium, lysol.[29]

In the United States, suicide by firearms and explosives accounts for more suicidal deaths than any other method. According to the 1964 United States Vital Statistics Report (Volume 2), the most frequent methods of suicide were the following: firearms or explosives were used in almost 48 percent of suicides; various types of poisoning (solid and liquid substances, and gases) were used in 27 percent of suicides; and hanging and strangulation accounted for almost 15 percent. Approximately seven of ten persons who committed suicide by poisoning themselves with analgesic or soporific substances, used barbituric acid and its derivatives. Motor vehicle exhaust gas was used in about nine of ten suicide deaths of gas poisoning.

The method chosen by suicide victims varies by different geographical locations, probably as a result of availability. For example, jumping from high places is not generally a popular means of suicide in the United States; however, in New York City—a city with numerous skyscrapers and high rise apartment buildings—this particular method accounts for over 15 percent of the reported suicides.[30] Accordingly, the New York City Police Department has set up a special suicide squad whose function it is to try to catch in a net individuals who jump from high buidings, thus breaking the fall and preventing a suicide.

Although the methods of suicide do differ according to race and sex, the differences between the white and nonwhite populations are small compared to those between males and females. Nonwhite suicide victims are more likely than white victims to use solid and liquid substances such as rat poison, lye, or denatured alcohol, and are more likely to jump from high places. However, the most frequent means of suicide—by firearms and explosives—is the same for nonwhites and whites. This is in sharp contrast to the fact that the most frequent method of suicide for females is poisoning by analgesic and soporific substances; men most often choose to kill themselves with firearms.[31]

Race, Sex and Age Differentials

As shown in Table 2-III, rates of suicide in the United States vary by race, sex, and age. In 1967, the most recent year for which detailed figures are available, the following variations are shown: 1) White male suicide rates increased with age to a peak of 56.0 per 100,000 at age 85 and above. 2) The rate for white females reaches a peak at the age range between 45 and 64 (12.7 per 100,000) and declines thereafter. 3) Both nonwhite males and females reached their peak suicide rates in the 25 to 44 age group, with a rate of 16.2 and 5.0 respectively, per 100,000.

The suicide rate among nonwhites seems to be increasing in recent years. In 1967, the ratio between rates for white males (16.8 per 100,000) was more than twice the figure for nonwhite males; the rate for white females was almost 2½ times as high as that of nonwhite females.[32] In 1960, the nonwhite population constituted 11 percent of the total United States population, yet they accounted for only 5 percent of the recorded suicides. The suicide rate of Blacks living in the United States is generally lower than that of Whites. In contrast, there are records of high suicide rates among certain Black tribes living in Africa.[33] With foreignborns, especially Chinese and Japanese people, suicide rates are higher than those of nativeborns; the rates tend to be comparable to those of the country of origin.

Suicide rates among American Indians are much higher than those for the general population in the United States. In 1967, there were 94 Indian suicides out of a total population estimated to be 550,000 (Indians, Aleuts, and Eskimos) residing in 24 states.[34] This is a rate of 17.0 per 100,000 as compared with 10.8 per 100,000 for all races in the United States. The suicide rate of the Blackfoot Indians of Montana is almost 47 percent higher than the national rate.[35] Suicide among Indians increases dramatically between twelve and twenty-one years of age, reaching its peak at twenty to twenty-one years of age.

TABLE 2-III

Variation of Suicide Rates per 100,000 by Age, Color, and Sex
United States, 1967

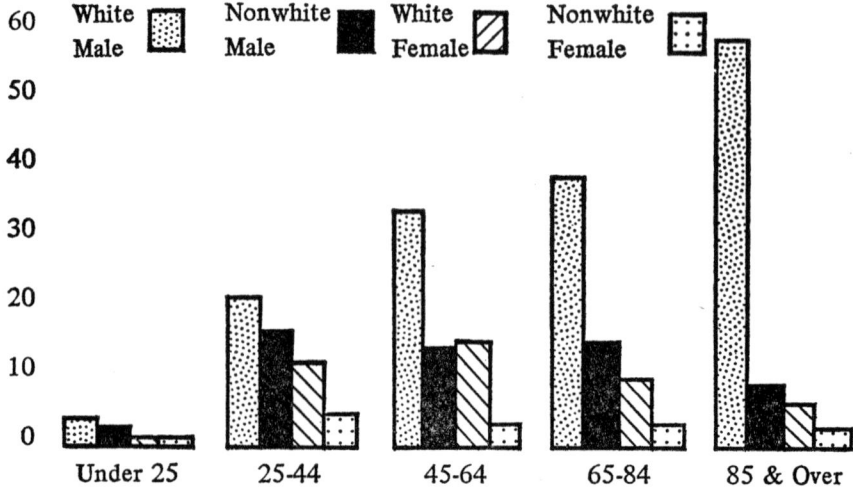

It has been reported that males comprise 70 percent of the completed suicide population. Since at every age level many more men than women kill themselves, suicide has been referred to as a masculine type of behavior.

It has been suggested that the success of male suicides has resulted from their tendency to choose more violent and lethal methods of self-destruction. Another popular explanation for the high suicide rate among white males is related to the higher expectation placed on them for occupational achievement and hence their increased chances to feel that they have failed. This explanation is derived from studies that report the highest suicide rates occurring among top executives, artists, and professional men—especially physicians.[36] In contrast, other studies report higher suicide rates among unskilled laborers and agricultural workers.[37] High suicide rates generally occur in occupations at the extremes of either high income and prestige, or low income and prestige.[38] The relation between suicide rates and occupation varies with different locations and economic conditions. In the present decade, with increased occupational equality and greater opportunities for females and nonwhites, their suicide rate is already beginning to rise.

In unsuccessful suicide attempts, women outnumber men by a ratio of over 2 to 1. Shneidman and Farberow were able to collect sex data on almost half of the 5,906 cases of suicide attempt they studied, revealing a sex ratio of 2.2 to 1.[39] Similarly, Dorpat and Boswell found a female to male ratio of 2.1 to 1, in their study of 121 suicide attempters who had been admitted to the King County Hospital in Seattle.[40] Edwards and Whitlock studied 680 suicide attempters in Brisbane, Australia and found a female to male ratio of 2.5 to 1.[41]

The suicide rates by sex vary in different countries. In the Philippines, the suicide rate for males exceeds the female rate by only 0.4 (0.7 for males and 0.3 for females per 100,000) while the difference in Iceland is 25.2 (31.4 for males and 6.2 for females per 100,000). An unusually marked distinction of the suicide variation by sex is evident in Nicaragua where the rate for males is 2.1 per 100,000 and for females 0.1 per 100,000 resulting in a male to female ratio of 23 to 1. In contrast, the suicide rates for males and females in Luxembourg are very much alike—11.0 and 10.3 per 100,0000 respectively. The proportionately lower rates of reported female suicides is further illustrated by the 1966 rates in Hungary and Finland. In Hungary, the male and female rates were 42.0 and 18.0 per 100,000 respectively. In Finland, the male and female rates were 30.1 and 9.1 per 100,000 or a ratio of 3.3 to 1.[42] These two countries have been referred to as suicide capitals of the world.

Suicide rates in the United States vary with age. It is fairly common knowledge that children rarely commit suicide; up to age fifteen, cases are comparatively rare. A dramatic increase in self-inflicted deaths occurs in the fifteen to nineteen age group—ranking as the second highest cause of death for this group, and topped only by accidents. In 1967, a rate of 4.7 per 100,000 was reported.[43] The suicide rate for males increases rapidly with age until the mid-eighties. For females, the rate reaches its peak at sixty and declines somewhat after that age.

With advancing years it becomes more difficult to adapt to

change; forced changes become especially disturbing. Mental and physical disabilities are more noticeable in the older population. Many elderly people suffer from psychosis (the most common psychosis among the aged is senile psychosis) others suffer from chronic depression, and from feelings of loneliness and uselessness as relations with family, friends, and involvement in productive employment diminishes.

Differences by Marital Status

In general, married persons are less prone to suicide than are those who never married or whose marriages have been broken by divorce or death. Appreciably lower rates for married persons, especially when compared with the suicide rates of the divorced, are reported in the United States, Canada, England, and Wales, Sweden, Switzerland, and the city of Vienna.

Among married men in all age groups (except the under 20 group) the suicide rate is markedly lower than it is for single men—in some age groups it is less than half. In contrast, rates for widowed and divorced males in certain age groups were almost seven times higher than those for married men of the same ages. In the group as a whole, about three times as many widowers as married men, and nearly five times as many divorced men are recorded as having taken their own lives.

In the United States, suicide is much less frequent among females than among males; the differences between the several marital groups, although less marked, are still considerable. Rates are lower for married than for single women in all age groups except the youngest (under 24 years of age) and the oldest (seventy-five and over). Rates for the widowed and divorced, especially the latter, are usually three to four times those for the married. These differences suggest that married people are less likely to commit suicide than the divorced, widowed, or never married (especially those people who are living alone).

Divorce and widowhood of themselves contribute to a wide range of social problems; familiar living habits are abandoned and new ones established. Usually, too, the adjustment is full of emotion, necessitating the formation of new relationships. Moreover, the divorced and widowed often live alone.[44] Loneliness may thus be considered a primary factor in this group's relatively high suicide rate. Ferdinand Tonnies has stated that "in the establishment of union (Gemeinschaft) with others, one expects sympathetic response."[45] This response is lost when a family break, as described above, occurs.

The well-adjusted family (primary group) has long been recognized as one of the most satisfactory groups for comfortable and happy living. Not only does the family provide the intimacy which most people crave, it also offers companionship, recognition, and security which foster the individual's well-being. It is the above attributes of family life which probably serve to prevent restlessness and social disorganization. According to Charles H. Cooley, "the primary group constitutes the unity and structure of the social mind. Social organization is this unity and structure."[46] Since a characteristic example of the primary group is the family,[47] we can then safely say that the previously discussed break in a family may lead to social problems such as suicide. The bond of the primary group relationship often helps the married individual to maintain stability and social organization, in contrast to the widower or divorcee who often loses this bond and as a result is more susceptible to the stress of social isolation and to committing suicide.

DIAGNOSTIC AND EVALUATIVE

What symptoms or clues will a person display which are indicative as danger signs of his suicide risk? What studies and guidelines have been completed which would be helpful to lay volunteers, professionals, and family physicians who frequently have the responsibility of assessing a suicide risk?

What is the suicide risk of the following groups of people: those who have a history of suicide attempts; those who are chronically depressed, or have a recent history of serious physical or mental illness; those who are confined in jails or prisons; those survivors who have lost a parent or spouse from suicide?

The basic symptoms and danger signals of suicide are not clearly understood. It is not a disease or a malignant growth. What, then, is the nature of suicide? It is the result of many varied and complex processes. Louis Dublin considered suicide as coming from within the individual, rather than from without; as such, it is considered as the terminal act in a complicated psychic drama.[48] Dublin viewed suicide as the final outcome of a series of psychic events. It is not a disease, but a symptom that may manifest itself in the course of any of several types of mental disorder—depression, either neurotic or psychotic episodes, schizophrenia, or hysteria.

In a booklet published by the United States Public Health Service, Shneidman and Farberow have strongly suggested that there are eight prevalent myths which should be corrected about suicide.[49] The following statements should be remembered by all practitioners and family members in order to recognize the danger signs of potential suicides:

1) *People who talk about suicide do commit suicide.* Eight out of every ten suicides had given definite warnings. Suicide threats and attempts *must* be taken seriously.

2) *Suicide does not happen impulsively.* Studies show that the suicidal individual gives many clues to his intentions. Alertness to these cries for help may well prevent suicidal acts from taking place.

3) *Suicidal people are not fully intent on dying.* It is wrong to say, "Why bother because we can't stop them anyway." Most suicidal people are undecided about living, and any suicide attempt is a desperate cry for help.

4) *People are not suicidal for life.* Hundreds of case histories reveal that a person brought through a suicidal crisis *can* go on to lead a useful life.

5) *Improvement following a suicidal crisis does not necessarily mean that the suicidal risk is over.* Many suicides take place in the three months following the beginning of "improvement," when the individual has the energy to put his morbid thoughts and feelings into effect. This is a time to be especially vigilant.

6) *Suicide strikes all socio-economic classes.* Suicide is very "democratic" in that it is represented proportionately throughout all levels of society.

7) *Suicidal behavior is not inherited.* Suicide is an individual matter, and can be prevented.

8) *Suicidal people are not necessarily mentally ill, or psychotic.* Numerous investigations of genuine suicide notes have shown that the suicidal person is extremely unhappy, possibly resulting from a temporary emotional upset, a long and painful illness, or a complete loss of hope.[50]

Mathew Ross, a Harvard psychiatrist, summarizes the importance of making physicians aware of the usefulness in preventing suicide of the standard tools of a complete history and physical examination. He suggests the following helpful tips for identifying patients with suicide risk:

> One's first observation may be of a pale-faced, sallow person sitting huddled in a waiting-room chair, evidencing little or no spontaneous activity. Further inspection reveals an accentuation of the facial wrinkles and eyelid folds, a lack-luster to the hair, some evidence of weight and sleep loss. Carelessness or even unkempt grooming also may be noted.
>
> When one shakes hands with the patient, he may become aware of the various stigmata of underlying emotional tone through psychophysiologic communications: warmth, dryness, dampness, cold, clammy, firm, listless, forceful, weak, and the like.
>
> The patient's chief complaint may be a generalized feeling that "something is wrong," an apprehensiveness or a generally alarmed state. This may be linked to an expressed fear of a dread disease or to complaints of regional aches and pains and, frequently, to various complaints of gastrointestinal dysfunction.
>
> Characteristically and commonly, there is a reported change of bodily feeling expressed as a decrease or loss of the feeling of wellbeing. Tiredness, fatigue, "heaviness" are presented in varying degrees....
>
> Sleep patterns are apt to be altered in quite characteristic, almost pathogenic, ways in depression. Most often the patient complains of awakening early in the morning, unable to return to sleep, but still too fatigued to face the new day.
>
> Loss of appetite is apt to be marked and sustained. But in other cases food may be used as a tranquilizer, leading to overeating and obesity. But, no matter which, increased or decreased intake, there is no true pleasure in eating because food seems to have lost its taste.
>
> Women patients may report various menstrual disorders and libidinal loss; men may complain of impotence and libidinal loss.
>
> Some people will indicate they are committing what can best be

described as "social suicide" through their behavior. This may be apparent in a history of alcoholism, sexual escapades, or business failure.[51]

Ross alerts professionals to the period of *highest suicide risk in a depressed patient—within a three-month period after the onset of improvement.* He suggests that it is at this time that the patient regains sufficient energy to put earlier plans for suicide into effect. Ross concludes: "When the danger of suicide is great, prompt hospitalization and, when available, psychiatric referral is indicated."[52]

Litman further expands our knowledge of diagnostic and evaluative measures by suggesting that practitioners gather the following types of information when evaluating a suicidal emergency: case history, including age and sex; onset of self-destructive behavior as determined by previous threats or attempts; method of possible self-injury; recent loss of a loved one through death, separation, and divorce; recent history of illness or surgery; and loss of resources (relatives, friends, and finances).[53]

Suicide Attempts

In the plentiful literature on suicide cited in a recently published comprehensive bibliography,[54] only a few studies examined the prevalence of suicide attempts. According to Shneidman and Farberow, "Data for attempted suicides are relatively difficult to come by, whereas statistics for committed suicides are relatively easy . . . to obtain."[55] In the few studies that have been completed, the sample of suicide attempts has come from hospital records, prison records, and more recently from survey data. Many of the people who have attempted suicide are treated in private hospitals, doctors' offices or at home, while others are not treated at all. This points out the sampling error in a study of suicide attempts which might simplistically purport that their data gathered from city hospitals is clearly representative of all attempted suicides in the population.

Shneidman[56] and Farberow,[57] and Stengel have pointed out some of the methodological problems in obtaining reliable data on suicide attempts. The tracing of patients and securing of accurate, rather than merely an abundance of fragmented, records is only part of the problem. The suicide attemptors "who do not lose their lives either cover up their own attempts or have their attempts covered up for them by others."[58] *These researchers caution against assuming that the characteristics of the population who commit suicide are the same as the suicide attempt group.*

One of Shneidman and Farberow's classic surveys reported on data gathered about persons who had attempted or committed suicide during the year 1957, in Los Angeles County. A total of 5,906 suicide attempts were found, of which 3,887 were reported by physicians, and 2,019 were obtained from the records of county and city hospitals. According to the official records of the Los Angeles County Coroner's Office, a total of 768 persons had committed suicide. Thus, the proportion of attempted suicides to committed suicides was found to be 7.69 to 1 (5,906 to 768) or almost 8 to 1.[59]

Although each psychiatric emergency must be assessed individually, knowledge of the following modal sociological comparisons between attempted suicides and committed suicides will enhance our understanding of this area.

> The *modal suicide attempter* is likely to be (a) female, (b) Caucasian, (c) in her twenties or thirties, probably the former, . . . (d) a housewife, and (e) native-born, and to (f) attempt suicide by barbiturates, (g) give as a "reason" marital difficulties or depression, and (h) live in an apartment in an apartment house area.
> By way of contrast, the *modal suicide committer* is likely to be (a) male, (b) Caucasian, (c) in his forties or older, (d) married, (e) a skilled or unskilled worker, and (f) native born, and to (g) commit suicide by gunshot wounds, hanging or carbon monoxide poisoning, (h) give as a reason ill health, depression, or marital difficulties, and (i) live in an apartment in an apartment house area.[60]

The survey research of Ronald S. Mintz was concerned with determining the true prevalence rate of persons who had attempted suicide in the city of Los Angeles. Between August, 1962 and January, 1964, 3,085 questionnaires were distributed serially door-to-door on randomly selected streets in the city of Los Angeles, to every person 14 years of age or older, residing in the dwelling units surveyed. Of the 3,085 questionnaires that were distributed, 2,018 were returned. Thus, the data sample consisted of 2,018 subjects, of which 78 persons, or 3.9 percent, stated that they had made one or more suicide attempts.

It was further indicated that almost four persons out of each 100 had made one or more attempts. Mintz applied the prevalence rate to the total population over 14 years of age in the city of Los Angeles, and concluded that 71,500 persons living in this city had made one or more serious attempts. His initial estimate, based on the above research and census data, is that the prevalence rate of suicide attempts in the entire United States is five million.[61] This preliminary study is an excellent beginning toward moving closer to finding the similarities and differences between attempted suicides and successful suicide victims.

Hospital Suicides

A number of varied and significant studies—dealing with characteristics of individuals who were hospitalized for a physical or mental illness and subsequently committed suicide have recently been completed. The content of these studies is broad based, encompassing medical, psychological, and sociological aspects of the problem.

In the study conducted by Farberow, Shneidman, and Leonard,[62] a sample of sixty schizophrenic patients who had been hospitalized, during the years 1955 to 1958, in thirty-seven mental hospitals in the United States was evaluated. Of the sixty schizophrenic cases studied, thirty had committed suicide, while the matching control group of thirty discharged patients (similar in age, religious affiliation, marital status, and year of discharge) did not commit suicide. By preparing a detailed abstract of each patient's history, conducting an intensive psychological autopsy on each case, and synthesizing the similarities and differences between suicide and control cases, a comprehensive Check List of Suicidal Potential for Hospitalized Schizophrenic Patients, with specific clues to suicide, was developed. This evaluation and Checklist are quite valuable and should be referred to by all hospital staff members working with schizophrenic patients.

An eight-year study of 966 hospital suicides which occurred during 1959 to 1966 was recently completed by Farberow and his associates.[63] Most suicides among the Veterans Administration patients studied had taken place after the patient was released from the hospital and was back in the community. The method of suicide seems especially significant when comparing the subjects studied with non-hospital suicides. In the general population, the most frequent method of suicide is firearms and explosives (mainly guns)—accounting for almost half of such reported deaths. In contrast, the most frequent method of suicide used in the hospital studied (where guns are not readily available) were jumping from a high place (40 percent), and hanging (32 percent); firearms accounting for only 4 percent.

The two studies cited above suggest the following recommendations for reducing suicide deaths: 1) terminal patients will be better able to make an acceptable adjustment to their illness if they find the staff to be understanding, sympathetic, not frightened of death themselves, and generally supportive; 2) careful evaluation should be made, including interviews with risk patients and their families, at the time of discharge; 3) continuing interest should be shown through frequent follow-up contacts, availability of medication and psychiatric care, and easy return to the hospital, if necessary for the discharged patient; 4) physical structure modifications should be made in hospitals, such as safety screens or stops on windows, and the enclosure of stairwells or installation of high guardrails which would be difficult to climb over.

Jones found, in his small but in-depth study of thirty cases of suicide, occurring over a seven year period, that a highly significant proportion of the people, when matched with a control group, had been hospitalized for physical and mental illness.[64] Kahne investigated seventy-nine psychiatrists, all engaged in psychotherapy with hospitalized patients, sixteen of whom committed suicide. His study revealed the danger of social disorganization within the hospital as well as its concomitants of insufficient patient contact, inability of residents to relate to the patient, and unavailability of experienced psychiatrists for ward therapy due to their involvement in administrative positions.[65]

Petrovsky studied thirty-two cases of attempted suicide in a general hospital. His findings concur with the studies mentioned above: the vigilant attention and clinical care of the hospital staff to suicidal patients is necessary to reduce the suicide rate. Stone and Shein[66] emphasize the frequency with which a family physician had seen a patient who eventually committed suicide in a mental hospital. They state that conventional psychotherapy is not enough, and recommend a specific active clinical approach.[67]

Prison Suicides

Interest and concern have been aroused over suicides that occur in prisons and jails. Studies have focused on the incidence, method, proximity to the date of entering the prison, and other contributing factors to prisoner suicides. The consensus is that the most prevalent method used in prison suicides was hanging, followed by jumping from high places. Unsentenced prisoners had the highest risk of suicide and most suicides occurred early in the period of confinement.

From time-to-time there have been newspaper reports on the prevalence of suicide in city and town jails and lock-ups. The most limiting factors on the accuracy of these reports, as well as suicides that are never officially reported, have been the inadequate records and lack of cooperation of many jail and lock-up administrators. The following small sample is an illustration of such a newspaper report. During the period from May through early July, 1972, four suicides—all by hanging—took place in Baltimore City police station lock-ups. All of these suicides took place during the first few hours of confinement. The first suicide victim had been awaiting trial on a disorderly conduct charge; the second had been charged with narcotics violations; the third with telephone misuse, and the fourth with drunken driving.[68] It should be noted that these men were *not* hardened criminals dangerous to society; they had not even been brought to trial. But they were dangerous to themselves and their suicidal acts were indicative of mental imbalance.

Data on prison/jail suicides that are more detailed than newspaper accounts, appear to come from studies such as those that will now be discussed. The following data were reported in professional periodicals.

Fully and his associates found 181 male suicides in the French penal system from 1955 to 1965: 148 of the 181 cases committed suicide by hanging; 109 were unsentenced prisoners, of whom twenty killed themselves within the first twenty-four hours, and another forty within the first month of incarceration.[69]

Rieger studied the records of fifty-eight federal offenders who had made one or more suicide attempts at the United States Penitentiary at Lewisburg, Pennsylvania. He classified attempts according to risk factors and seriousness of self-injury. Among the twelve cases that were considered in the more serious attempt category (severe self-injuries and unequivocal attempt at self-destruction) eight had suffered a loss of either a parent or a spouse through either death or divorce just prior to the attempt. There was no information available on two of the remaining four individuals.[70]

Similar to Rieger's findings on the effects of the loss of a loved one on prison suicide, Koller and Castanos found that 65 percent of the prisoners they studied who had attempted suicide came from families in which one or both of the parents committed suicide when the prisoner was ten to fifteen years of age.[71]

In Rieger's study, thirty-five of the forty-six attempts that were classified as non-serious attempts had inflicted superficial cutting wounds on their wrists.[72] Although 53 percent of the suicide attempt group had a prior record of "violent" crimes (aggravated assault, armed robbery, kidnapping, murder, and sexual crimes) it is not a significant factor because an estimated 50 percent of all prisoners at the Lewisburg penitentiary have a record of one or more violent crimes.[73] Rieger recommended that the more serious attempters needed short-term intensive crisis intervention psychotherapy.[74]

Danto, in his study of suicides which took place between 1967 and 1970 at the Wayne County Jail, indicated that the method used by all of the suicides was hanging. He pointed out that seven of the ten inmates who committed suicide either had been remanded to jail for trial without the prospect of bond being granted, or high bond of $10,000 or more was imposed.[75] It is understandable why these emotionally unstable inmates may have lost all hope for the future. Suicide for such inmates provides an escape from the overcrowded, rat-infested, punitive conditions preponderant in most jails in the United States.

Roberts, in his comprehensive work on penology reveals the nature of prisoner problems and suggests rehabilitation methods:

> Incarceration, and its attendant regimentation to prison life, is often boring, frustrating, and at times depressing to the inmate. . . . This regimentation can create serious institutional problems, such as hunger strikes, escapes, suicides, and prison riots unless some type of healthy outlet is provided.[76]

In order to counteract the feelings of extreme despair, hopelessness, and social isolation which lead to prison suicides, recommendations such as the following should be heeded by jail officials:

> This small study might be used to encourage an experimental program which would train inmate trustees to form rescue patrols to be available at night to talk with the lonely prisoners and to spot those attempting to hang themselves. Assigning groups of depressed and suicidal patients into ward structures with sensitive staff might also help to reduce the number of those who commit suicide.[77]

Survivors of Suicide

Children are especially vulnerable to severe emotional problems resulting from the loss of a loved one. The loss of a parent by natural death can lead to ambivalent feelings of resentment, guilt, shame, and abandonment. When the cause of a parent's death has been found to be suicide, the problems cited above are often compounded. The legacy of the loss of a loved person that appears to predispose survivors to severe emotional stress, including suicidal behavior, is prevalent not only among children and adolescents. Depression and a heightened danger of suicide are apparent among older people, too, as they grieve the loss of a spouse, sibling, or close friend. This is particularly true among widows in the forty-five to sixty-four age group. Thus, follow-up psychiatric treatment and aftercare services are needed not only by released hospital patients who have been treated for injuries inflicted during a suicide attempt, but also, frequently, by the families of suicide victims and suicide attempters.

Several studies have explored the pathogenic impact of suicide upon the spouse as well as upon the children of the victim. The primary objective of these studies is to encourage a more realistic awareness of the pathogenic ramifications that the suicide of a parent or marital partner can have on the child or spouse. An additional objective is to foster a much needed clinical sensitivity of the child's or spouse's disturbed reactions to the sudden death of a loved one. Studies of this type will hopefully lead the way to sensitizing clinicians to post-suicide preventive and therapeutic interventions needed by the bereaved survivors of suicide.

Cain and Fast have explored pathological patterns of behavior in the surviving spouse—the marital partner of the suicide victim. In this clinical study, the following pathogenic disturbances, precipitated by suicide by one's spouse, were revealed: 1) There were frequent, extremely unpleasant meetings with the police, who overtly or implicitly considered homicide as the alternative possibility to suicide. 2) In addition, there were similar encounters with the coroner's office and insurance representatives. 3) Often, there were unpleasant contacts with clergymen who would not conduct traditional burial services and there were several cases where burial was refused in consecrated church grounds. 4) Most destructive was the blame often thrust upon the suicide's surviving spouse by the community, neighbors, and family—especially in-laws. The bereaved spouse was denied emotional support from neighbors; the general reaction of the community members was finger-pointing and gossip about the couple's recent marital discord or statements such as "she drove him to it." These types of insensitive community reactions heighten the shame and guilt of the surviving spouse and family. It was also revealed that many of these surviving individuals had serious personality problems long before their spouse's suicide.[78]

There has been a recent investigation of the legacy of suicide on the children of a suicide victim. Cain and Fast's in-depth study of forty-five disturbed children, most of whom were seen at the University of Michigan Children's Psychiatric Hospital, indicated the profound psychological impact of a parent's suicide upon the the children studied. These children whose parent committed suicide had to cope with additional guilt and burdens produced by their surviving parent.

> ... their surviving parent's shock, grief, preoccupied withdrawal, guilt, and blaming; their own heightened separation problems and deep sense of loss; misconceptions and fears of death; irrational guilts; anger over desertion; distorted intertwining of the bereavement reactions of the child and the surviving parent; realignments of family dynamics necessitated by the loss; stressful changes made in basic living arrangements; ... Definitive assessment of the unique impact of parent suicide ... will require ... quantitative comparative studies involving groups of children who have experienced different forms of parent loss.[79]

Oscar Hill's study of a group of 1,483 depressed inpatients who had been at the Maudsley Hospital in London, England, strongly indicates an association between death of a parent in childhood and a subsequent suicide attempt in adult life.

> Suicide is significantly more common in depressed women who lost their fathers when aged ten to fourteen and, to a lesser extent, at fifteen to nineteen. Men and women whose mothers died in the first ten years of life also tended to attempt suicide more often.[80]

The loss of a loved one by natural or accidental death has been considered an important predictive clue to mental illness as well as suicide in the survivors. However, very few experimental studies utilizing rigorous methodological procedures have been conducted on the effects of bereavement.

Two studies on bereavement are now underway which may provide valuable data on the effect suicide has on survivors. The first is a three-year study of families mourning accidental vehicular death. Researchers are considering the possibility that the nature of the bereavement and mourning process will differ as a function of the expectations of death among family members. This study is attempting to develop gross prognostic criteria for subsequent personal and familial adjustment to death, and to identify clues indicative of a family's adaptive or maladaptive capacity for coping with bereavement.[81]

The other study is a demonstration project in preventive psychiatry at Montefiore Hospital in the Bronx, New York. Psychotherapy is being given to a group of bereaved families by psychiatric social workers under the supervision of psychiatrists. Two control groups—one of bereaved families who received no psychotherapy, and other a group of matched families who experienced no bereavement during a three-year period prior to the study's inception—will be followed-up and compared to the experimental group in terms of the incidence of maladjustment and mental illness several years after the initiation of the study. The findings will help to determine the need for the duplication of similar preventive intervention programs for survivors in other locations.[82]

The effect of losing one or both parents during childhood has been shown to result in some degree of disorganization in the emotional environment of the child. One question that can be asked is, does a parental death at an early age increase the probability of a surviving child committing suicide? Not necessarily. Death of a parent can best be considered an indirect influence effecting the individual child's development. The quality of care the grieving child subsequently receives is of paramount importance.

Summary

The vital need for therapeutic intervention aimed at preventing suicide in chronically depressed patients is revealed by the following summary statements:

1) Dr. Milton Rosenbaum, Chairman of the Department of Psychiatry at Albert Einstein Medical College stated that:

> It is not to be forgotten that patients almost always cry out for help before attempting suicide. It is when the cry is unheeded that the likelihood of a suicide attempt is at its height.

2) Dr. Robert E. Litman, Co-director at the Los Angeles Suicide Prevention Center, stated that:

> Investigations of suicide deaths reveal that, in the great majority of cases, suicide did not occur suddenly, impulsively, unpredictably, or inevitably, but was, on the contrary, the final step or outcome of a progressive failure of adaptation.

3) Dr. Stanley F. Yolles, Professor of Psychiatric Medicine at the State University of New York at Stonybrook stated:

> It is obvious that man's unique question is still "To be or not to be," and it is our task to provide him with an affirmative answer.

Needless to say, many suicides committed by adolescents and the aged, by hospital patients, prisoners, and survivors of suicide, and by the divorced and widowed, could have been prevented if adequate mental health and crisis intervention services were available to treat the individual in times of crisis.

SUICIDE PREVENTION ACTIVITIES

The magnitude of the suicide problem has been discussed. Efforts at remedying the problems must be in the area of prevention. Some individuals at risk can financially afford, and are motivated to seek, long-term psychiatric treatment and that type of intervention may be effective for them. However, the majority of persons in crisis are in need of less costly intervention. Many recent, organized efforts at preventing suicide have come about through the establishment of specialized suicide prevention centers, emergency room psychiatric services in general hospitals, community mental health centers, and mental hygiene clinics, pastoral counseling centers, anti-suicide bureaus, and poison control centers.

Other less formalized preventive efforts come from persons often called "gatekeepers" or "significant others." A gatekeeper is any person to whom a person in distress turns for help—a family member, a friend, a neighbor, a clergyman, a family physician, a corner druggist, a beautician, or a policeman. The gatekeeper generally needs to be a good listener, supportive, and capable of directing the troubled individual to the proper community resource or self-help behavior. In England, the rapidly expanding Samaritan movement publicizes its local telephone numbers throughout the country; persons tempted to commit suicide may call these numbers anytime, day or night. The caller in crisis is given understanding, advice, and friendship by either clergy or intelligent laymen. In the United States, 820 of 1,405 Holiday Inns provide readily accessible spiritual counseling for guests. Reverend W. A. Nance is employed by Holiday Inns, Inc. and oversees a growing national network of clergymen. These clergymen claim to have talked about 235 people out of committing suicide. Sensitive and dedicated volunteers such as the above are illustrations of gatekeepers.

The organizational study of suicide prevention agencies will review the structure and function of these specialized agencies as well as professional and non-professional resources in the community.

ORGANIZATIONAL STUDY OF SUICIDE PREVENTION AGENCIES[83]

The large number of calls for help reaching suicide prevention agencies each year, and the growing number of these agencies, suggests that they fill urgent needs. They appear to offer a valuable service not only to the suicidal persons who call upon them, but also to the public service agencies of the community. Yet few sociological investigations have been conducted of suicide prevention agencies. Therefore, to obtain information on how they function, Albert R. Roberts undertook an exploratory study in 1966 of such agencies, located in urban areas. The purpose of this survey research was to learn the specific activities of the agencies that were directed at crisis intervention, the relationship of these activities to the prevention of suicide, how the emergency telephone service operated, what initial procedures were used in crisis intervention, the publicity methods, the types of resources to which clients were referred, and the strengths and weaknesses of each agency's services.

Constructing the Sample

In each of the 212 Standard Metropolitan Statistical Areas of the United States, the telephone information operator was asked to check the local directory for suicide prevention organizations. A questionnaire of twenty-two items was then mailed to the thirty-one organizations identified. A few suicide prevention agencies may have been missed; a directory of suicide prevention centers in the United States, published in March, 1969[84] lists thirty-three such centers in operation in 1966. Nevertheless, the sample was constructed in such a way that it constitutes a substantial crosscut of the agencies in the United States which were providing emergency suicide prevention services in 1966.

Two months after the initial mailing to the thirty-one agencies, the post office had returned only three questionnaires because the addresses of the agencies were unknown. By then, replies had been received from seventeen of the remaining twenty-eight agencies; (these 28 constituted the study sample). A follow-up letter and another copy of the questionnaire were sent to the other eleven agencies. By two months after this second mailing, replies had been received from seven more suicide prevention organizations. Thus, replies were eventually received from twenty-four of the twenty-eight agencies (86 percent) in the sample. All twenty-four replies indicated that the purpose of the agency was emergency suicide prevention.

Methods

Since most of the questions in the questionnaire were of the checklist type, they could be handled quantitatively. In a few open-ended questions, however, the respondents were asked to give their opinions, for example, of the initial procedures their agencies used in helping an emergency patient. Replies to such questions required analysis to delineate the similarities and differences in the various agencies' programs.

In addition, in-depth interviews were conducted with personnel on the staff of the two suicide prevention agencies located in the New York metropolitan area (Harry M. Warren, Jr. President of the National Save-A-Life League in Manhattan, and a number of resident physicians of the Suicide Prevention Service of Kings County Hospital in Brooklyn).

When the replies to the questionnaires and the information obtained in the interviews were received, certain key characteristics of the suicide prevention agencies were apparent which became the primary categories for the analysis—the emergency telephone service, the initial procedures used in crisis intervention, ways through which callers were referred to the agencies, publicity methods used, the resources to which patients were referred, and the agencies' self-evaluation of the strengths and weaknesses of their services.

Organizational Structure

The organizational structure of the suicide prevention agencies consists of the board of directors, the advisory board, and the director-coordinator. The directorate body of each agency usually plans and directs the activities of the agency. This body is assisted by professional consultants and a community advisory board. The coordinator of the agency is usually the executive director and has a seat on the board of directors. When it is necessary, the director-coordinator assists the prevention workers and volunteers in solving any problem they encounter. The director-coordinator also is the chief administrator of the prevention activities of the agency.

THE BOARD OF DIRECTORS: The overwhelming majority of the agencies studied answered *yes* to question 13, "Do you have a Board of Directors?" Three of the agencies answered *no*, because they are managed by the County Department of Health or Mental Health Association. The board of directors is ultimately responsible for achieving the following aims: securing financial funds for the agency; applying for and receiving county, state, and federal grants; and planning the budget of the agency. The members of the board at the National Save-A-Life League in New York are ministers, psychiatrists, and legal counselors.

THE ADVISORY BOARD: Seven of the agencies indicated that they did not have an advisory board for the following reasons: they are in the process of reorganizing; the board of directors acts as an advisory board; or, no reason given. The advisory board consists of persons specially chosen because of their position in the health and welfare network of the community. The advisory board includes any combination of the following health and welfare officials:

> Psychiatrist
> Psychiatric Social Worker
> Clinical Psychologist
> Research Sociologist
> County Medical Examiner
> Director of County Health Department
> Hospital Administrator
> Police Chief
> Sheriff
> Director of County Welfare Department
> Director of Family Service Agency
> Director of Vocational Rehabilitation Center
> Representatives of the Clergy

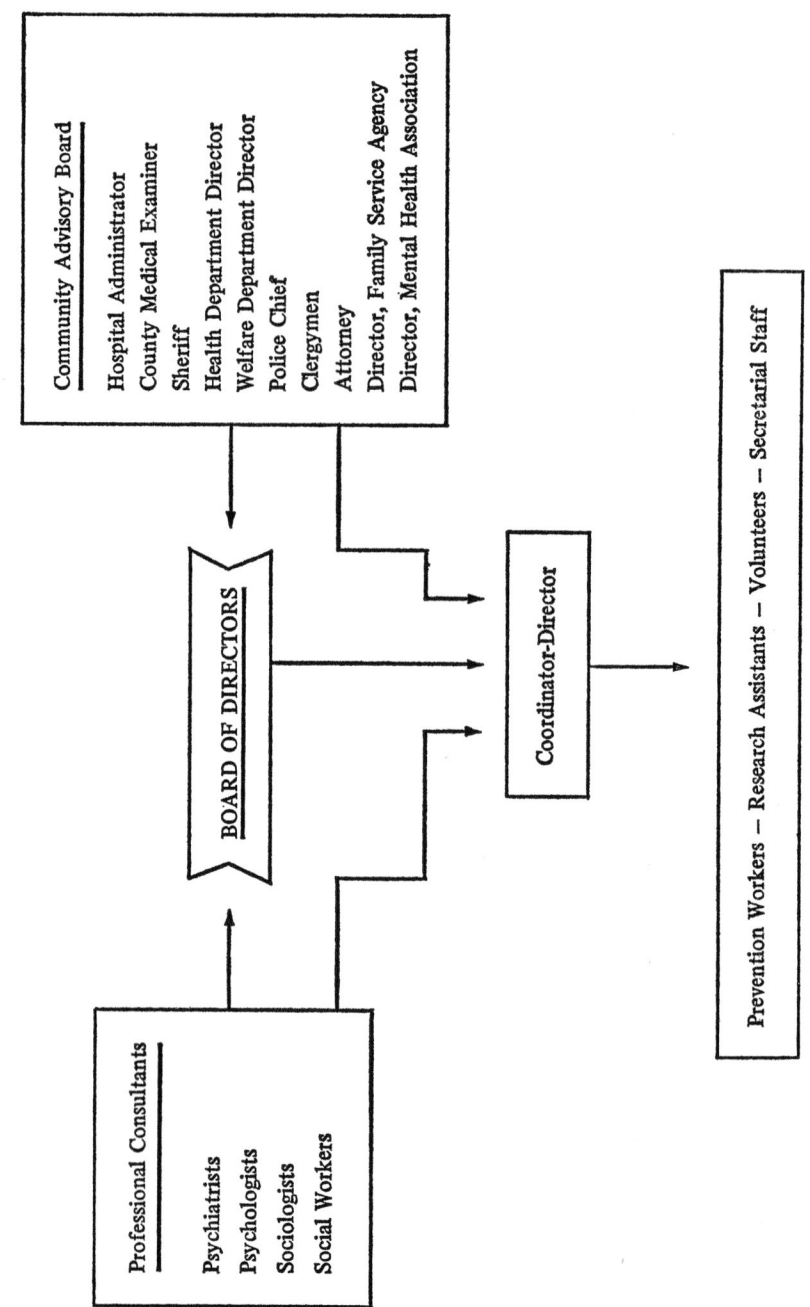

DIRECTOR-COORDINATOR: The coordinator gives most of the administrative guidance for the suicide prevention agency programs. These director-coordinators have varied backgrounds: seven are psychiatrists, five are social workers, five are clergymen, four are clinical psychologists, and three are lay personnel directors with a background in community service work. The agencies with a psychiatrist as a coordinator are usually backed by a long list of psychiatric consultants. The agencies with a social worker as coordinator had a greater number of referrals to social workers and public health nurses. But as a whole, all the agencies had ready access to hospital beds and extensive medical services.

LACK OF BUREAUCRATIC STRUCTURE: The internal strife and hostility, often found in a bureaucracy, are not typical of suicide prevention agencies. This may be partly the result of the lack of well-developed hierarchical organization and the non-salaried nature of the personnel of these agencies. Although there are a large number of specialists working for the agencies, they are not placed in a hierarchical order. There is no detailed delegation of authority through long chains of command. The members of the advisory board, along with the prevention workers, interact in a close network of mutual cooperation and have the goal of helping people, that is, of saving lives and of assisting them in adjusting to, and coping with life; this further supports the above point.

Functions of Suicide Prevention Agencies

All of the agencies maintain a 24 hour telephone service. This service provides a lifeline to help the crisis caller release severe stress. When the prevention worker at an agency answers the cry for help, his primary duty is to initiate crisis intervention services. In essence, crisis intervention service includes making an evaluation of the lethality of the case and developing a plan of action which mobilizes the individual to some responsible self-help activity. In most instances, the caller with suicide risk is encouraged to meet the prevention worker for an interview at the agency, in a local hospital, or in the caller's home.

The most frequent outcome of cases is that they are transferred to one of the other agencies in the community. The pre-

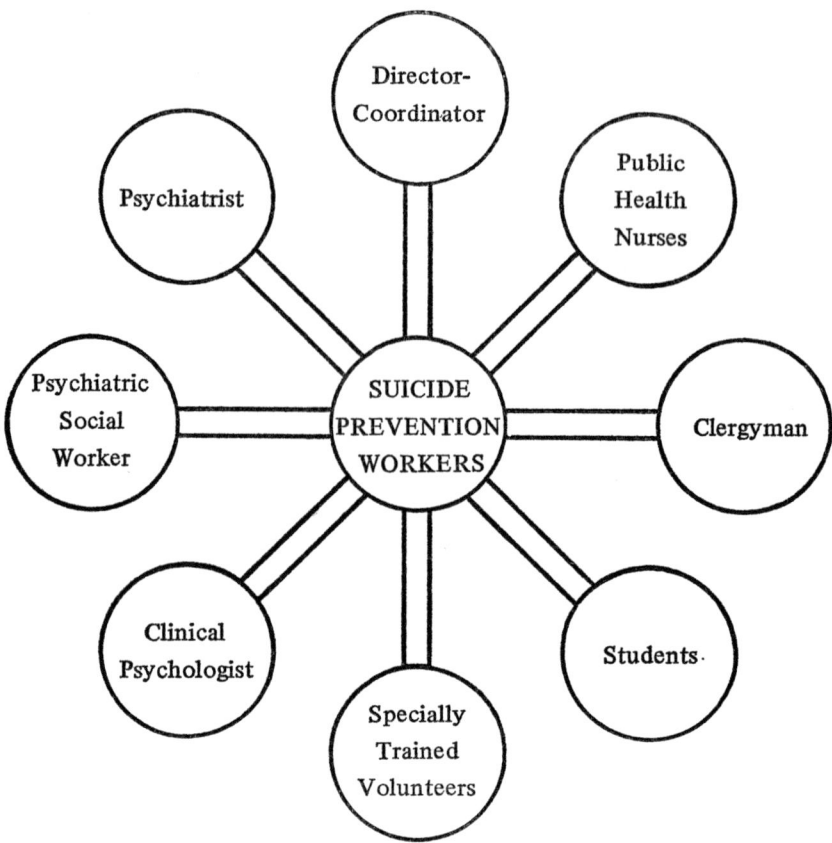

vention workers do not continue on long-term counseling relationships with any of the callers. Immediate referral or eventual transfer to general hospitals, social casework agencies, psychiatrists and out-patient clinics, or other professional services is accomplished in more than 50 percent of the agency's contacts. The suicide prevention agencies have found every agency in the community ready and willing to accept callers referred by the the prevention workers. The Suicide Prevention Service in Orlando, Florida, operates with the philosophy that once the telephone is answered the agency has assumed the responsibility for the case; it cannot be handled by mere referral but must be followed until complete transfer of responsibility has been accomplished by some other agency assuming the responsibility. The prevention worker makes several follow-up calls to the caller until it is ascertained that he has made effective contact elsewhere. The agencies also refer callers to non-professional resources such as the caller's family, friends, doctors, or police. The ultimate goal of all the agencies and services is to strive to relieve stress and help the crisis caller to adjust and cope with his situation.

EMERGENCY TELEPHONE SERVICE: All the agencies studied had 24 hour hour emergency telephone service 7 days a week to provide help quickly to persons at risk of suicide. The service was listed in the telephone book and with the police. Specially trained personnel handled all telephoned requests for help in which suicide was a danger, often backed by professional consultants—psychiatrists, physicians, psychologists, psychiatric social workers, public health nurses, and sociologists. A person calling in a crisis was never told: "It is now 5 o'clock, so will you call back tomorrow?" In contrast to some mental health associations, at least one trained suicide prevention worker was on duty at all times.

Although more than half of the agencies reported they had no written plan for handling callers at risk of suicide, their workers did have operational principles to guide them. In responding to a caller in a crisis, the worker sought to show patience and to provide a sympathetic ear. While none of the agencies followed exactly the same procedures in their initial contacts with a suicidal person, all of the replies indicated that the worker tried to abate the caller's stress and help him cope with the crisis.

Concerning the daily distribution of total calls received by the agencies, Tuesday, Wednesday, and Thursday had an equally low pattern of calls. Monday and Sunday, in that order, appeared to be the busiest. The statistics in Figure 2-1 have some limitations as indicators of days when suicide is most likely to be contemplated because six of the twenty-four agencies did not have a record of the busiest day, and eight of the agencies reported two or three days as equally the busiest. Other variables were also introduced. For example, the Suicide Prevention agency in St. Louis publicizes their agency's service in the weekend edition of the local newspaper. This probably increases the number of Sunday and Monday calls.

Despite these limitations, this study concurs with a seven-year study by Rescue, Inc., of Boston, which substantiates the findings of this study, that Monday is the busiest day for suicide calls. Rescue, Inc., reported, however, that no clear-cut explanation for "Blue Monday" had emerged. The reasons these days are the busiest days for suicide calls may result from the following: on Monday most people return to work, usually after a week-end of leisure, to begin a week of the same boring routine, sometimes resulting in "Monday blues."

Durkheim contended that an individual's social isolation accompanied by his or her feeling of aloneness, was a condition affecting the occurrence of suicide.[85] On Sunday a depressed individual may be alone because this is a day which most families spend together, and the lonely divorcee, widow, or widower may feel the desolation of no longer having a family. Even the parents of married children may not have them around, and unmarried

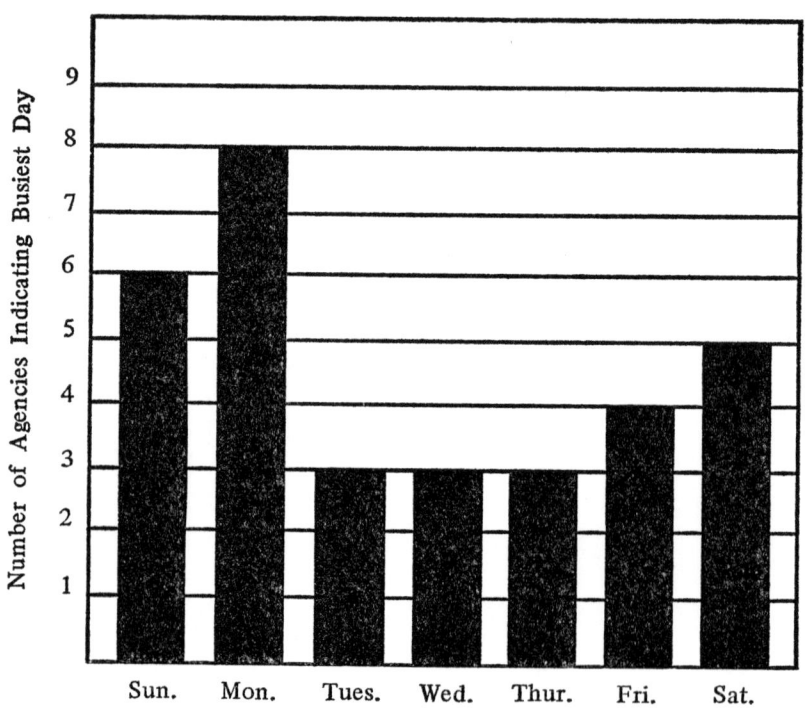

children may be living away from home, and so forth. Being alone, such people have too much time to think about their loneliness and depression, and, as a result they entertain the thought of suicide.

INITIAL INTERVENTION IN A CRISIS: When a worker at one of the agencies studied responded to a cry for help, his primary duty was to initiate crisis intervention services. The first step was to establish rapport with the person at risk and to communicate to him the worker's willingness to help. Listening to the client in a concerned and hopeful way, the worker would indicate that the person had done the right thing in calling. The caller was given an opportunity to relieve his stress by talking out his problem. An informal, personal, and noninstitutionalized interaction was sought.

As the worker listened to the client, he evaluated his suicidal potential. If the caller had the means for suicide, for example, a lethal weapon or a specific plan, then he would be evaluated at high risk. On the other hand, a caller would be evaluated as only lightly suicidal if he talked about ending his life but had not as yet planned the specific details.

The evaluation completed, the worker decided on an appropriate course of action for helping the caller to help himself. In general, this course of action should help the caller understand his own needs better and how he might meet them. The worker tried to help the caller mobilize his individual capacities. When necessary, however, the client was also shown how to call upon appropriate resources in the community in order to achieve a better adjustment between himself and his total environment.

The specific initial procedures that suicide prevention agencies take to prevent a crisis caller from committing suicide were indicated in the response of the agencies to a request on the twenty-two item questionnaire to "briefly explain the initial procedures used in helping to prevent the emergency caller from committing suicide." Sixteen agencies responded to this request and listed their initial procedures (see box). Every step was not noted by all sixteen agencies, but a general pattern emerges, namely, establishment of rapport, evaluation of the caller's suicidal potential, and deciding on the course of action to be taken.

Initial Procedures Used in Preventing the Caller from Committing Suicide

Suicide Prevention Center, Los Angeles, Calif.
1. Establish contact and rapport.
2. Evaluate lethality by talking to patient about suicide (plan, specificity of time and method, prior attempts, etc.) and evaluating resources (intrapsychic and interpersonal).
3. Involve significant others.

Fulton-DeKalb Suicide Prevention Center, Atlanta, Ga.
Establishment of rapport, encouragement to discuss and delineate the precipitating events, urging to participate with the worker in finding alternatives, referring to treatment resources if available.

We Care, Inc., Orlando, Fla.
Crisis intervention worker tries to draw out the caller, to find out his problem; reassures caller that we do want to help, feel that we can if caller will tell worker what is bothering him; if caller is determined to go ahead with suicide, regardless of our help, we dispatch police or sheriff's department to intervene, take gun, etc., then we follow up.

Citizens for Mental Health, Buffalo, N.Y.
The caller is evaluated as to the seriousness or emergency nature. Depending on this, the caller would be:
1. Counseled over phone
2. Visited in person
3. Taken by police or rescue squad to hospital
4. Referred to clinic, hospital, social service agency, or clergyman.

Wyandotte County Guidance Center, Inc., Kansas City, Kans.
A quick assessment of the suicidal potentiality is the first approach to every call. What action is to be taken depends on the seriousness of the situation.

Emergency Mental Health Service, Phoenix, Ariz.
Keep them on the line and keep them involved. Find out if friends or relatives are close by. If no one is there, notify police, who will make a check. They (the police) are much more mobile than any other group or organization.

Santa Clara County Suicide Prevention Center, San Jose, Calif.
Obtain information, assess and evaluate information, and propose action.

Suicide Prevention Center, San Francisco, Calif.
Ours is a telephone "first aid" service for suicidal people. In emergency situations, our staff calls the necessary emergency facilities in the community to give the caller immediate aid. In all cases we win the caller's confidence in order to make the most appropriate referral for his particular problem.

Contra Costa County Suicide Prevention Center, Walnut Creek, Calif.
We ask, "May I help you?" and then play it by ear. Each caller responds somewhat differently depending on many variables.

Suicide Prevention Service, Eau Claire, Wis.
Personal attention, psychotherapeutically oriented.

Suicide Prevention, Inc., St. Louis, Mo.
Sympathy, attempt to understand, evaluation of risks, referral to appropriate resources, follow up to see they enter treatment.

Suicide Prevention Center, Denver, Colo.
When a call comes, we attempt to program a plan of action, whether it is to see the person in our program or to call on some other agency.

Mental Health Center, Suicide Prevention Service, Pasadena, Calif.
Name, telephone number. How do you plan to kill yourself? Why do you want to kill yourself? How will that help? Have you thought of something else to solve your problem other than killing yourself—death is forever.

Friends Organization, Miami, Fla.
We provide sympathetic listening, then evaluate the seriousness of the caller, and direct the caller to an agency or person where he can be helped.

National Save-A-Life League, New York, N.Y.
Your wish to help them; willingness to make possible contacts with relatives, friends, etc.; supportive help of all kinds; pastoral counseling, psychiatric, etc.

Suicide Prevention of Tarrant County, Fort Worth, Tex.
The question "Can I help you?" first; one requirement for prevention worker is a warm friendly voice; by skillful questioning and listening in particular, stress is reduced. If suicide is in progress—poison taken, etc.—trained police are called.

The pattern of initial procedures reflected in the agencies' responses will probably continue, but certain modifications of the pattern will undoubtedly result when appropriate research has been carried out.

SOURCE OF REFERRALS USED TO CONTACT THE AGENCY: Who calls the agency concerning a potential suicide? Usually the person committing the act, or some close friend or relative who interacts with the caller in a primary relationship. These relatives and friends may be emotionally involved, but feel that a professional suicide prevention agency may be more qualified to help the caller. This may well be, or it may not be so—depending upon the nature of the intimacy and personal involvement in this primary relationship.

The source of referrals used to contact the agencies as reported in the study indicated that the overwhelming majority of referrals to the agency were made in the following order: the source of the most referrals was self-referrals, and referrals from concerned relatives and friends. The rest of the contacts are referred by a great many sources such as: professionals in the clergy, education, medicine, mental health, psychiatry, law enforcement, social work, and pharmacy. These referral sources from individuals interacting in a secondary relationship with the caller were very few in number.

MOST REFERRALS

Self-referrals ⟶ Primary
Relatives and friends ⟶

Police and fire
Social agencies
Physicians and psychiatrists in private practice
Hospitals
Clergy
Schools
Pharmacist

LEAST REFERRALS

RESOURCES TO WHICH REFERRALS WERE SENT: The resources to which referrals were sent are indicated in Table 2-IV. Often, a combination of these was used to deal with a situation. The types of referrals indicated by the completed questionnaires reflected inter-agency community cooperation with the suicide prevention agencies.

When a person calls a suicide prevention agency, he is usually referred to a professional therapeutic service, such as a psychiatric clinic. Sometimes, it is recommended that he come in contact with non-professionals, such as a particular member of the family.

Professional Sources to Which Referrals Were Sent

GENERAL HOSPITALS: All but three of the agencies had a good working relationship with a local hospital. The hospitals provide ready access to emergency treatment for callers referred to them by the suicide prevention agency. Some hospitals, such as Los Angeles County General Hospital, and Jackson Memorial Hospital (Miami, Florida) cooperate with the suicide prevention agency to such an extent that they provide medical care, ready access to hospital beds, and ambulance service to bring in patients who are in very serious condition.

PSYCHIATRISTS IN PRIVATE PRACTICE OR OUT-PATIENT CLINIC: Often, calls will be received from people who are looking for

TABLE 2-IV
RESOURCES TO WHICH REFERRALS ARE SENT

1. *Professional Services:*
    A. General Hospitals;
    B. Psychiatrists in Private Practice or Out-Patient Clinic;
    C. Social Service Agencies (Family service agencies, marital counseling agencies, county health and welfare departments, mental health clinic, Alcoholics Anonymous, alcoholic rehabilitation clinic, half-way house for drug addicts, home for transients, Salvation Army, Travelers Aid Society, Vocational Rehabilitation Center, Guidance clinic, Veterans' Administration);
    D. Clergy;
    E. Physicians.
2. *Non-Professional Services:*
    A. Police
    B. Family
    C. Friends

psychiatric treatment. The person can be referred to a private therapist, if the worker is familiar with any, or the caller can be asked to call the suicide prevention agency during the next regular office hours (9 a.m. - 5 p.m.) for a referral. The Suicide Prevention Center in St. Louis Missouri, has a list of thirty-one psychiatrists and physicians who have agreed to see the agency's referrals on a next day basis.

SOCIAL WORK AGENCIES: In those cases, where the suicide danger is not high, or perhaps not even the primary problem, and the underlying problem is marital discord, family conflict, or chronic personal and social maladjustment, a referral to a family service agency or a psychiatric clinic is considered. The Suicide Prevention Council at Ancora State Hospital in Ancora, New Jersey, refers callers with marital problems to the local Marital Counseling Agency. Callers recognized by the agency as alcoholics, drug addicts, mental patients or unwed mothers, are often referred to an alcoholics anonymous group, a half-way house, a psychiatric hospital, or a home for unwed mothers. President Harry M. Warren Jr. of the National Save-A-Life League in New York states that the League refers mentally ill or psychotic callers to Bellevue Hospital. "It might be necessary to have family or friend take the emergency caller to Bellevue Hospital, if the patient himself is incapable of getting there." The Suicide Prevention Center in Fort Worth, Texas, refers unwed mothers to a special home which provides care for unwed mothers.

CLERGY: If the caller is close to a church, the prevention worker answering the emergency telephone can encourage him to discuss his situation with a minister, priest, or rabbi. The Suicide Prevention Service of Dayton, Ohio, provides pastoral counseling. This service refers the caller to the appropriate church or synagogue wherein continued counseling can take place.

PHYSICIANS: People often turn to their family doctor for help, and physicians can be very supportive and helpful authority figures. The patient usually has a good relationship with his doctor and should be encouraged to discuss his problems with him. However, some physicians are strictly business, and are unwilling to give personal attention to their patients in the form of emotional and supportive guidance.

Non-Professional Sources to Which Referrals Are Sent

POLICE: Police are utilized in cases of clear and immediate emergency, for example, if a suicide attempt is about to occur or has occurred. When the caller needs prompt medical attention, the police or someone else capable of taking the responsibility of bringing the caller to the hospital will need to be involved. In general, the police are used if the caller is helpless and hurt. We Care, Inc., the suicide prevention agency in Orlando, Florida, will dispatch police or sheriff's department to intervene and take the gun or other weapon when the caller is determined to go ahead with suicide.

FAMILY: The family is neglected by many agencies as a resource, but the Los Angeles Suicide Prevention Center indicates that the family is most valuable in times of crisis. This agency encourages the caller to discuss his situation and problems with his family. Also, the agency saw to it that families of callers were involved in accepting responsibilities for emergencies, and seeing to it that the caller received the help which the agency recommended.

FRIENDS: Close friends are often used the way families are, as described above. In addition, the caller is encouraged to have a friend stay with him during a particularly bad night. Also, the caller usually talks things over with a close friend.

PUBLICITY METHODS: The primary goal of suicide prevention agencies is to save lives. To achieve this general aim, the agencies must inform the public of the emergency services they offer through public education activities. They also must publicize the significant work of the suicide prevention agency. This goal of agency work is to transform public apathy into acceptance and active support. The agencies try to awaken every member of society to his potential role in preventing suicide. For example, Rescue Inc., the suicide prevention agency of the greater Boston area, publicizes its 24-hour-a-day service through daily broadcasts on 20 different radio stations. The emergency number is also listed on the first page of every Boston telephone directory along with police, fire, and other emergency numbers. The President of Rescue Inc., Kenneth B. Murphy, has indicated that the number of callers has increased considerably from a few hundred during its first year of operation in 1959, to over 3,000 callers in 1970. He feels that a major reason for the increased number of callers is the effective publicity of the daily radio broadcasts.

Each agency uses several methods to publicize its suicide prevention activities. Most agencies publicize through the mass media—newspaper, radio, and television (public service announcements). But many agencies do not take full advantage of the other available methods, which are enumerated in the comprehensive list shown in Table 2-V.

The Suicide Prevention Center in Denver, Colorado, advertises its service in the church page of the *Rocky Mountain News* and the *Denver Post* every Saturday. The Director of this agency points to Saturday and Sunday as the busiest days of the week

TABLE 2-V
TYPES OF PUBLICITY MEDIA BY AGENCY USE

Types of Publicity Media:	Number of Agencies Using each Media; in order of Prevalence
1. Newspapers and magazines	18
2. Television and Radio (public service announcements)	14
3. Talks and speeches by staff to civic groups and students	8
4. Telephone book (yellow pages)	5
5. Booklets and professional publications	3
6. Training seminars with professionals in all related fields (clergy, social science, law enforcement, medicine, etc.)	4
7. Information cards circulated to the public	2
8. Church bulletins and newsletters	2
9. Common knowledge and general information	2
10. Letters circulated to community agencies	2
11. Police by speaking engagements	1
12. Social service and religious organizations	1
13. Film specials	1
14. American Medical Association	1
15. Placards in buses	1

for emergency callers because of the effective publicity of their newspaper advertisements on Saturdays. The staff of the Suicide Prevention Agency in Kansas City publicizes through speaking engagements made to civic and student groups. The Crisis Clinic in Seattle, Washington, broadcasts spot announcements on local radio stations: "Suicide is not the answer, call EA 5-5550 when you need one. Help is available 24 hours a day." The Suicide Prevention Agency in Buffalo, New York has a weekly television and radio show on which Joseph A. Vetter, the Director of the agency, interviews people who have attempted suicide in the past, and are presently leading successful and contented lives. The people interviewed usually have made not only a satisfactory adjustment to life, but have also become community leaders in a number of instances. This agency distributed over 100,000 pieces of literature to the public in 1967 on the emergency services it provides. Mr. Vetter believes that the publicity the agency has received from radio, television, newspapers, and brochures and pamphlets has resulted in the agency receiving over 11,000 emergency calls annually. The Buffalo agency receives its financial support through voluntary donations from physicians, social service, church and business groups. Funds are solicited through mail appeals. The Contra Costa County Suicide Prevention Center in California, and the Suicide Prevention Center of Tarrant County in Fort Worth, Texas publicize their services by circulating information cards throughout their respective counties. The Community Mental Health Center in Washington, D.C. publicizes its service by circulating small informative pamphlets throughout the Washington, D.C. area. These pamphlets state that: "If help is needed for yourself or others for pressing emotional problems such as—suicidal feelings, depression, tension, loneliness, feelings of hopelessness and helplessness, feelings of confusion, sexual problems, family crisis (e.g. divorce, or loss of a loved one), or if you do not know where to turn for emotional help, a staff of trained people will help you; call anytime—day, night, or weekend, open twenty-four hours every day."

Public education and a greater dissemination of information about suicide and the availability of suicide prevention services is essential in the prevention of suicide. The agencies' efforts to give effective suicide prevention treatment are often counteracted by prejudice, the stigma that mental illness is disgraceful. People often feel that those who commit suicide are weak, worthless people. To achieve their aims, these agencies should utilize every means of publicity enumerated in Table 2-V, to inform people about the danger signals of suicide and the emergency services available for preventing suicide. As mentioned earlier, the suicide prevention agencies do use some forms of mass media to publicize their service, but an all-out effort is needed whereby each agency will use more of the modern promotional techniques of publicity. For example, a full-scale publicity program should include: radio and television broadcasts every hour on a number of different stations; newspaper advertisements on the emergency suicide prevention service available; newspaper and magazine editorials on the life saving work of the agency; speeches by the staff of the agencies to civic and social groups; and film specials and plays on suicide prevention.

Films and plays on suicide prevention are beginning to provide a viable means for informing practitioners and community members of the clues of suicide and the best ways to help the person through their crisis. One excellent film is entitled, "Suicide Prevention: The Physician's Role."* This film was produced to assist doctors in recognizing and dealing with suicidal tendencies in their despondent patients. It was produced by Newton E. Meltzer with the cooperation of the Los Angeles Suicide Prevention Center. A reading copy of the script and discussion guide for "Quiet Cries," a play on suicide and its prevention is available upon request to the Center for Studies of Suicide Prevention.† This play is about three individuals experiencing suicidal crises: a widower who has turned to drink, a desperate woman recently separated from her husband, and an adolescent in a sexual identity crisis. The three characters each have an Alter Ego, a technique which allows the audience to view the ambiv-

---

* This 20 minute 16-mm. film is available from Hoffmann-LaRoche Inc., at Nutley, New Jersey or Visual Projects Ltd., 67 Yale Street, Roslyn Heights, New York.
† Send requests to: Center for Studies of Suicide Prevention, Information Services, National Institute of Mental Health, Chevy Chase, Maryland 20015.

alent feelings which often precede suicide attempts. The discussion guide will help a group leader to stimulate an exchange of ideas about suicide prevention, particularly the suicide clues exhibited by the three characters.

The problem remains that to have increased publicity, each agency will not only need more financial support, but more essential is the need for research on the effect of increased publicity on the suicide rate. Follow-up studies must determine whether people who commit suicide ever contact suicide prevention agencies. In any case, people must be made aware of the activities of these agencies, if they are going to use their facilities and services in a time of emergency.

CONCLUSION

In general, suicide prevention and other crisis intervention services have the potential for serving the unmet mental health needs of people who are overwhelmed by multiple crises. These mental health services are flexible and cooperative; they have developed workable and humane techniques for handling crises in the lives of people with suicidal risk. Their services are available to everyone who seeks them.

A large number of the agencies in Roberts' study reported their strongest feature as the consistent round-the-clock service and immediate attention available for anyone who calls. For instance, the Crisis Clinic in Seattle, Washington, stated that they provide "instant concern" to all callers, twenty-four hours a day. Suicide Prevention, Inc., of St. Louis, Missouri, reports that the strongest feature of its agency is the professional Board of Directors and the support of local medical groups and facilities. The Suicide Prevention Center of Los Angeles, places emphasis on both research and training, which continually augment each other.

In contrast, the agencies saw their greatest problem as the need to expand existing programs. Eight agencies saw their major problem as the need for gaining the community's support; to do this a strong publicity program was seen as essential. For example, the Suicide Prevention Agency (SPA) in Dade County, Florida felt that it needed increased financial backing to enlarge its professional staff. The S.P.A. in Phoenix, Arizona, stated that full-time psychiatric services were needed for physicians to make suicide evaluations at city jails and hospitals. The strong desire on the part of the agencies for an extensive public education program can be explained as follows: First, the public must be informed of the agency's existence. Second, the public must be made aware of the significance of the vital work suicide prevention agencies can perform for the community. The study indicated other weaknesses of present suicide prevention programs which increased financial backing could help overcome. If more money was made available to specific suicide prevention agencies, the following changes would be made: 1) The S.P.A. in Atlanta would add clerical staff and research aids, and implement an expanded public information and training program. 2) The Community Mental Health Center in Washington, D.C. would enlarge its visiting psychiatric nurse team to make home visits to distressed people in all areas of the city. 3) The S.P.A. in San Francisco would expand and deepen its research program to improve the techniques used in dealing with crisis callers.

An annual total of 41,020 calls for help were handled by the agencies in Roberts' study. The number of "cries for help" received by these agencies indicates the urgent need for specialized crisis intervention facilities aimed at preventing suicide. But not every caller is a potential suicide victim. For example, a center in Buffalo reported that approximately 50 percent of its calls were from persons seeking information only, while the other 50 percent were from persons assessed to have suicide risk and serious emotional problems requiring immediate attention. The Suicide Prevention Center in Eau Claire, Wisconsin reported that approximately 50 percent of the calls they received came from persons seeking information, were prank calls, or were from callers who hung up. The Contra Costa County Suicide Prevention Service in Walnut Creek, California reported that 40 percent of their callers were non-suicidal and had alcoholic, marital, and other problems. This agency usually referred alcoholics to an Alcoholics Anonymous group or to an alcoholic rehabilitation clinic and referred persons with marital difficulties to a marital or family counseling agency. In a different study of suicide prevention centers in several cities, James Wilkens indicated that 60 percent of the total calls received were directly related to suicide risk.[86]

If, however, even half of the 41,020 calls reported in Roberts' study are considered to represent suicide risks, the importance of these emergency crisis intervention services are still vital, because they are concerned with saving the lives of a large number of people on the brink of self-destruction.[87] Anyone who places a value on human life can see that crisis intervention services are needed when people threaten or attempt to take their own lives.

Roberts' study was the first comprehensive organizational study on the suicide prevention movement. Since the completion of this study, there has been a tremendous growth of suicide prevention and crisis intervention services. The number of such agencies grew to nearly 200 between 1968 and 1972 because of the following two factors: 1) the growing number of crisis callers to existing hotlines; and 2) the Center for Studies of Suicide Prevention's (funding source for hotlines seeking N.I.M.H. support) expanded definition of crisis intervention services to include individuals on the verge of suicide as well as youths with drug-related or alcohol problems. Sheila A. Fisher's doctoral dissertation collected data on 192 suicide prevention and crisis intervention services. Of the 192 agencies studied, she tabulated data on 142 suicide prevention or crisis services for people of all age groups, and 50 hotlines which provided crisis intervention for youths (usually in the 10 to 25 year old range).

Recent estimates by experts in the mental health field suggest that there are now between 650 and 700 hotline services throughout the United States. These telephone services for people in crisis are designed to provide short term intervention and referral to appropriate community resources. As of 1974 (when this chapter was written) there had not been any research projects of a national scope which surveyed or evaluated the services provided by crisis intervention hotlines.

Since the research to date has provided only limited evidence that suicide prevention programs actually prevent suicide, the programs of all suicide prevention and crisis intervention agencies must be evaluated to determine the effectiveness of their goals and methods.

SUGGESTIONS FOR FURTHER RESEARCH

Follow-up studies at each suicide prevention agency should
ine:
in better results as initial prevention work-
ntion agencies—specially trained profes-
d lay volunteers.

..₀ᵣ the emergency callers followed the suicide prevention agency's advice and went to the hospital, alcoholics anonymous meetings, a psychiatrist, a vocational rehabilitation center, a home for unwed mothers, or not.

(3) Whether the emergency callers eventually committed suicide or made a satisfactory adjustment to life, two or three years later.

Each agency should plan the following:

(1) An all-out publicity campaign by television, radio, periodicals, newspapers and magazines, and public notices on suicide prevention. What would be the effect on the number of calls to the suicide prevention agency? What would happen to the suicide rate?

(2) Investigations on how stigmatization and prejudice towards suicidal persons can be removed. These popular prejudices weaken the efforts of crisis intervention workers to reach the general public and therefore hinder them from effectively achieving their goal of saving lives.

(3) Research to determine common socio-psychological characteristics of persons who have made previous suicide attempts or who have been considered as high suicide risks by the suicide prevention agency. These investigations should be designed to enhance the family physicians and suicide prevention agencies' ability to identify those persons who are serious suicidal risks in order that more extensive attention may be given them.

(4) Investigations on identifying the areas from which suicide callers come. Over a period of time, this technique should reveal the existence of "high suicide" neighborhoods, just as one finds areas of high delinquency and high crime rates. Then examinations of the characteristics of the "high suicide" neighborhoods

may provide a valuable insight into some of the general environmental, as well as social, correlates of suicide.

Life insurance and accident insurance companies should grant large sums of money for long-range research programs on suicide prevention. Federal and local mental health organizations throughout the world could greatly aid suicide prevention agencies by giving more financial aid to help support these agencies' vital work of removing suicide from the list of major causes of death.

The increasing development and strong reinforcement of present research and action programs on suicide and suicide prevention is an excellent first step into the larger field of sound public health, in an increasingly complex and anomic society.

REFERENCES

1. *Statistical Bulletin,* New York: Metropolitan Life Insurance Company, May, 1970, Vol. 51, pp. 10-11; *Demographic Yearbook, 1970,* New York: United Nations, 1971.
2. Shneidman, Edwin S.: Suicide prevention and the nation: a new program, Washington, D.C. Center for Studies of Suicide Prevention, National Institute of Mental Health, mimeographed, no date indicated.
3. *Ibid.,* p. 1
4. Resnik, H. L. P.: Suicides and aging. *J. Am. Geriatr. Soc., 18*: 154, 1970.
5. Flint, Jerry M.: Suicides by young reported on rise. *The New York Times. 4:* 12, 1972.
6. Farber, M. L.: Suicide and the Welfare State. *Men. Hygiene, 49*: 371-373, 1965.
7. Farrar, C.: Suicide. *J. Clin. Expe. Psychopathol. 12*: 79-88, 1951.
8. Felix, Robert H.: Suicide: A Neglected Problem. *J. Public Health, 55*: 16-17, 1965.
9. Litman, Robert E., and Tabachnick, Norman: Fatal one car accidents. *36*: 248-259, 1967, and Cutter, Fred: Suicide: the wish, the act, and the outcome. *Life-threatening Behavior. 1*: 125-137, 1971.
10. Cutter, Fred: *op. cit.* p. 127; and Pokorney, A. D. A follow-up study of 618 suicidal patients. *Am. J. of Psychiatry, 122*: 1109-1116, 1966.
11. Durkheim, Emile: *Suicide.* Translated by Spaulding, John R., and Simpson, George. Glencoe, The Free Press, 1951; original publication, *Le Suicide.* 1897.
12. Similar statements have been made by Sainsbury, Gibbs, Martin, and Johnson. See Sainsbury, Peter. *Suicide in London: An Ecological Study.* London, Chapman and Hall, 1955, p. 22; Gibbs, Jack P. Suicide.

In Merton, R. K., and Nisbet, R. *Contemporary Social Problems,* 3rd ed. New York, Harcourt-Brace, and Jovanovich, 1971, p. 305; Martin, Walter T.: Theories of variation in the suicide rate. In Gibbs, J. P.: *Suicide.* New York, Harper & Row, 1968, pp. 74-96; and Johnson, Barclay D.: Durkheim's one cause of suicide. *Am. Sociol. Rev. 30*: 875-886, 1965. For a statement in defense of Durkheim (i.e. Durkheim's concepts can be distinguished) see: Dohrenwend, Bruce P.: Egoism, altruism, anomie, and fatalism: a conceptual analysis of Durkheim's types. *Am. Sociol. Rev. 24*: 466-473, 1959.
13. Durkheim, Emile: *Suicide. op. cit.* p. 209.
14. Gibbs, Jack P.: Suicide, in *Contemporary Social Problems. op. cit.* p. 306.
15. Douglas, Jack D.: *The Social Meanings of Suicide.* Princeton, Princeton University Press, 1967, p. 203.
16. Sainsbury, Peter: *Suicide in London. op. cit.;* and Stengel, Erwin: *Suicide and Attempted Suicide.* Middlesex, England, Penguin Books, 1964; and Dublin, Louis I.: *Suicide: A Sociological and Statistical Study. op. cit.*
17. Henry, Andrew F., and Short, James F., Jr.: *Suicide and Homicide: Some Economic, Sociological, and Psychological Aspects of Aggression.* Glencoe, The Free Press, 1951.
18. *Ibid.,* Chapter 7: and Henry, Andrew F., and Short, James F., Jr.: The Sociology of Suicide. In Shneidman, E. S., and Farberow, N. L. (Ed.): *Clues to Suicide.* New York, McGraw-Hill, 1957, pp. 58-69.
19. Freud, Sigmund: *Mourning and Melancholia.* In *Collected Papers, Volume IV.* London, England, Hogarth Press, 1925. Originally published in *Zeitschrift fur Psychoanalyse,* Band IV, 1917.
20. Zilboorg, Gregory: Differential diagnostic types of suicide. *Archives of Neurology and Psychiatry.* Vol. 35. January, 1936, pp. 270-291; and Zilboorg, Gregory: Suicide among civilized and primitive races. *Am. J. Psychiatry. 92*: 1347-1369, 1936.
21. Bender, L., and Schilder, P.: Suicidal preoccupation and attempts in children. *Am. J. Orthopsychiatry, 7*: 225-234, 1937.
22. Palmer, D. M.: Factors in suicide attempts: a review of 25 consecutive cases. *J. of Nerv. Men. Dis. 93*: 421-442, 1941.
23. Menninger, Karl A.: *Man Against Himself.* New York, Harcourt, Brace, 1938.
24. Hendin, Herbert: *Suicide in Scandinavia.* New York, Grune and Stratton, 1964.
25. Jackson, Don D.: Theories of suicide. In Shneidman, E. S., and Farberow, N. L.: *Clues to Suicide, op. cit.*
26. Meerloo, Joost A. M.: *Suicide and Mass Suicide.* New York, Grune and Stratton, 1962.
27. Zilboorg, Gregory: *op. cit.*

28. Shneidman, Edwin S.: Suicide: psychological aspects, *International Encyclopedia of the Social Sciences*. New York, Crowell, Collier and Macmillan, 1968, p. 389.
29. National Center for Health Statistics, *Vital Statistics of the United States*. Washington, D.C.: U. S. Government Printing Office. 1964. Annual volumes previously published as Mortality Statistics, U. S. Department of Commerce. Bureau of the Census, Washington, D.C.: U. S. Government Printing Office.
30. Hendin, Herbert: Psychiatric emergencies. In A. M. Freedman, and H. I. Kaplan (Ed.): *Comprehensive Textbook of Psychiatry*. Baltimore, Williams and Wilkins, 1967, p. 1170.
31. National Center for Health Statistics, Series 20, Number 5. *Suicide in the United States, 1950-1964*. United States Public Health Service. August, 1967.
32. *Statistical Bulletin*. Metropolitan Life Insurance Company, May, 1970, p. 10.
33. Frenay, Adolph: *The Suicide Problem in the United States*. Boston, Gorham, 1927, pp. 150-152.
34. Ogden, M., Spector, M. I., and Hill, C. A.: Suicides and homicides among indians. *Pub. Health Reports*. Vol. 85. January, 1970, pp. 75-77.
35. Suicide among the Blackfeet Indians. *Bul. Suicid.* No. 7. Fall, 1970, pp. 42-43.
36. On suicide. *Time*. November 25, 1966; and Physician suicides cause concern. *Med. World News*. June 9, 1967, p. 28.
37. Powell, Elwin H.: Occupation, status, and suicide: toward a redefinition of anomie. *Am. Soc. Rev.* 23: 137, 1958, and *The Registrar General's Decennial Supplement, England and Wales, 1951 Occupational Mortality*. Part I. London: H.M.S.O., 1954, p. 11; and Hendin, Herbert *op. cit.*
38. Gibbs, Jack P.: Suicide. In *Cont. Soc. Prob. op. cit.*, p. 294.
39. Shneidman, E. S., and Farberow, N. L.: Statistical comparisons between attempted and committed suicides. In Farberow, N. L. and Shneidman, E. S. (Ed.): *The Cry for Help*. New York, McGraw-Hill 1961, pp. 19-47.
40. Dorpat, T. L., and Boswell, J. W.: An evaluation of suicide intent in suicide attempts. *Compr. Psychiatry*, 4: 117-125, 1963.
41. Edwards, J. E., and Whitlock, F. A.: Suicide and attempted suicide in Brisbane. *Med. J. of Aust.* 1: 932-938, 989-995, 1968.
42. *Demographic Yearbook, 1967*. New York, United Nations, 1968, Table 24.
43. National Center for Health Statistics. *Vital Statistics of the United States, Volume 2*. U. S. Public Health Service. Washington, U. S. Government Printing Office, 1968.

44. Cavan, Ruth S.: *Suicide.* Chicago, University of Chicago Press, 1928, p. 320.
45. Martindale, Don: *The Nature and Types of Sociological Theory.* Boston: Houghton-Mifflin, 1960, p. 271.
46. *Ibid.,* p. 346.
47. *Ibid.,* p. 345.
48. Dublin, Louis: *Suicide: A Sociological and Statistical Study.* New York, The Ronald Press, 1963, p. 153.
49. Shneidman, Edwin S., and Farberow, Norman L.: *Some Facts about Suicide: Causes and Prevention.* Washington, D.C.: U. S. Government Printing Office, Public Health Service Publication No. 852, 1965.
50. *Ibid.,* p. 3-7.
51. Medical News, *JAMA. 194*: 25, 1965.
52. *Ibid.,* p. 25; and Ross, Mathew: The presuicidal patient: recognition and management. *South. Med. J. 60*: 1094-1098, 1967.
53. Litman, Robert E.: *J. Mich. State Med. Soc. 62*: 68-72, 1963.
54. Farberow, Norman L. (Ed.): *Bibliography on Suicide and Suicide Prevention.* Bethesda, Maryland: National Institute of Mental Health, Public Health Service Publication No. 1979, 1969.
55. Shneidman, Edwin S., and Farberow, Norman L.: Statistical camparisons between attempted and committed suicides. In Farberow, N. L., and Shneidman, E. S. (Eds.): *The Cry for Help. op. cit.* p. 20.
56. *Ibid.,* pp. 19-47.
57. Stengel, Erwin: *Suicide and Attempted Suicide.* Baltimore, Penguin Books, 1964, pp. 79-84.
58. Shneidman and Farberow. *op. cit.* p. 20.
59. *Ibid.,* p. 24.
60. *Ibid.,* pp. 45-46.
61. Mintz, Ronald S.: Prevalence of persons in the city of Los Angeles who have attempted suicide: a pilot study. *Bull. Suicidol.,* 1970, pp. 9-16.
62. Farberow, Norman L., Shneidman, Edwin S., and Leonard, Calista V.: Suicide among schizophrenic mental hospital patients. *The Cry for Help.* New York, McGraw-Hill, 1965, pp. 78-109.
63. Farberow, Norman L., Ganzler, Sidney, Cutter, Fred., and Reynolds, David: An eight-year survey of hospital suicides. *Life-threatening Behavior, 1*: 184-202, 1971, for a review af the literature which notes some of the discrepancies in the suicide rate among various groups of schizophrenics see: Warner, H.: Suicide in schizophrenia. *Dis. Ner. Sys.* 29-5: 35-40, 1968.
64. Jones, Kingsley: Suicide and the hospital service—a study of hospital records of patients who subsequently committed suicide. *Brit. J. of Psychiatry.* London, V. 37: 625-630, 1965.
65. Kahne, Merton J.: Suicide among patients in mental hospitals. *Psychiatry, 31*-1: 32-43, 1968.

66. Petrovsky, C. C.: Suicide in a general hospital. *Med. J. Aust.*, 2-15: 669-672, 1967.
67. Stone, Alan A., and Shein, Harvey M.: Psychotherapy of the hospitalized suicidal patient. *Am. J. of Psychotherapy*. 22-1: 15-25, 1968.
68. Prisoner Hangs Self. *The Baltimore Sun*. June 21, 1972, p. A2; Clerk, Held as Drunk, Hangs in Jail. *The Baltimore Sun*. July 4, 1972, p. C12.
69. Fully, G., Hivert, P. E., and Schaub, S.: Suicides en milieu carcéral: edtude de 183 cases constates en France depuis 1955. *Ann Med Leg*, 45: 108-115, 1965.
70. Rieger, W.: Suicide attempts in a Federal Prison. *Archives of General Psychiatry*, 24: 532-535, 1971.
71. Koller, K. M., and Castanos, J. N.: Parental deprivation and attempted suicide in prison populations. *Medical Journal of Australia*.
72. Rieger: *op. cit.* p. 534.
73. Tuckman, J., and Youngman, W. F.: A scale for assessing suicide risk of attempted suicides. *J. Clin. Psych.*, 24: 17-19, 1968.
74. Rieger. *op. cit.* p. 535.
75. Danto, Bruce: Suicide at the wayne county jail: 1967-1970. *Police Law Quarterly*, 1: 34-42, 1972.
76. Roberts, Albert R.: *Sourcebook on Prison Education: Past, Present, and Future*. Springfield, Thomas, 1971, p. 153; for further information on prisoner rehabilitation programs see: Albert R. Roberts (Ed.): *Readings in Prison Education*. Springfield, Thomas, 1973.
77. Danto. *op. cit.* p. 40.
78. Cain, Albert C., and Fast, Irene: The legacy of suicide: observations on the pathogenic impact of suicide upon marital partners. *Psychiatry*, 29: 406-411, 1966.
79. Cain, Albert C., and Fast, Irene: Children's disturbed reactions to parent suicide. *Am. J. Orthopsychiatry*, 36: 874-875, 1966. An earlier work points out the methodological difficulties of studying the object-loss reactions in the bereaved child: Cain, Albert C., Fast, Irene, and Erickson, Mary E.: Children's disturbed reactions to the death of a sibling. *Am. J. Orthopsychiatry*, 34: 741-752, 1964.
80. Hill, Oscar W.: The association of childhood bereavement with suicidal attempt in depressive illness. *Br. J. Psychiatry*, 115: 301-304, 1969. The following study found a significant association between the absence of either parent and a subsequent suicide attempt, especially if the absence started in the first five years of life: Greer, S., Gunn, J. C., and Koller, K. M.: Aetiological factors in attempted suicide. *Br. Med. J.*, 2: 1352-1355, 1966.
81. For further information contact Flesch, Regina F., Ph.D. Eastern Pennsylvania Psychiatric Institute. Philadelphia, Pennsylvania.
82. For further information contact Weiner, Alfred, M.D. Department of Psychiatry, Montefiore Hospital and Medical Center, Bronx, New York.

83. This section is adapted from Roberts, Albert R.: *The Structure and Function of Suicide Prevention Agencies in the U. S.* Unpublished Master's Thesis submitted to the Graduate Faculty of Long Island University, August, 1967; Albert R. Roberts: An organizational study of suicide prevention agencies in the U. S. *Police, 14*: 64-72, 1970; Albert R. Roberts, and Joseph Grau: Procedures used in crisis intervention of suicide prevention agencies. *Public Health Reports, 85(8)*: 691-697, 1970.
84. Directory of suicide prevention facilities, *Bulletin of Suicidology*, pp. 47-58, 1969. In July, 1968, it was reported that there were 63 suicide prevention centers in the United States which all provide 24-hour emergency telephone service: Anson Haughton: Suicide prevention programs in the United States—an overview. *Bull. Suicidol.*, July, 1968, pp. 25-29; More recently, it was estimated that there are more than 200 suicide prevention and crisis intervention centers: Center Comments, *Bull. Suicidol.* Fall, 1970, p. 2; a total of 192 suicide prevention/crisis intervention services were reported in *Behavior Today Newsletter. 3*: June 19, 1972.
85. Durkheim, Emile: *op. cit.*, pp. 258-276.
86. Wilkens, James: Suicide Prevention Centers: Comparisons of Clients in Several Cities. *Comprehen. Psychiatry. 10*-6: 443-451, 1969.
87. Roberts: *op. cit.* 1967.
88. Fisher, Shiela A.: *Suicide Prevention and/or Crisis Services: A National Survey.* Doctoral Dissertation, Case Western Reserve University, Cleveland, Ohio, 1972, p. 11.

CHAPTER 3

DYSCONTROL AND SUICIDAL BEHAVIORS

THEODORE L. DORPAT

MANY PEOPLE—PERHAPS MOST PEOPLE—at one time or another have self-destructive thoughts or wishes which are not acted out in suicide. Despite strong self-destructive impulses, the majority of depressed patients do not commit suicide. Reviewing the twenty-one patients I am now treating in psychoanalysis or psychotherapy, I find that all have spontaneously reported suicide impulses or wishes. None of the twenty-one have lost control of their self-destructive impulses and made a suicide attempt. Our more comprehensive understanding of suicide should include not only consideration of the dynamics of suicidal motivation, but also knowledge of the factors which lead to the loss of control over suicidal motives. My aim is to discuss our very incomplete knowledge about the psychological, social and physical factors involved in this dyscontrol. In a discussion on the psychodynamics of suicide, Grinker[1] asked "What differentiates the wish from the act?" We may postulate that suicide stems from two factors: one is the suicidal motivation, and the other is the failure or impairment of the controls which normally inhibit the acting out of such motives. Previous studies emphasize the conscious and the unconscious psychodynamics of suicide wishes. Meerloo[2] has described fifty-two motivations for suicide. Few have been concerned with the psychological functions that control or fail to control one's acting upon suicidal impulses.

The following case vignette illustrates some psychic mechanisms involved in suicidal dyscontrol.

CASE VIGNETTE

The patient was a 42-year-old married woman with a childlike demeanor that made her appear younger than her age. A birth injury had left her with a moderate weakness on the left side of her body. Partially because of her physical handicap, she was closely attached to and dependent on her mother. One day while stepping off a street corner she and her mother were suddenly struck by an automobile. The mother died. The patient's grief was inconsolable and she developed severe depressive and phobic symptoms, including the fear of crossing the street alone. Her insomnia was especially distressing. She often told others of her wish to die and her longing for her mother. One year after her mother's death she ingested over twenty barbiturate sleeping pills in about an hour. Her husband, a seaman, unexpectedly returned from a voyage and found her comatose. He took her to the hospital and she survived but remained depressed and suicidal. She told the analyst that if she found herself on a street with a car bearing down on her, she would not move. Her fondest desire was for death and reunion with her mother "in heaven." She said of her symbiotic tie to her mother, "We were never separated; we were like one person."

As a member of a fundamentalist religion, the patient considered "deliberate" suicide sinful and a sure way of going to hell. Here, then, was her dilemma. Only in death could she rejoin her mother, but to die by a deliberate self-destructive act meant eternal damnation and continued separation from her mother in heaven.

Immediately after describing her wish to die and telling the analyst how she had taken the sleeping pills, she said "I *can't*[*] think I deliberately did it." Her statement of denial reveals how

---

[*]All italics in this chapter are the author's.

she was able to make the suicide attempt and still avoid feeling guilty. She could do it because she denied doing it "deliberately." The denial of the intentionality of the act, as shown by her use of the word *can't*, was done in the service of avoiding the fear of punishment for attempting suicide.

The patient was aware of suicidal wishes before, during and after her attempt. The act was planned, intentional and voluntary. Still, she denied that she had tried to kill herself. The denial was not a conscious lie, for she was a rigidly truthful person. Nor was it a conscious effort to conceal the nature of her act from others. Rather, it was a denial unconsciously determined by her fear of punishment for attempting suicide.

Defenses of denial and isolation brought about a "split" in her ego, with part of herself consciously and actively seeking to kill herself, while at the same time another part denied that she had intended to take her own life. By means of the defensive split in the ego she had sought to die by means of the sleeping pills and at the same time avoid eternal punishment and separation from her mother. Freud[3] was the first to describe denial and splitting of the ego in the defensive process.

The patient was conscious of her wish to die and of her wish to commit suicide. What was unconscious was her defense against the awareness that she had tried to kill herself. Not every defense acts in such a way as to bar destructive wishes from access to consciousness. When such defenses as denial and projection are used, the wishes that are being defended against can enter into consciousness and discharged in action.

She had isolated the wish to commit suicide from the execution of the wish in her suicide attempt. These unconscious defensive maneuvers allowed her to avoid responsibility for her act and relieved her anxiety over being punished for carrying out the suicidal wish. Her statement that she would not move if a car was bearing down on her describes her continuing desire to die passively without responsibility for her death.

In all of her behavior her sense of active intention, deliberateness and planning for the future was markedly impaired. This mode of experience formed the basis of her defensive operations. These defenses involved an externalization of responsibility for the decisions and conduct of her life. Related to this were the prominent qualities of impulsivity and passive-dependence on others, chiefly her mother.

Her extensive employment of denial of suicide intentionality led to the loss of control over suicidal impulses. The split in the ego between the part that wishes and plans suicide and another part that denies the intentional nature of the suicidal act was aptly illustrated in Eugene O'Neill's play, *Long Day's Journey into Night*.[4] Mary, the depressed and addicted heroine, says "I hope, sometime, without meaning it, I will take an overdosage. I never could do it deliberately. The Blessed Virgin would never forgive me, then."

DENIAL REACTIONS IN SUICIDAL BEHAVIOR

In a study of 121 suicide attempts, the author[5] found that approximately one-fourth had denied either the fact of self-injury or their intention to kill themselves. This denial was most often observed in those whose suicide attempts involved drug ingestion. A clue to the denial of suicide intention or suicide motivation may be revealed by statements such as: "I didn't do it deliberately;" "I didn't know what I was doing;" "I felt confused and not sure of what would happen;" or, finally, "I accidentally took an overdosage."

Physicians often underestimate the suicidal risk in such patients and sometimes unconsciously collude with the patient in denying the lethal intention of their suicide attempts. "Drug overdose" or "drug automatism" and similar euphemistic expressions are sometimes used by mental health professionals to deny and dismiss genuine suicide attempts in their patients.

Modell[6] described a patient who made a serious suicide attempt but who denied any suicidal intentionality or wish to kill himself at the time of the act. The patient ". . . made a serious, but entirely unconscious, suicidal attempt. He overingested sleeping medication, conscious only of a powerful desire to sleep; there was no thought of suicide and it was only upon his subsequent recovery that he recognized with horror the danger of self-destruction which had been denied." The stimulus for his massive use of denial was separation anxiety. Denial was related to a profound ego regression in which he denied his separateness from others and sought through death to achieve an objectless stage and fulfillment of his wish for reunion with his mother.

Denial reactions take different forms in different suicidal persons. Some, like Modell's patient, deny not only the intentionality of their suicidal act but also their suicidal motivation. In my research and clinical experience, nearly all suicidal persons deny the meaning of death as a final loss and irrevocable separation. Rather, they represent death in terms of continued existence superior to the baneful life they want to leave. For most people death means the end of life and separation from loved and needed objects. Those who are suicidal reverse these usual meanings of life and death. Continued living in this world means "death" for them, but dying is for them a gateway to a better life. The denial of death as the end of life is implicit in their frequent conscious and unconscious suicidal fantasies of rebirth or reunion with lost loved objects. Such wishful and pleasant fantasies are used to disavow the painful meaning of death and the fear of death. Hendin[7] warns that the erotization of death, as exemplified in fantasies of suicide involving a sexual reunion with a lost object, is an ominous sign presaging suicidal dyscontrol. The suicidal person may deny one or more of the following: the meaning of death as loss of life, the fear of death, the guilt over killing himself, the wish to kill himself, the intentionality or the fact of his suicidal actions.

In the symbols for death there is an ever-present ambivalence and ambiguity. Death can mean loss, separation and the end of life. On the other hand, it can have a pleasurable or even erotic meaning when it is equated with a peaceful sleep, immortality and union with the "good" mother of one's infancy, or with a reunion with lost loved ones. The suicidal deny the former meaning of death and cling to its pleasurable meanings.

How do these denials bring about suicidal dyscontrol? Ordinarily a suicidal impulse will elicit some fear of death or guilt over the anticipated destructiveness. The ego normally responds to such danger signals as fear or guilt by initiating defensive and adaptive tactics to control the self-destructive impulse itself. As Jacobson[8] has shown, the more primitive defense of denial functions differently. Denial defenses act against the fear or other danger signal but do not act against the self-destructive impulse itself. When denial defenses are functioning, suicidal wishes may enter and be carried out in action unopposed by defenses or other conscious or unconscious ego controls. Here the ego reacts to the danger signal—e.g. the fear of death—by an immediate attempt to ignore the fear. It is this immediate, initial denial of fear or guilt which prevents the ego from instituting controls over the impulse and over the execution of the impulse.

Denial tends to short-circuit ego defensive and adaptive functions. Also, it interferes with other ego functions such as cognitive controls, the synthetic function, reality sense and reality testing. Impairment of these ego functions leads to the loss of conscious and unconscious controls over self-destructive wishes.

OTHER CAUSES OF DYSFUNCTION

Psychic factors other than the defense of denial may affect the ego or superego functions necessary for the control over self-destructive impulses. Defects in these functions may stem from developmental failure or from disease processes as in psychosis. The developmental failure of these control and synthetic functions is found most typically in impulsive and passive-dependent characters similar to the woman described in the case vignette. Shapiro[9] explained how the attenuation of the feeling of deliberateness forms the nucleus of the impulsive personality and serves as the basis for their characteristic defensive disavowal of personal responsibility. In the patient described above this characterological lack of deliberateness and defective capacity for anticipation in conjunction with her denial reactions brought about the breakdown of her psychic control functions.

Nearly all persons who commit suicide suffer from psychiatric illness and severe ego and superego defects. It seems reasonable to assume that these ego defects are causally related to their dyscontrol over self-destructive impulses. In both the author's[10] study of 114 cases of suicide and in another psychiatric study of an unselected and consecutive series of 134 cases done by Robins, et al.,[11] it was found that nearly all subjects suffered from a severe psychiatric disorder. A majority of cases in both studies had either some type of psychosis or alcoholism. More research is needed to clarify the relationship of the ego and superego defects in these disorders to dyscontrol.

In a study of fifteen men involved in fatal one-car accidents and fifteen men who committed suicide, Litman and Tabachnick[12] suggested that the crucial factor which accident-prone and suicide prone states have in common is a defect in the ego's synthesizing function. In suicide-prone states passive, masochistic and immobilizaton defenses predominate. A suicidal action occurs when there is a functional failure of these defenses. In the accident-prone state denial, counter-phobic and action defenses predominate. Accidents occur when these defenses fail and there is a breakthrough of passive wishes expressed in a withdrawal of attention and regressive fantasies.

GENERAL SYSTEMS THEORY

Concepts derived from Bertalanffy's *General Systems Theory*[13] may be used to provide a conceptual framework for understanding the interrelationship between psychological, social and physical causes of dyscontrol in self-destructive behavior. In this theory the human organism is regarded as a multi-leveled hierarchy of relatively autonomous systems. The organism in its structural aspects is not simply an aggregration of elementary parts such as atoms. Rather, each system has a structure or organization of its own—one that is relatively independent or autonomous from other systems. Each system is an *open* system which interacts dynamically with other systems and takes in elements and gives off products.

Starting from the top of a vertical hierarchy, these systems include: 1) the social system, 2) the psychic system, 3) the body organ system, 4) the cellular system, 5) the molecular system. Each system can, of course, be divided into subsystems e.g. the ego, id and superego of the psychic system. Since the previous discussion has centered around the psychic system, I will focus my study on factors in the other systems and transactions between the various systems which lead to dyscontrol.

SOCIAL SYSTEMS AND OBJECT LOSS

The patient and her mother in the case vignette constituted a social subsystem—a symbiotic relationship in which the mother assumed many ego and superego functions for her daughter. The mother's death led to the loss of the mother's external controls over the patient's behavior. Most typically, suicidal persons have a kind of dependent and more-or-less symbiotic relationship with another person who may be a lover, parent or spouse. Suicidal drives may be acted out when they are separated from the symbiotic partner. In contrast to the symbiotic relationship, both members of a mature object relationship maintain autonomy and employ their own ego and superego functions.

The psychoanalytic and psychiatric literature is replete with studies demonstrating the salient significance of threatened, actual or symbiotic object loss in precipitating both attempted and completed suicide. As used in psychoanalysis the term "object loss" refers to the loss of anything of value to the individual.

An actual or threatened object loss was a major precipitating factor in eight subjects who committed suicide immediately after killing a loved one.[14] A comparison of the psychodynamics and social context of the fatal act in these eight subjects with other studies of suicide following murder revealed a consistent pattern. The murderer was a psychotic or severely disturbed man who killed himself immediately after murdering his mistress or wife. The murder came as a reaction to a real or threatened separation in a relationship marked by prolonged turmoil. The clinical evidence favored the hypothesis that the threat of object loss brought about an ego regression in which rage was directed at both of the subjects, and that the murder-suicide was an acting out of fantasies of reunion.

A typical case was that of a 61-year-old man who had become increasingly suspicious and withdrawn. Psychiatrists had previously made the diagnoses of alcoholism and paranoid schizophrenia. A few days before his suicide his wife had called her daughter saying that she was frightened. The wife had planned to seek a divorce. She said that her husband had warned her he would not tolerate a separation. Her body was found near the door to their trailer, as if she were about to leave, and he was found shot to death on a couch.

Suicidal behavior may also follow a partial object loss in which the subject's relations with other persons are altered. For example, a 50-year-old man became depressed and killed himself after a stroke changed his relationship to his wife from one of strength to one of helpless dependence—a partial loss. Dorpat, et al[15] and others have found a high frequency of childhood parental loss in subjects who attempted or completed suicide. Current loss events which precipitate suicidal behavior emotionally revive and symbolize unresolved repressed reactions to childhood parental losses.

In their previous studies of attempted and completed suicides, Dorpat and Ripley[16] found that the most frequent kinds of object loss were, first, losing a loved one, and, secondly, loss of health. Others killed themselves because of loss of money or employment. Out of 114 subjects who committed suicide, approximately half had a serious and chronic illness which was judged to have contributed to their suicide. The loss or disruption of interpersonal relationships caused by illness was in a majority more significant in bringing about suicidal behavior than the actual physical distress or disability.

In some cases depression and suicide were the result of the cumulative effects of several losses. The case of a middle-aged man with rheumatoid arthritis illustrates the effect of a series of losses in bringing about suicide. His arthritis began soon after his wife died, and it was believed to be part of his reaction to the loss. With the progressive deformation of his joints he suffered further losses through the deterioration of his physical appearance. His disability brought about the loss of his job. Unable to leave home, he sorely missed his friends and aquaintances. His chronic depressive reaction became exacerbated, and he committed suicide after his daughter left home to be married.

An object loss may be more symbolic than real. A post-menopausal nurse, whose life-long preoccupation was having or caring for babies, and who had lavished maternal care on her patients and family, committed suicide after a hysterectomy. The symbolic loss of her child-bearing capacity triggered her self-destruction.

In a study of six suicidal subjects treated in long-term psychoanalysis or psychoanalytically oriented psychotherapy, Dorpat[18] found that their suicidal behavior grew out of an arrested grief reaction. The subjects were unable to complete the process of mourning for the lost object. Their mourning reaction was stalemated in one or more of the three states of grief: 1) shock, 2) protest, 3) detachment from the lost object.

Unlike the suicidal person, the normal mourner gradually relinquishes his ties to the lost object, and he is able to master the stages of the grief process. In doing so he also attains two precious achievements, the development of new object relationships, and a higher degree of individuation. Sandler, et al.[19] have shown how individuation is one of the constructive outcomes of mature mourning.

Everyone experiences loss. Why, then, do some people become depressed and even suicidal whereas others are able to mourn and find new objects? The suicidally depressed patients in Dorpat's studies[16, 17, 18] were unable to master loss because they experienced the lost object as an essential part of themselves and as indispensable to their existence. They depended on the lost object for the direction of their lives and for the regulation of their self esteem. Loss of the needed object brought with it a breakdown of meaning and purpose in their lives. Their subjective sense of being unable to live without the lost object was also true in an objective sense. They had lived in a symbiotic relationship with the lost object, who supplied such ego and superego functions as thinking, decision-making, self-control and self-esteem for both members of the dyad. Most prominent were their superego defects, especially in capacities for loving and caring for themselves. The loving aspect of the superego is formed by identification with the parents' loving and caring functions. By means of these identifications the child develops the capacity to love, to protect and to comfort himself and his children after him.

The core personality defects which predispose serious depressions and suicide behavior were deficiencies in the capacity for self-love and pride. The suicidal subjects had an infantile kind of dependence on others for approval and regulation because they had not learned how to care for themselves. Their psychiatric histories revealed the genesis of their personality defects.

The absense of empathic and loving care by their parents at critical times of their development provided the malformative roots of their ego and superego defects.

A variety of sociological studies have described the role of social isolation, social disorganization and loss of social integration as social causes of suicide. The sociologist Rushing[20] concluded that "Extensive research findings suggest that suicide is associated with physical illness, mental illness, alcoholism, homicide and economic failure, all of which tend to result in disruptions in social relations . . . . The most general conclusion is, then, that interpersonal elements, particularly disruptive social relations, are crucial etiological factors in suicide."

In their study of 114 consecutive suicides, Palola, et al.[21] found that their subjects had a decrease in social integration before committing suicide. A Scale of Change in Social Integration was constructed which covered the year prior to the suicide and included measures of changes: (a) employment, (b) residence, (c) religious activity, (d) formal organizations, (e) health, (f) interpersonal relationships, (g) financial status, (h) family status, (i) use of alcohol, drugs and gambling. The direction of change for each item was measured. A plus score designated an increase in social integration and a minus score a decrease. When these plus and minus scores were added for each subject, it was found that the cumulative direction score was in a minus direction for nearly all subjects.

What sort of bridge is there between various sociologic theories having to do with "social integration" and suicide and psychoanalytic studies of self-destructiveness? In what way does a decrease in social integration impinge on the individual? Particularly suggestive leads in this connection are provided by a correlation of psychoanalytic studies by French[22] on the theme of "hope" with a sociological study by Meier and Bell[23] on the subject of "anomia" and its relation to differential access to the achievement of life goals.

Meier and Bell use the concept of anomia in its psychological sense of despair and hopelessness. In their study individuals who had a high "index of means for the achievement of life goals" had low anomia scores, whereas those with low index scores had high anomia scores. Meier and Bell's conclusions are congruent with those of French. Writing of the role of hope in goal-directed behavior, French said, "Hope is based on present opportunity and on memories of recent success." He emphasized the channelizing or integrating influence that hope has on behavior.

Farber[24] called suicide a "disease of hope." Schmale[25] has summarized many studies on the significance of object loss in bringing about hopelessness and depression. Object losses and their resultant decrease in social integration for the subject may lead to a suicidal depressive reaction in which the subject feels hopeless over attaining his goals. The loss of hope and its integrating effect on goal-directed behavior facilitates dyscontrol. When hope disappears through lack of opportunities to reach life's goals, self-destructive drives previously subordinated to other goals become discharged. The patient described in the case vignette felt hopeless over achieving any of her goals after the loss of her mother. Her capacity to pursue any goal was contingent upon the presence and help of her "auxiliary ego," her mother.

Although complaints of hopelessness are prominent aspects of the *conscious* feelings of the suicidal person, psychoanalytic studies show that such persons do not relinquish hope for union or reunion with their love objects.

The psychoanalyst Rubenfine[26] maintains that the depressive person never gives up hope for union with an idealized "good" object. He wrote, "By making himself 'bad' and keeping the object 'good' he maintains hope." Rubenfine emphasizes that although depressives wear the guise of hopelessness, they never relinquish the hope of attaining the object. He said, "Even in instances of actual suicide the act is not one of hopelessness but contains the fantasy 'this will make her realize how much I love her and she will love only me again.' This fantasy is apparent in the very thinly disguised contents of suicide notes, in the public nature of those suicides in which the subject waits, sometimes for hours, for the appearance of a particular rescuer who may no longer even exist, and in analytic studies of those who have made unsuccessful suicide attempts."

The suicidal subject's sense of uncontrolled and disintegrating hopelessness screens a more-or-less unconscious hope for union with an idealized object. Suicidal persons are characterized by the relative absense of appropriate and reality-based feelings of both hope and hopelessness. Their failure to develop realistic and controlled means of dealing with feelings of hopelessness stems from their deficient learning of how to mourn lost objects.

One of the signs of emotional maturity and adaptive acceptance of life's limitations is the mastery, acceptance and tolerance for mourning emotions such as sadness, helplessness and hopelessness. Such emotions are integral aspects of the mourning process and they assist the mourner in the painful but necessary relinquishment of his bonds to unattainable objects.

To "turn off" one's ties and longings for lost objects through small and controlled quantities of feelings of hopelessness is a necessity, not only for completing the "work" of mourning, but also for the formation of new object relations and for individuation. The suicidal person is unable to terminate his strivings for lost or otherwise unobtainable objects through realistic feelings of hopelessness over attaining his goal of relation with the object.

SOCIAL CONTROLS

Thus far, we have mainly discussed dyadic subsystems, and how object loss, particularly loss of a symbiotic partner, may lead to dyscontrol and suicidal behavior. Now, my aim is to briefly consider the influence of larger social subsystems of self-destructive dyscontrol. Using the concepts of Durkheim and other sociologists who have studied suicide, Maris[27] has derived a major thesis on the relationship between social controls and suicide. His thesis states, "The suicide rate varies inversely with external restraint." External restraint is low when an individual is not regulated either by other people or by shared ideas. Specific cases usually take the form of social isolation or of role failure, in the work role for men, and in the family role for women.

The breakdown of social controls over aggressive behavior plays an important role today in the increased suicidal behavior and other forms of violence found in groups characterized by social turmoil and/or social disorganization. Recent studies of suicide behavior among young people highlight the role of cultural changes and the failure of social controls. The past decade is marked by a striking increase in the suicide rate in young people (ages 15 to 30). Psychosocial studies indicate that the traditional forms of social restraint and control over aggressive behavior no longer have as much meaning or force for today's youth. The present generation does not internalize or obey parental controls to the extent of previous generations. Today young people tend to look more to their peers than to their parents for values and directives.

In his study on suicidal behavior of black people living in New York City, Hendin[28] observed that suicide there is twice as frequent in Black men between the ages of twenty and thirty-five as it is among white men of the same age group. Young militant blacks have turned against the "Uncle Toms" in their community. The "Uncle Toms" controlled and coped with their aggression by passive kinds of compliance and obedience. Since this pattern of aggression control is no longer acceptable, the young black has fewer socially sanctioned means of controlling his aggression. The resulting dyscontrol has led to the increasing rate of suicide behavior and other forms of violence.

Hendin offers a convincing explanation of the psychic and social genesis of black self-hatred and its crucial role in suicide reactions. The black's self-hatred was formed partly by internalizing the white culture's rejection and oppression. However, the clinical one-to-one interviewing method used in Hendin's study and other similar studies imposes limits on the kind of data available for the investigation of the effects of social systems, the culture and the family on individual psychopathology.

Research in suicidology today is comparable to the situation in schizophrenia research prior to the advent of family studies. Before Lidz,[29] Laing,[30] and others studied the families of schizophrenics, psychiatrists had many clues derived from treating individual schizophrenics about schizophrenogenic family constellations. It was only after family studies were made, however, that knowledge became available about what family patterns led to the development of schizophrenia and how they did so.

Integrative and inter-disciplinary studies of the effects of various social subsystems on individual suicide psychopathology are much needed. This task will require not only psychoanalytic methods and perspectives but also the tools of sociology and cultural anthropology to examine the relations between culture, the family and the self-destructive individual.

PHYSICAL SYSTEMS

Further down this hierarchy of systems are the organ systems such as the central nervous system. Gross functional or structural defects in body organ systems such as the circulatory, respiratory or nervous systems can indirectly lead to the loss of psychic controls over self-destructive impulses. Prolonged sleeplessness in the patient discussed in the case vignette impaired her central nervous system functioning and secondarily weakened her ego and superego controls.

The role of central nervous system defects in suicidal dyscontrol is illustrated in the case of a fifty year old construction worker who fell thirty feet from a building site. He was comatose for several weeks and he sustained moderately severe brain damage. When he regained consciousness he had a number of neurological deficits, including memory loss and motor incoordination. He became depressed over his physical impairment, since both his livelihood and his self-esteem depended on his ability to use his body effectively.

Three months after the accident he committed suicide. Both the depressive reaction and the brain damage impaired his ability to control his feelings, thoughts and behavior. The resulting loss of control over his self-destructive impulses led to his suicide.

At the end of this hierarchy of systems are the cellular and molecular systems. Diseases, poisons or drugs which attack the integrity of these systems may indirectly lead to suicidal dyscontrol, since effective mental functioning depends in part on the normal functioning of brain cells and upon innumerable chemical reactions, both within cells and in the extracellular space. It is probable that the ingestion of sleeping pills by the patient discussed in the case vignette further impaired her psychic controls. There are many published reports of individuals who have committed suicide while they were under the influence of sedatives, narcotics and psychedelic drugs such as LSD.

Other studies suggest that alcohol ingestion may lead to loss of controls over suicidal impulses. Clinical evidence presented by Moore[31] and others indicate that most alcoholics are intoxicated when they attempt suicide. In the study by Litman and Tabachnick,[12] nine of the fifteen men who had fatal one-car accidents and twelve of the fifteen suicide cases had been drinking heavily before their deaths. Palola, et al.[21] found that 28 percent of a group of 114 consecutive suicide cases had been drinking at the time of their suicide.

In a study of all suicides occurring in one California county during a five-year period, Krieger[32] found that 21 percent of the male suicides and 9 percent of the female suicides at postmortem had blood alcohol levels above 0.05 percent. Selzer studied alcoholics involved in auto accidents and he provided persuasive evidence that excessive drinking just before the accident had led to the loss of their controls over self-destructive impulses.

The findings of recent experimental intoxication studies also support the impression that intoxication per se may be a crucial factor in dyscontrol of self-destructive impulses. Several studies have shown that alcoholics experience increasing anxiety and depression with continued heavy drinking. Tamerin and Mendelson[34] observed the development of severe depression to suicidal proportions after two weeks of experimental intoxication.

There are, of course, many other structural and functional defects in the body's physical systems which can cause various degrees and kinds of dyscontrol. The psycho-physiological mechanisms through which such defects affect dyscontrol are beyond the scope of this paper. *General Systems Theory*[13] can enrich our understanding of dyscontrol in suicide behaviors by integrating the contributions of the biological, social and psychological sciences.

SUMMARY

Suicidal behaviors occur when there is a loss of control over self-destructive impulses. This paper uses the case study of a depressed woman who attempted suicide with barbiturates after the death of her mother. Her denial that she had performed the act "deliberately" was unconsciously determined by her fear of punishment for attempting suicide. Previously this fear had mobilized her controls over her suicidal wishes. The denial of her suicide intentionality led to her dyscontrol. Her suicidal depressive reaction stemmed from her inability to grieve for and relinquish her symbiotic relationship with her mother.

This paper uses the case vignette to illustrate and explain some of the psychological, physical and social factors involved in dyscontrol. Concepts based on general systems theory are discussed, especially the relationship between object loss, the mourning emotions (hopelessness, helplessness and sadness) and suicidal dyscontrol. General systems theory provides a conceptual framework for understanding the loss of control over suicidal wishes and broadens our understanding of dyscontrol by integrating the contributions of the biological, social and psychological sciences.

REFERENCES

1. Grinker, Roy R.: The psychodynamics of suicide and attempted suicide. In Yochelson, L. (Ed.): *Symposium on Suicide.* Washington, George Washington University, 1967.
2. Meerloo, Joust A. M.: *Suicide and Mass Suicide.* New York, Grune and Stratton, 1962.
3. Freud, Sigmund: Splitting of the ego in the defensive process (1938). *Standard Edition, 23:* 275-278. London, Hogarth Press, 1964.
4. O'Neill, Eugene: *Long Day's Journey Into Night.* New Haven, Yale University Press, 1956.
5. Dorpat, Theodore L., and Boswell, John W.: An evaluation of suicide intent in suicide attempts. *Comp Psychiat, 4:* 117, 1963.
6. Modell, Arnold H.: Denial and the sense of separateness. *J Am Psychoanal Assn, 9:* 533, 1961.
7. Hendin, Herbert: *Suicide and Scandinavia.* New York, Grune and Stratton, 1964.
8. Jacobson, Edith: Denial and repression. *J Am Psychoanal Assn, 5:* 61, 1957.
9. Shapiro, David: *Neurotic Styles.* New York, Basic Books, 1965.
10. Dorpat, Theodore L., and Ripley, Herbert S.: A study of suicide in the Seattle area. *Comp Psychiat, 1:* 349, 1960.
11. Robins, Ely, Gassner, J., Kayes, J., Wilkinson, R. H., and Murphy, George E.: The communication of suicidal intent: a study of 134 consecutive cases of successful (completed) suicides. *Am J Psychiat, 115:* 724, 1959.
12. Litman, Robert E., and Tabachnick, Norman: Fatal one-car accidents. *Psychoanl Q, 36:* 248, 1967.

13. Bertalanffy, Ludwig: *General Systems Theory.* New York, George Braziller, 1968.
14. Dorpat, Theodore L.: Suicide in murderers. *Psychiatry Digest, 27:* 51, 1966.
15. Dorpat, Theodore L., Jackson, Joan K., and Ripley, Herbert S.: Broken homes and attempted and completed suicide. *Arch Gen Psychiat, 12:* 213, 1965.
16. Dorpat, Theodore L., and Ripley, Herbert S.: A study of suicide in King County, Washington. *Northwest Medicine, 61:* 655, 1962.
17. Dorpat, Theodore L., Anderson, William F., and Ripley, Herbert S.: The relationship of physical illness to suicide. In Resnick, H. L. P. (Ed.): *Suicidal Behaviors—Diagnosis and Management.* Boston, Little, Brown, 1968.
18. Dorpat, Theodore L.: Suicide, loss and mourning. *Life-Threatening Behavior,* 1973 (in publication).
19. Sandler, Joseph, and Jaffee, W. G.: Notes on pain, depression and individuation. *Psa Study Child, 20:* 394, 1965.
20. Rushing, William A.: Individual behavior and suicide. In Gibbs, J. P. (Ed.): *Suicide.* New York, Harper and Row, 1968.
20. Rushing, William A.: Individual behavior and suicide. In Gibbs, J. P.
21. Palola, Ernest G., Dorpat, Theodore L., and Larson, William R.: Alcoholism and suicide behavior. In Pittman, D. J., and Snyder, C. R. (Eds.): *Society, Culture and Drinking Patterns.* New York, John Wiley and Sons, 1962.
22. French, Thomas M.: *The Integration of Behavior.* Chicago, University of Chicago Press, 1952, vol. I, p. 53.
23. Meier, D. L., and Bell, W.: Anomia and differential access to the achievement of life goals. *Am Sociol Rev, 24:* 189, 1959.
24. Farber, Maurice L.: *Theory of Suicide.* New York, Funk and Wagnalls, 1968.
25. Schmale, Arnold H.: Relationship of separation and depression to disease. *Psychosom Med, 20:* 259, 1958.
26. Rubenfine, David L.: Notes on a theory of depression. *Psychoanal Q, 37:* 400, 1968.
27. Maris, Ronald W.: *Social Forces in Urban Suicide.* Homewood, Dorsey Press, 1969.
28. Hendin, Herbert: *Black Suicide.* New York, Basic Books, 1969.
29. Lidz, Theodore: *The Origin and Treatment of Schizophrenic Disorders.* New York, Basic Books, 1973.
30. Laing, Ronald D., and Esterson, A.: Sanity, madness and the family, vol. I. *Families of Schizophrenics.* Lonon, Tavistock, New York, Basic Books, 1965.
31. Moore, M.: Alcoholism and attempted suicide: report of 143 cases, *New Eng J Med, 221:* 691, 1939.

32. Krieger, George: Suicides in the San Mateo County. *Calif Med, 107:* 153, 1967.
33. Selzer, M. L., and Payne, C. E.: Automobile accidents, suicide and unconscious motivation. *Am J Psychiat, 119:* 237, 1962.
34. Tamerin, J. S., and Mendelson, J. H.: The psychodynamics of chronic inebriation: observations of alcoholics during the process of drinking in an experimental group setting. *Am J Psychiat, 125:* 886, 1969.

CHAPTER 4

THE SELF-INJURY PATIENT: SOCIOLOGICAL AND MEDICAL PROFILES AND IMPLICATIONS FOR PREVENTION

ROBERTA G. FERRENCE, GEORGE K. JARVIS,
F. GORDON JOHNSON, AND PAUL C. WHITEHEAD

SELF-DESTRUCTIVE BEHAVIOR IS USUALLY tragic, wasteful, and we feel, largely preventable. Such behavior may have varied manifestations such as suicide, alcoholism, or engaging in very high risk activities. One of its forms, sometimes called "sub-suicidal," is "self-injury behavior." As we use the term, self-injury includes all cases of self-inflicted overdosage, asphyxiation, and injury, whether or not there is evidence of suicidal intent. This definition is comparable with those used by other researchers in this field.[26, 41] Recent investigations of the incidence of self-injury behavior indicate that it has assumed major proportions and there are reasons to believe that it will continue to increase in the future.[56]

In order to institute measures of prevention that are apt to be effective it is necessary that we understand the nature of the

---

This project was supported by grants from the following sources: the Ontario Mental Health Foundation (#241), the Public Health Research Grants Division of the Department of National Health and Welfare (#605-7-585), and the Canada Council (#573-0294-51). Support was also received from the Lake Erie Region of the Addiction Research Foundation, London, Canada.

phenomenon with which we are dealing and that we have our programs attuned to characteristics of the population that need to be reached. The purpose of this chapter is to examine some current research findings concerning persons who self-injure and to discuss the implications of this research for practical application in the area of prevention.

Three sub-types of prevention can be distinguished conceptually namely, primary, secondary, and tertiary prevention.[5] *Primary* prevention addresses itself to changing those conditions (e.g., social) that produce an environment known to be associated with the occurrence of a particular phenomenon. *Secondary* prevention aims to identify those individuals who are highly "vulnerable" or in the early stages of developing a particular condition in order that appropriate intervention can take place so as to ward off further development of the condition. *Tertiary* prevention is the same as what we usually call "treatment" in that it involves an intervention with those who are already afflicted and the goal is either to prevent them from getting worse or to prevent a recurrence of the phenomenon.

Our research on self-injury behavior indicates that an examination of sociological and medical factors may be useful in developing approaches to prevention. In this chapter we will examine such factors in terms of both the community and the individual.

SOCIOLOGICAL PROFILE

CHARACTERISTICS OF THE COMMUNITY: Information about the social and geographic distribution of self-injury provides valuable clues regarding its etiology and essential information for the planning and evaluation of treatment programs and facilities. A variety of studies—both retrospective and prospective—have reported rates of self-injury varying from 80 per 100,000 to 300/100,000 population per annum in a number of different countries.[31, 48, 20, 40, 53, 50, 45, 41, 17, 14] Most of these studies focussed on only one or a few of the potential sources of information about self-injury cases. Typically these have consisted of hospital records and, in some cases, police statistics or reports of physicians. However, a recent study of self-injury in London, Canada* sought data from a broader range of sources including psychiatric, veterans and extended care hospitals, social and other health care agencies, primary care physicians, local clergy and the county jail and reports a crude rate of 730/100,000 population per annum.[56] Further research suggests that differences in methods of data collection and reporting explain most of the variation to be found in incidence rates.[19]

SEX AND AGE STRUCTURE: Two factors responsible for much of the variation within communities are gender and age. An excess of females over males on the order of 2:1 is most commonly found in self-injury cases from the noninstitutionalized population, although this ratio varies considerably with age. Females begin to self-injure somewhat earlier than males, but the general pattern for both sexes is similar; rapid increase to a peak during young adulthood followed by a decline through later ages.[34, 50, 45, 23] Although the recorded incidence of attempts may considerably underrepresent the elderly[36] it is also likely that older persons do not survive attempts as well as younger persons for reasons of isolation, poorer general health and a greater use of more lethal drugs such as barbiturates.

Many explanations have been offered for the sex difference and the most compelling involve differences in cultural expectations of problem-solving behavior, i.e. that suicide is prescribed to a greater extent for males than for females, whereas attempted suicide is tolerated more for females than for males.[32] Reports that self-injury among young males is increasing more rapidly than among young females may reflect the growing similarity in sex-role behavior among young persons.

ECOLOGY: Ecological research indicates that rates of self-injury are generally highest in depressed areas of the city.[44, 25, 50] This relationship is maintained even when age and sex are standardized.[4, 23] More specifically, rates of self-injury are inversely correlated with the average socio-economic status for the area, the proportion of owner-occupied homes and with the distance from the city centre.[23] Female to male ratios are also smaller for

---

* Unless otherwise specified, London, Canada will henceforth be referred to as London.

lower status areas of the city especially among the population twenty-five years of age and older. This suggests the relative disadvantage suffered by males in low status areas relative to such factors as the job market may produce higher rates of self-injury for these individuals.[23] Social isolation does not appear to be related to nonfatal self-injury, but various measures of social disorganization have been shown to be highly correlated with rates of self-injury.[34]

CHARACTERISTICS OF INDIVIDUALS: A number of studies have investigated the social histories of self-injury patients with particular emphasis on such variables as parental deprivation in childhood, religion and ethnic origin, education and employment history, and the stability of interpersonal relationships in adulthood.[34, 14, 17, 58, 51, 40, 45, 22] Despite the diversity of these and other social history items they do appear to form configurations of variables that may act as a basis for the formulation of a small number of general hypotheses.

The first is a "value hypothesis" which suggests that certain attitudes and values increase the likelihood of self-injury behavior and are associated with particular ethnic and religious groups. Those groups with higher rates of self-injury would tend to be those that adhere most closely to those values and attitudes.

A "rejection hypothesis" is the second general hypothesis. It is based on the psychological notion of "internalized rejection" and incorporates such variables as parental deprivation, parental rejection, and marital breakup. Individuals experiencing such rejection may come to evaluate themselves in a negative way. As a result they may seek to negate themselves or punish themselves by self-injurious behavior.

A third hypothesis examines the role played by "social status" as measured by education, occupation, and employment status. In a way this hypothesis is a corollary to the preceding one in that those who are rewarded by society and have high status will tend to develop a favorable self-image, while those who are not similarly rewarded will suffer self-rejection and be more likely to attempt suicide.

Fourth, change *per se*—rather than the position or direction of change—may be related to a high risk of self-injury. This may be viewed as an "instability hypothesis." Instability is operationalized in terms of changes in marital status, residential mobility, migration and other variables that are commonly known as "life events."

Value hypothesis. Contrary to the well-known finding for completed suicide,[13] Roman Catholics tend to be overrepresented in self-injury populations.[35, 21, 58, 43, 49, 22] The "value" explanation for this finding would be that differences in response patterns are produced by religious values, for example, Catholics may be more likely to express hostility inwardly. However, Morphew[38] investigated intrapunitiveness among Catholics and Protestants and found no significant difference in this regard. Alternative explanations would include a spurious relationship explained by the association between religion and social class (i.e. Catholics tend to be overrepresented in lower socio-economic status categories); or, a rejection response caused by social disapproval of Catholics by other religious groups.

Ethnic origins account for little variation in rates of self-injury except for certain highly differentiated groups which are characterized by significantly greater rates of self-injury: Blacks in the United States,[51] Asians and Africans in Israel[37] and Canadian Indians in London. Since these cultural groups are those that experience a greater degree of social and economic deprivation, it is likely that socio-economic status differences rather than particular cultural patterns would explain most of the excess.

On the basis of religion and ethnicity, then, little support has been obtained to date for the "value hypothesis." Further investigations using different measures of values and attitudes might yield different results.

Rejection hypothesis. To test the "rejection hypothesis," we examined situations in which self-injurers experienced interpersonal rejection. Most studies report that an excessive incidence of separation from parents results in greater propensity to self-injury in subsequent years. There is some indication that the relationship is more important for marital separation and divorce than for parental death.[33, 2, 28, 40] Nevertheless, as the association often fails to reach statistical significance or to differentiate self-injury cases from other patient groups, it is possible that parental deprivation is a somewhat inaccurate index of some other associated variable. Bruhn[2] suggests that social disorganization as indicated by recent evidence of household instability, unemployment of head of household, residential mobility and marital disharmony bears a more direct relationship to self-injury than separation from parents in childhood. Adam, et al.,[1] argue that early parental loss combined with recent disruptions in interpersonal relationships predispose to suicidal behavior.

In the London Study, 42 percent of the patients had been separated from one or both parents for at least three months before they were sixteen. Significantly more patients had lost both parents, suffered a loss at an early age or been separated for reasons other than death than a group of "normals" in another study.[29] This suggests that persons raised with a step-parent or in a foster home or institution are more likely to self-injure. The subsequent environment, however, is probably of greater importance than the initial separation.

On the basis of the London Study, perceived parental rejection appears to be even more significant than actual separation from parents. Fifty-one percent of patients felt they had been seriously rejected by their parents or guardians and 5 percent were unsure. Of the former, 45 percent felt rejected by both parents. Paternal rejection was more important for males whereas only slightly more females felt rejected by their mothers than their fathers. Despite the lack of a normal control group, the large proportion of self-injury patients who felt rejected suggests that this is a more sensitive measure of internalized rejection than parental deprivation. To test this idea, we examined the relationship between separation from parents and perceived rejection. The association was significant, but we still found that a high proportion of those from intact homes felt rejected by their parents.

STATUS HYPOTHESIS: The use of indexes of social status such as education, employment status and occupation makes findings easier to analyze because comparable data are available for large "normal" populations such as those reported in the census.

Except for our own study, little data exist on the level of education achieved by self-injury patients. In London, where subjects had a mean age of 26, only 27 percent of those not currently in school had completed high school before leaving. A random sample of the London community (mean age=38) indicates that twice as many of the general population (54%) had completed their high school education.

Perhaps more cogent is the high rate of failure in school, particularly in the elementary grades. Fifty-eight percent of male and 43 percent of female self-injury patients in London had failed one or more grades in school. Of these, 41 percent of males and 30 percent of females had failed two or more grades. It is not surprising, then, that fewer than 20 percent of patients left school because they felt they had completed their education. Emotional problems, poor performance at school, pregnancy and problems at home were frequently cited as reasons for having left.

Related to these findings are the subsequent employment patterns of self-injury patients. Unemployment rates for self-injury patients vary by community. These rates are invariably several times greater than those recorded for the general population.[14, 40, 22, 45] Physical and psychiatric disabilities contribute substantially to the unemployment rate among self-injury patients.[14] The London sample experienced extremely high rates of unemployment among males with 34 percent of males out of work. Among females it also appears that more were unemployed and looking for work than in the normal population. While economic fluctuations would affect the overall proportion who are unemployed, persons who self-injure appear to lose their jobs primarily because of personal difficulties. In the London Study, about two thirds of persons out of work experienced longterm psychiatric disabilities, problems with employers or were otherwise unable to hold a job. The remainder were laid off, were between jobs or had marginal skills.

Using occupation as a measure of social class, we find that most reports place the majority of self-injury patients in the lower strata.[58, 22, 53] When London patients were compared with a random sample of the community, only half as many self-injury patients came from professional or semi-professional occupational backgrounds, whereas a much higher proportion came from households where the head was semi-or unskilled. The pattern was more visible for male patients than for females and suggests the possibility that family status position, as measured by occupation, has a greater effect on the adjustment of men than it does for women.

In terms of the "social status" hypothesis, it appears that occupying a lower position in society is significantly related to self-injury behavior. The direction of this relationship has not been fully investigated and it is yet to be determined whether psychologically vulnerable individuals remain or drift into lower status positions, or whether lower socio-economic status involves hardships and deprivations which predispose one to self-injury. While there is undoubtedly evidence to support both hypotheses, certain facts favor the second (social causation) model. For example, rates of self-injury are highest among young persons who because of their age effectively occupy a low status position. With increasing age, however, rates decline dramatically. The same reasoning can be applied to sex differences in self-injury rates. Neither age nor sex differences can be explained by the drift hypothesis, and therefore provide strong support for a social causation explanation.

Instability hypothesis. The "instability hypothesis" rests on the assumption that change in itself rather than the particular character of events is stressful for the individual and that as the level of stress increases, so does the probability of self-injury. Since most changes involve the disruption of interpersonal relationships this may be the component that has greatest impact on the individual. Data related to changes in marital status and place of residence are commonly reported in the literature.[3, 16] Others such as illness, children leaving home, retirement and criminal conviction are rarely dealt with.

A high rate of divorce and separation is frequently reported among cases of self-injury,[14, 53] although the findings are equivocal. The London Study measured the number of changes in marital status and found that 31 percent of patients had experienced two or more changes in marital status. The youthfulness of the sample indicates that most of the changes would not involve the death of a spouse. Comparable data for the general population are not available, but it is very likely that self-injury patients experience excessive changes of this type for their age. One should remember in this context that divorce rates in Canada are relatively low compared to other industrialized countries.

Changes in residence comprise another type of change that self-injury patients frequently undergo. Bruhn[3] reported that 38 percent of respondents had moved at least once during the past year whereas 22 percent of psychiatric controls matched for age, sex and occupation had done this. Among London patients, 46 percent of females and 54 percent of males had two or more addresses during the previous year. More than half of these had lived at their present address less than three months.

Considering types of changes that are less commonly reported, we found that two thirds of patients had experienced three or more significant changes in their lives during the previous year. Most frequent for males were: demotion or loss of job, 41 percent; serious illness of self or significant other, 37 percent; legal problems involving self or significant other, 35 percent; and a major change in getting along with a significant other, 26 percent. In addition, 21 percent separated from their spouses, 20 percent experienced the death of a close friend or relative, 16 percent were arrested and 6 percent were released from penetentiary. About the same proportion of females experienced serious illness and deaths, but more, 41 percent, had a major change in getting along with a significant other, while fewer were demoted or lost jobs, 26 percent; separated from their spouses, 12 percent; encountered legal difficulties involving themself, or a significant other, 23 percent; or were released from jail, 1 percent. Comparisons with normal subjects are difficult, particularly because most surveys inquired about different numbers of events, but we have good reason to believe that our subjects experienced an unusually high incidence of significant changes in the year prior to their self-injury. Thus, self-injury patients are not necessarily inadequately coping with a "normal" amount of change; they in fact seem to experience a greater number of stressful events, at least during the period prior to injuring themselves. Their self-destructive behavior may be closely associated with the amount of change they do experience. The self-injurious individual may be partly responsible for creating certain kinds of events, for example, loss of job, unsatisfactory relationships leading to divorce or separation, but one investigation of social status and events which controlled for the degree of control which the individual had over each event suggests that this is not a crucial factor.[12]

We have examined four hypotheses relating the sociological characteristics of individuals to subsequent self-injury. The first, although lacking support, cannot be firmly rejected. The remaining three receive some support both from the literature and from our findings. But more important, perhaps, are two themes that appear repeatedly. The first is that the patient's position is frequently characterized by decreased control over the environment and a limiting of viable options. The second usually precedes or accompanies the first and it is the disruption of meaningful relationships with significant other persons. In this context, the act of self-injury may be viewed as a positive act because it has impact on the environment and at times restores impaired relationships.

MEDICAL PROFILE

Characteristics of the community.

Although self-injury is a reflection of the characteristics of individuals and their problems, it must also be viewed in the context of community patterns of drug prescribing and usage, and of treatment approaches and facilities. Social attitudes toward the use of drugs not only affects the incidence of self-injury but also the degree of recidivism that occurs.

The dramatic increase in overdoses during the past decade[48] has been facilitated and perhaps encouraged by a similar increase in the availability of drugs, particularly those that are psychoactive. By and large the type of drugs used by patients who overdose reflects the larger patterns of drug use in the community. When we compared the distribution of drugs used by self-injury patients in London with mood-modifying drugs used by the general public in two Canadian communities,[52, 8] we found little difference in the proportion using sedatives and hypnotics, tranquilizers and stimulants. Drugs prescribed for purely physical reasons, for example, antibiotics, are rarely used for overdoses. Other authors[31] have noted that the decrease in prescriptions for barbiturates has resulted in a smaller proportion of barbiturate overdoses. Since barbiturates have a low margin of safety when compared with other drugs, their decreased use has probably lowered the fatality rate for self-injury.

The phenomenal increase in the use of illicit psychoactive drugs during the past decade has also affected the rate of self-injury. Tranquilizers and barbiturates are now commonly used by young persons[57] and are becoming less strongly identified as female behavior.

The overall sex difference in the use of drugs for self-injury (2:1 for females) closely parallels the sex ratio for the prescribing of drugs in the general population. Cooperstock[7] provides evidence that physicians prescribe more mood-modifying drugs for their female than for their male patients, regardless of diagnosis. This suggests that societal expectations of sex role behavior affects both the prescribing of more psychoactive drugs for women and their greater use by women, including greater use of overdoses.

The way in which a community manages those who engage in deviant behavior can dramatically affect the rate of self-injury it reports. For example, residents of jails and mental institutions show excessive rates of self-injury behavior when compared with the non-institutionalized population.[56, 36] Here again, societal expectations for behavior combined with a severe limiting of the ways of expressing dissatisfaction increases the probability of self-destructive behavior occurring among residents and inmates. As a further example, the recent liberalization of bail laws in Ontario contributed to the decline in rates of self-injury among inmates of the London County jail.[56]

It is well-known that suicide rates among former mental patients are highest during the month following discharge.[18, 30] One would expect that the provision of intensive support and follow-up could considerably reduce the probability of suicide during this period.

For nonhospitalized persons with emotional difficulties, self-injury provides one of the quickest routes to sources of help. In most communities, hospital emergency departments provide one of the few services that operate on a twenty-four hour basis, and, as a rule, they discourage admissions that are not considered urgent. The attitudes of hospital staff toward self-injury patients are often negative,[54] and this may result in hostile treatment, quick discharge and perhaps increased recidivism. On the other hand, more positive attitudes might serve to reward self-injury as a method of help-seeking and increase this type of behavior accordingly. Attitudes of treatment staff regarding the legitimacy of particular self-injuries could also affect recidivism by encouraging patients to "do it properly" in order to prove their sincerity. Thus, the way in which a community responds to the problems and actions of its residents has major implications for the nature and extent of their self-destructive behavior as well as for the consequences of such behavior.

Characteristics of individuals.

Self-injury has traditionally been viewed as a medical problem that is best treated by physicians with the use of hospitalization, chemotherapy and psychotherapy. For this reason, the medical profile of self-injury patients is of importance as a potential source of clues and techniques for prevention.

The help-seeking patterns of self-injury patients* provide one of the most useful dimensions of this profile. In the London Study, 79 percent of self-injury cases reported that they used at least one medical source in seeking help for their problems in the six months prior to their self-injury. Psychiatrists were utilized most and comprised 32 percent of all helpers; 28 percent were other physicians and 8 percent were staff of hospital Emergency Departments.

Fifty-five percent of the London patients reported having seen a physician during the month prior to their self-injury and 82 percent had seen a physician during the previous six months. These reports were corroborated by the physicians. Fifty-two

---

*Parts of this section are adapted from Johnson, et al., "Self-Injury: Identification and Intervention," *Candadian Psychiatric Association Journal*, 18: 101-105 (1973).

percent of the physicians given as family doctors reported having seen their self-injury patients during the month prior to self-injury and 79 percent in the past six months. These rates are comparable to those found in other studies.[39, 15] Thus, physicians can play a crucial role in the diagnosis of potential self-injury and subsequent prevention because they are the chief source of help used by persons who eventually self-injure and go to the hospital.

Most patients in the London Study (72%) sought some type of help for their problems, but 52 percent of these felt that they received little or no help during their last contact; nevertheless, 86 percent feel that they can still be helped and 63 percent of the sources they would try would be medical.

The most common reasons for visiting a physician were a physical disease or an emotional problem: 29 percent of the patients reported that they sought help for a specific physical disease, 28 percent for an emotional problem, 17 percent for a checkup, 16 percent for a somatic symptom, 6 percent sought medication and 4 percent sought help for some other family member. There is no significant difference in the overall proportion of reasons given by the patients and those reported to us by their physicians.

There are gender differences in these help-seeking patterns: significantly more males (50%) than females (35%) sought help from hospital Emergency Departments and psychiatrists ($p<.01$), whereas females more often chose their regular physician (31% vs. 23%). Since physicians reported that they considered 65 percent of the female cases but only 44 percent of the male cases surveyed to be regular patients, it appears that male patients have weaker ties with personal physicians and are less likely to seek their help.

The use of drugs was involved in 85 percent of all self-injuries reported in London: in 40 percent of the cases they had been prescribed for the patient, in 25 percent they were either prescribed for others or were nonprescription drugs; and for the remaining 35 percent, information was lacking on the status of the drug. Physicians reported that they prescribed 48 percent of the drugs used by their patients who injured themselves. It appears that patients having family physicians are more likely to use drugs as a method of self-injury ($p<.01$) as 92 percent of the cases reported by physicians involved drugs. Since patients sometimes go to more than one physician, the use of prescribed drugs is probably greater than 48 percent.

London patients were also asked about their use of illicit drugs. Eighteen percent of males and 6 percent of females were currently using these drugs on a regular basis. However two thirds of the males and more than 80 percent of the females had never used illicit drugs. On the basis of these findings it appears that self-injury patients are no more likely to use illicit drugs than those of comparable age in the general population. However, a higher proportion of those who have ever used these drugs are regular users.

In terms of the patients' medical history, four types of experiences were shown to be highly associated with self-injury in the London Study: previous psychiatric treatment, previous self-injury, depression and the heavy use of alcoholic beverages.

The majority of self-injury patients (64%) reported previous psychiatric treatment and actual figures are probably even higher. A surprisingly large percentage of patients (45%) reported previous *in-patient* treatment with 91 percent of these involving a stay of at least one week. Physicians reported that they had previously referred 31 percent of the self-injury patients for psychiatric treatment. Other studies[15, 27, 49] report rates of previous psychiatric treatment ranging from 42 percent to 58 percent.

A high incidence of previous self-injury (60%) for all patients was discovered. However, physicians were aware of previous self-injuries in only 20 percent of their self-injury patients and unsure in an additional 28 percent.

There was considerable underreporting of previous self-injury on the part of the London patients—46 percent reported at least one previous self-injury, but additional information from hospital records, physicians, and police files raised this figure to 60 percent. Where information was available from both patients and physicians, the latter denied or were unaware of self-injury reported by the patient in 18 percent of the cases, but 9 percent of the patients denied previous self-injury, although some of these were reported by the physician. It is quite likely that many more self-injuries were not reported. Thus, self-injury appears to be chronically repeated rather than being an acute episode in an otherwise stable personality.

These rates of previous self-injury are almost double those usually reported in the literature, for example, Leicester 28 percent;[15] Edinburgh 39 percent;[27] Southern Tasmania 34 percent;[20] and Newcastle-on-Tyne 35 percent.[49] This is probably due to the fact that more sources of information were used in the London Study than in those studies previously conducted.

Despite the high incidence of psychopathology among those who self-injure, no single diagnosis characterizes these persons, nor do they all show evidence of psychiatric disorder. If self-injury it not a result of mental illness as such, there is no doubt that all patients were distressed[25] and that the majority exhibited depressive symptoms. In the London Study, more than half the patients were worried about their mental health. The predominant concerns were anxiety, depression, and fear of going insane, as well as physical symptoms such as insomnia, fatigue, weight gain or loss, and fear of illness. Only 26 percent of the patients had positive self-images while over 50 percent had a poor opinion of themselves which is a usual accompaniment to depression.

The excessive rates of psychiatric treatment and previous self-injury among these patients gives the impression that they are defective individuals, unable to cope with their particular life situation. However, when we investigated psychiatric treatment and previous self-injury among the families of self-injury patients, we found that they too exhibited high rates of these phenomena. Almost one third of self-injury patients had members of their immediate families who had received psychiatric treatment. Eighteen percent had family members or close relatives who had self-injured. Furthermore, 6 percent reported that a member of their extended family had committed suicide. These findings suggest that self-injury behavior may to some extent take the form of a learned response to distress which is associated with certain styles of family interaction. Future research should be addressed to unravelling the dynamics of these familial contexts.

The fourth factor, the heavy use of alcohol, was highly associated with self-injury. At least 50 percent of the males and almost one quarter of the females were heavy drinkers—six or more drinks at a sitting.[10, 8] An additional 4 percent of males had been heavy drinkers in the past.

In this section, we have examined the medical profile of self-injury patients and discovered a number of factors that are highly associated with self-injury. The value of these findings lies in their role as predictors of self-injury behavior, and prediction is the first step towards prevention.

IMPLICATIONS FOR PREVENTION

Primary, secondary and tertiary prevention, which were outlined at the beginning of the chapter, can be implemented in both the social and medical spheres.

PRIMARY PREVENTION: Primary prevention activities of a social nature would involve attempts to alleviate those social conditions known to be associated with elevated rates of self-injury. A high incidence of overcrowding, children being taken into care, school truancy, divorce and juvenile delinquency are some of the related problems which could be tackled.[34] Some efforts in this direction have already been made in Edinburgh, Scotland, where community action programs attack social problems using such means as liberal cash awards to needy families and conscious attempts to stimulate community pride and concern.[34]

The growing number of citizens groups and the increase in popularity of the concept of guaranteed income offer encouraging prospects for prevention, by reducing the proportion of persons in positions of extremely low status and severely limited power. Given the high rate of self-injury among the unmarried and formerly married, we might encourage patterns of interaction that rely less heavily on the married couple as the prime social unit. To lessen the impact of role failure in the conventional roles of spouse, student and employee, we might provide more alternatives to traditional patterns of marriage, education and work and encourage the adoption of less stringent norms

The Self-Injury Patient: Sociological and Medical Profiles 113

for achievement within these roles. These changes, however, may not improve conditions for a major group of self-injury patients—adolescents between fifteen and nineteen years of age. They have a history of school failure, psychiatric disturbance and general unmanageability that is often related to an irregular unsatisfactory home environment. What may be needed in these cases is a higher quality performance by those who do opt to take on the role of parent. Perhaps the greater freedom in selecting alternative family or non-family roles may be structured so as to result in a better, more willing performance by a selective group of parents.

Changes in the management of deviant behavior provide another potentially promising route. For instance, it may be possible to reduce the size of our institutionalized populations without adversely affecting current levels of social control. This is the direction being taken relative to mental patients where an increasing emphasis is being placed on keeping persons in their community and if hospitalization is required, moving toward reintegration into the community as quickly as possible. Such changes can also be brought about in prisons. Between 1965 and 1969 Canada dramatically increased its proportion of prisoners who, when eligible, were granted parole without producing a concomitant increase in the rate of parole revocations.[9] However, much can also be done within institutions by decreasing isolation, by reducing institutional dependence, and by providing more opportunities for interaction with the noninstitutionalized population.

Rates of self-injury could be somewhat reduced by addressing programs of primary prevention to those syndromes that are associated with high rates of self-injury. Alcoholism and abuse of other drugs are two of these; mental illness might be another. Thus, programs effective in reducing per capita consumption of alcohol and other drugs might reduce the incidence of alcoholism[11,55] and drug abuse[47,46] and concomitantly reduce the incidence of self-injury behavior.

Medical efforts at primary prevention could focus on changing current patterns of the use of licit drugs. Fewer prescriptions particularly for drugs with a low margin of safety, more complicated packaging and the promotion of non-drug treatment methods such as biofeedback are some of the possibilities.

SECONDARY PREVENTION: Secondary prevention would involve the identification of those individuals with a sizeable risk of self-injury and effect appropriate intervention to reduce that risk. In the social sphere, schools and employers have access to sufficient information to identify high risk individuals and refer them for assessment and, if necessary, treatment. Social agencies could also identify those most likely to self-injure and plan appropriate programs that focus on effective referrals for the purpose of assessment.

Courts regularly deal with people in the throes of such life events as marital separation, divorce, evictions, and criminal charges. Opportunities to channel the potentially most serious cases are available at this level. One drawback to this approach occurs when false positive identification is made, i.e. persons who are not self-destructive are singled out for treatment. The labelling which occurs at this stage may well tag the individual for life. Society also has a responsibility to rethink these events and attempt to restructure them in ways which will reduce their negative effect on individuals. For instance, how can divorce be rendered less shattering in its effect on all participants?

The general public has been seriously neglected as a vehicle for prevention. A massive educational program via the media might enable nonprofessional persons—especially friends and family members of potential self-injurers—to recognize the associated characteristics and initiate remedial action.

Physicians become aware of much relevant information about their patients and presently constitute the major front line where intervention can begin. In the London Study, most patients manifested one or more of the predictors of self-injury, so that on the basis of history, presenting problems and previous experience with the patient, physicians have considerable information available to them to help them diagnose potential for self-injury. Perhaps additional education about self-injury would assist physicians to use this information to recognize and refer those with high potential for self-injury.

An assessment of the situation suggests certain inadequacies in this area. At least two thirds of London patients had either injured themselves previously or undergone psychiatric treatment. This may suggest that the help given to them was ineffective or that there was a lack of proper follow-up in which case some of the responsibility must be placed with the psychiatric and social agencies of the community rather than with primary physician care. Two thirds of London patients previously sought help from physicians and one-half felt they did not get it. When the majority of patients following their self-injury still felt they could benefit even though their previous help-seeking efforts were largely unsuccessful, this suggests that extensive reorganization of the help-giving facilities in the community is indicated.

TERTIARY PREVENTION: Tertiary prevention, which refers to the actual treatment of those who self-injure is also inadequate in most communities. Many of the means discussed under the previous types of prevention are appropriate here. However, since the target population is known and at hand, more specific tactics can be implemented. Some authors[25, 34] suggest that prolonged contact which allows the patient to develop satisfying relationships and more positive self concepts reduces the risk of repeated self-injury. Such contact could arise in traditional psychotherapy or within a therapeutic community setting. In addition they recommend the provision of crisis facilities which are easily accessed on a twenty-four hour basis.

As far as medical practitioners are concerned, it seems that physicians simply do not have the time to deal with these problems even if the inclination is present. As in the case of the alcoholic, the self-injury patient is often viewed as having a self-induced problem which is liable to be dishearteningly repetitive. There is a growing tendency to shift the load directly to psychiatry through referral to the general hospital emergency department—a service which can usually only give first aid, without good follow-up. As evidence of this, a follow-up of London self-injury patients indicated that psychiatric treatment in hospital was not associated with reduced recidivism.[42] What seems to be required is the ability of the person in trouble to refer himself directly, or to be referred by a physician to a readily identifiable facility in the community. Such a facility must give assessment and treatment or act as a clearinghouse so that treatment can be given elsewhere. Adequate follow-up is essential for the self-injury patient to give the continued support and encouragement that is needed by the patient to reestablish equilibrium.

The rationale for the prevention of self-destructive behavior is rarely considered, particularly since prevention measures are usually viewed in terms of saving lives, a basic tenet of the medical ethic. When we look at prevention of self-injury rather than suicide, the mandate is less clear-cut. Most of those who self-injure survive (97% in London) and in many cases, the crisis results in changes in interpersonal relations that, at least for a time, are somewhat beneficial to the patient. Alternative forms of help-seeking such as counselling, may be inadequate because they lack the power and immediacy of a crisis. For this reason primary and tertiary forms of prevention may prove more effective in the long-run. In view of the current emphasis on secondary prevention as evidenced by the rapid increase in suicide prevention centres, it may be wise to devote equal efforts to changing environmental conditions known to be associated with self-injury and overhauling current patterns of hospital management and community follow-up.

REFERENCES

1. Adam, K., Lohrenz, J. G., and Harper, D.: Suicidal ideation and parental loss: a preliminary research report. *Canad Psychiatr Assoc J, 18:* 95-99, 1973.
2. Bruhn, J. G.: Broken homes among attempted suicides and psychiatric out-patients: a comparative study. *J Ment Sci, 108:* 772-779, 1962.
3. Bruhn, J. G.: Comparative study of attempted suicides and psychiatric out-patients. *Br J Prev Soc Med, 17:* 197-201, 1963.
4. Buglass, D., Dugard, P., and Kreitman, N.: Multiple standardization of parasuicide (attempted suicide) rates in Edinburgh. *Br J Prev Soc Med, 24:* 182-186, 1970.
5. Caplan, G.: *Principles of Preventive Psychiatry.* New York, Basic Books, 1964.
6. Cahalan, D., Cisin, I. H., and Crossley, H. M.: American drinking practices: a national study of drinking behavior and attitudes. New Brunswick, Rutgers Centre of Alcohol Studies, Monograph No. 6, 1969.

7. Cooperstock, R.: Sex differences in the use of mood-modifying drugs, an explanatory model. *J Health Soc Beh, 12:* 238-244, 1971.
8. Cooperstock, R., and Sims, M.: Mood-modifying drugs prescribed in a Canadian city: hidden problems. *Am J Pub Health, 61:* 1007-1016, 1971.
9. Cousineau, D. F., and Veevers, I. E.: Incarceration as a response to crime: the utilization of Canadian prisons. *Canad J of Criminol and Correct, 14:* 10-31, 1972.
10. De Lint, J. E.: Alcohol use in Canadian society. *Addictions, 15:* 14-28, 1968.
11. De Lint, J. E., and Schmidt, W.: Consumption averages and alcoholism prevalence: a brief review of epidemiological investigations. *Br J of Addict, 66:* 97-107, 1971.
12. Dohrenwend, B. S.: Social status and stressful life events. *J of Pers and Soc Psychol, 28:* 225-235, 1973.
13. Durkheim, E.: *Suicide.* New York, The Free Press, 1951.
14. Edwards, J. E., and Whitlock, F. A.: Suicide and attempted suicide in Brisbane. *Med J Aust, 1:* 932-938, 989-995, 1968.
15. Ellis, G. G., Comish, K. A., and Hewer, R. L.: Attempted suicide in Leicester. *Practitioner, 196:* 557-561, 1966.
16. Evans, J. G.: Deliberate self-poisoning in the Oxford Area. *Brit J Prev Soc Med, 21:* 97-107, 1967.
17. Farberow, N. L., and Shneidman, E. S.: *The Cry for Help.* Toronto, McGraw-Hill, 1961.
18. Farberow, N. L., Shneidman, E. S., and Neuringer, C.: Case history and hospitalization factors in suicides of neuropsychiatric hospital patients. *J Nerv Ment Dis, 142:* 32-44, 1966.
19. Ferrence, R. G., and Johnson, F. G.: Factors affecting reported rates of self-injury. *Life-Threatening Behavior, 4:* 1, 1974.
20. Freeman, J. W., Ryan, C. A., and Battie, R. R.: Epidemiology of drug overdose in Southern Tasmania. *Med J Aust, 2:* 1168-1172, 1970.
21. Gold, N.: Suicide and attempted suicide in Northeast Tasmania. *Med J Aust, 2:* 361-364, 1965.
22. Jacobson, S., and Tribe, P.: Deliberate self-injury (attempted suicide) in patients admitted to hospital in Mid-Sussex. *Brit J Psychiatr, 121:* 379-386, 1972.
23. Jarvis, G. K., Ferrence, R. G., Johnson, F. G., and Whitehead, P. C.: Sex and age patterns in self-injury. London: *Addiction Research Foundation,* 1974.
24. Johnson, F. G., Ferrence, R. G., and Whitehead, P. C.: Self-injury: identification and intervention. *Can Psychiatr Assoc J, 18:* 101-105, 1973.
25. Kessel, N.: Self-poisoning. *Brit Med J, 2:* 1265-1270, 1136-1340, 1965.

26. Kessel, N., and Lee, E.: Attempted suicide in Edinburgh. *Scottish Medical Journal, 7:* 130-135, 1962.
27. Kessel, N., and McCulloch, N.: Repeated acts of self-poisoning and self-injury. *Proc Roy Soc Med, 59:* 89-92, 1966.
28. Koller, K. M., and Castonos, J. N.: The influence of childhood parental deprivation in attempted suicide. *The Medical Journal of Australia,* March, 1968.
29. Koller, K. M., and Castonos, J. N.: Family background and life situation in alcoholics. *Arch Gen Psychiat, 21:* 602-610, 1969.
30. Krupinski, J., Stoller, A., and Polke, P.: Attempted suicides admitted to the mental health department, Victoria, Australia: a socio-epidemiological study. *Int J Soc Psychiat, 13:* 5-13, 1966-1967.
31. Lawson, A. A. H., and Mitchell, I.: Patients with acute poisoning seen in a general medical unit (1960-71). *Br Med J, 4:* 153-156, 1972.
32. Linehan, M. M.: Toward a theory of sex differences in suicidal behaviour. *Crisis Intervention, 3:* 93-101, 1971.
33. McConaghy, N., Linane, J., and Buckle, R. C.: Parental deprivation and attempted suicide. *Med J Aust, 1:* 886-892, 1966.
34. McCulloch, J. N., and Philip, A. E.: *Suicidal Behaviour.* Oxford, Pergamon Press, 1972.
35. Middleton, G. D., Ashby, D. W., and Clark, F.: An analysis of attempted suicide in an urban industrial district. *Practitioner, 187:* 776-782, 1961.
36. Mishara, B. L.: Correlates of self-injuries behaviour in the institutionalized elderly. No date.
37. Modan, B., Nissenkorn, I., and Lewkowski, S. R.: Suicide in a heterogeneous society. *Br J Psychiat, 116:* 65-68, 1970.
38. Morphew, J. A.: Religion and attempted suicide. *Int J Soc Psychiat, 14:* 188-192, 1968.
39. Motto, J. A., and Greene, C.: Suicide and the medical community. *Arch Neur Psychiat, 80:* 776-781, 1958.
40. Oliver, R. G., Kaminski, Z., Tudor, K., and Hetzel, B. S.: The epidemiology of attempted suicide as seen in the casualty department, Alfred Hospital, Melbourne. *Med J Aust, 1:* 833-839, 1971.
41. Parkin, D., and Stengel, E.: Incidence of suicidal attempts in an urban community. *Br Med J, 2:* 133-138, 1965.
42. Price, M. P.: The effect of intervention on the recurrence of self-injuring behaviour. Paper presented at the Suicide Symposium, Woodstock, Ontario, Canada, October, 1973.
43. Ropschitz, D. H., and Ovenstone, I. M. K.: A two-years' survey on self-aggressive acts, suicides and suicidal threats in the Halifax district between 1962 and 1964. *Int J Soc Psychiat, 14:* 165-187, 1968.
44. Schmid, C. F., and Van Arsdol, Jr., M. D.: Completed and attempted suicide: a comparative analysis. *Am Sociol Rev, 20:* 273-283, 1955.

45. Sims, M., Purdy, M., and Devenyi, P.: Drug overdoses in a Canadian city. *Am J Public Health, 63:* 215-226, 1973.
46. Smart, R. G., and Whitehead, P. C.: The consumption patterns of illicit drugs and their implications for prevention of abuse. *U.N. Bulletin on Narcotics, 24:* 39-47, 1972.
47. Smart, R. G., Whitehead, P. C., and Laforest, L.: The prevention of drug abuse by young people: an argument based on the distribution of drug use. *Bulletin on Narcotics, 23:* 11-15, 1971.
48. Smith, A. J.: Self-poisoning with drugs: a worsening situation: *Br Med J, 14:* 125-128, 1972.
49. Smith, J. S., and Davidson, K.: Changes in the pattern of admissions for attempted suicide in Newcastle-Upon-Tyne during the 1960's. *Br Med J, 4:* 412-415, 1971.
50. Termansen, P. E.: Suicide and attempted suicide in Vancouver. *B C Med J, 14:* 125-128, 1972.
51. Tuckman, J., Youngman, W. F., and Bleiberg, B. M.: Attempted suicide by adults. *Public Health Reports, 77:* 605-614, 1962.
52. Vobecky, J., Kelly, A., and Munan, L.: Population health care practices. *Can J Public Health, 63:* 304-310, 1972.
53. Weissman, M. M., Paykel, E. S., French, N., Mark, H., Fox, K., and Prusoff, B.: Suicide attempts in an urban community, 1955 and 1970. *Soc Psychiatry, 8:* 82-91, 1973.
54. Welu, T. C.: Psychological reactions of emergency room staff to suicide attempters. *Omega, 3:* 103-109, 1972.
55. Whitehead, P. C., and Harvey, C.: Explaining alcoholism: an empirical test and reformulation. *Journal of Health and Social Behavior* (forthcoming), 1974.
56. Whitehead, P. C., Johnson, F. G., and Ferrence, R. G.: Measuring the incidence of self-injury: some methodological and design considerations. *Am J Orthopsychiat, 43:* 142-148, 1973.
57. Whitehead, P. C., Laforest, L., and Smart, R. C.: Les tranquillisants: drogues ou medicantes? *Toxicomanies, 41:* 225-241, 1970.
58. Whitlock, F. A., and Schapira, K.: Attempted suicide in Newcastle-Upon-Tyne. *Br J Psychiat, 113:* 423-434, 1967.

PART II
AUTOMOBILE FATALITIES, DRUGS, ALCOHOL AND OBESITY

CHAPTER 5

SELF DESTRUCTION AND THE AUTOMOBILE

Alex D. Pokorny

INTRODUCTION

THIS CHAPTER REVIEWS WHAT APPEAR to be some of the most relevant studies of the relationship between suicide and other self-destructive behaviors and the automobile. It then summarizes two studies in which the author was personally involved. Finally, there is a discussion of possible preventive and remedial measures.

I. LITERATURE REVIEW

Moseley[1] has been a pioneer in stressing the possibility that some driver fatalities represent suicides. He has presented many convincing case histories of such subjects, some of whom have made previous suicide attempts using different methods. In other case histories, the drivers were observed by passengers to crash their vehicles deliberately. Moseley stresses that the emotional problems seen in the death cases tend to occur in conflict-ridden people, with troubles of many years' duration. Such individuals then appear to enter a type of suicidal crisis; one of his cases had made two other suicide attempts within the preceding few weeks. Moseley brings out the important contribution of alcohol intoxication in many of these cases. He also points out that some pedestrians appear to commit suicide by stepping into the pathway of automobiles, but this is outside the scope of the present chapter.

MacDonald[2] pointed out that death by automobile offers special opportunity for concealment of a suicide, so as to protect a family from disgrace or perhaps to insure payment of life insurance. MacDonald did a study of a three month period in Colorado, during which no official suicides by motor vehicle were recorded, but during which time sixty-two drivers were blamed for accidents causing either their own death or the death of others. On investigation, it was found that three of these drivers were former patients of the Colorado Psychopathic Hospital and all three had died under circumstances which suggested suicide. This would mean about a 5 percent rate in this series of motor vehicle deaths. MacDonald also compared the rate of subsequent automobile fatalities among the 1,725 patients who had been admitted to the Colorado Psychopathic Hospital during a 19 month period, to the automobile death rate for the state as a whole; he found that the incidence of fatal accident drivers among the ex-hospital patients was more than thirty times greater than was true for the state population as a whole. He concluded that this disproportionate representation of former psychiatric patients may be related to the greater risk of suicide among former psychiatric patients. MacDonald then studied forty patients of whom thirty had attempted suicide, three had attempted homicide, and seven who had attempted both suicide and homicide, all by use of an automobile. He found that half of the patients had made their attempts impulsively following arguments and other acute emotional upheavals. He found that twenty-five of these patients had also attempted suicide by other means and one later committed suicide with poison. The automobile had apparently been chosen because of its immediate availability. MacDonald concludes that suicide as well as homocide by automobile are attempted much more frequently than is generally recognized.

Selzer[3, 4, 5] has studied this phenomenon in a series of investigations. Selzer and associates[3] point out that they found four depressive variables to be significantly related to automobile accidents, including those which indicated there had been prior suicidal preoccupation or prior suicide attempts. They state that the automobile is an almost ideal instrument for self-destruction on grounds of availability, frequency of use, plus the generally inherent hazards of driving. The automobile offers the driver an opportunity to imperil his life or even end it, perhaps without conscious awareness of suicide attempt. Furthermore, the automobile may offer to the depressed and frustrated alcoholic an opportunity to "end his life in what he may perceive as a burst of glory."

Selzer and associates[4, 5] investigated ninety-six drivers causing fatal accidents and a matched control group. They found that 20 percent of the fatality drivers had acutely disturbing experiences during a period of six hours preceding the fatal accident. Nine of the ninety-six fatality drivers were classified as suicidal or approximately 10 percent, whereas only one control case was classified as suicidal. Similarly, twenty of the fatality drivers were judged to be clinically depressed in contrast to only seven of the control group. In addition to suicidal trends, fifteen of the ninety-six fatality drivers had histories of violent behavior, but this was true of only nine of the control subjects. There was also a heavy component of alcoholism in the fatality group. These authors feel that such potential fatality drivers could be identified by their alarming traffic records and by their excessive use of alcohol. Thirty-seven percent of the fatal accidents were caused by alcoholics, almost all of whom had been drinking at the time. Therefore, a relatively small group of drivers accounts for an excessive number of fatal accidents. Selzer and associates have several constructive suggestions including the greater use of suspension or cancellation of licenses, prevention of the sale of a motor vehicle to unlicensed drivers, and better and more immediate attention to emotionally disturbed individuals and those under immediate social stress.

Edland[6] of the Forensic Pathology and Toxicology Section of the University of Missouri School of Medicine, points out that nearly all of the 50,000 plus fatalities on American highways each year are certified as accidental deaths. He believes that a definite percentage of these have actually committed suicide. He bases his observations partly on a study of accident fatalities in the Kansas City, Missouri, area and on a survey of psychiatric patients. Following a study, Dr. Edland considers that thirteen of eighty-six traffic fatalities which had occurred during the previous year were the result of eleven purposely caused collisions. Furthermore, four of the eleven drivers had prior histories of suicidal threats or attempts; in addition, one had gross psychiatric illness and one driver had previously committed homocide by automobile. In spite of this, only one of the eighty-six fatalities was certified as a suicide. Dr. Edland also reported a study of sixty male psychiatric patients in whom automobile accidents were associated with suicidal trends; thirty-three of the patients admitted to suicidal thoughts or attempts, and this same group had had more than twice as many motor vehicle accidents as the remainder of the group. Dr. Edland feels that automobile suicides are grossly underreported because officials tend to rule all auto crash deaths as accidental unless there is compelling reason to do otherwise.

Hamburger[7] states that some cases of death by automobile accident may actually be conscious, goal-directed suicide. He bases this on two years of work in the Emergency Psychiatric Unit at the University of Colorado Medical Center, during which time he examined forty-one patients whose primary reason for psychiatric evaluation was suicidal ideation and/or gesture. Hamburger presents several illustrative cases. In six of the forty-one suicidal patients, an automobile accident had been contemplated by the patients as a means of suicide. Their case histories and personal situations resembled those of other subjects who were contemplating suicide by other means.

In a related area, Siegel[8] has pointed out that suicidal motivation may play a part in many plane crashes. This may include a certain percentage of deliberate volitional crashes, possibly about a dozen per year in the U.S.A. Furthermore, there are a number of crashes due to poor judgement and to emotional upheaval which induces a pilot to undertake hazardous activities.

Schmidt and associates[9] described a method for investigating driver fatalities by means of a retrospective, in-depth psychological investigation. They studied all of the twenty-two driver fatalities associated with single car accidents which had occurred in

Baltimore County, Maryland, between August 1968 and June 1969. As a comparison group, they investigated victims of multiple vehicular accidents, on the theory that the single car accident victims would more likely have been suicidal. It was found that the multiple car drivers were on the average significantly older. On the basis of a psychological autopsy, sixteen of the twenty-two single car drivers were rated as having significant psychopathology with a definite psychiatric diagnosis. In contrast, significant psychopathology was considered to be present in only three of eleven multiple vehicle accident drivers, with a definite psychiatric diagnosis applicable to only two of them. Two of the single car drivers were suspected of being suicides. A third driver who threatened to kill himself by running his vehicle into a truck was later killed in this manner and was therefore rated as a suicide. If it is considered that one of these twenty-two subjects was a suicide, this would yield a rate of 4 percent, but if three of the drivers are judged as suicides this means that 14 percent of the single-car fatalities were suicides.

These authors also talk about the possibilities and the problems involved in identifying such high risk drivers. They mention the possible use of history of prior convictions, indicators of acute and/or chronic stress, suicidal trends, etc. They urge that others be sensitized to suicidal signs and messages, since a known useful suicide prevention technique is to remove the means of self-destruction during a suicidal crisis. This same type of intervention might be applied to the automobile.

Huffine[10] compared drivers involved in equivocal (possibly suicidal) traffic accidents with drivers involved in other fatal traffic accidents. She stressed that many deaths which are in actuality suicide may not be categorized as such, and a good example of this is death from an automobile accident involving only one vehicle. She states that traffic experts estimate that from 1 to 10 percent of all traffic fatalities are suicides. Huffine compared 782 single vehicle, driver-alone accidents with 4,381 other non-pedestrian fatal traffic accidents (multiple-vehicle accidents and driver not alone). In the single-vehicle driver-alone cases the driver was more apt to be male, to have been drinking, and to be driving as speeds in excess of 60 miles per hour.

Huffine then selected, from the single-vehicle cases, 115 "equivocal accidents," those in which no clear cause for the crash was found. These had occurred in clear weather, on good roads, etc. Drinking drivers were excluded from this "equivocal" group. The equivocal accidents were found to differ from other accidents in several ways which were suggestive of suicide: many occurred on freeways, at high rates of speed, the drivers tended to be older, etc.

One of the most active research groups in this field has been Norman Tabachnik and his associates at the Los Angeles Suicide Prevention Center.[11, 12, 13, 14, 15, 16] In one of their earliest studies,[11] these investigators compared fifteen situations of accidental death with fifteen cases of suicidal death. Both groups had been drinking prior to their deaths and had appeared to utilize drinking as a means of dealing with upsetting situations. However, subjects who had died by accident had not encountered a clear traumatic situation just prior to their deaths, whereas subjects who died by suicide had encountered the loss of an important person, or a feeling of failure, or of being unloved just prior to their deaths. Furthermore, they had depressive and self-punishing features in their life style.

Tabachnik and Litman[12] studied sixty cases of near-fatal accidents, and concluded that there was little question that using the automobile was merely a mode of committing suicide in many situations. This might be because of a desire to conceal the suicide for insurance gain, or perhaps because of improved self-image. They also thought that there might have been an "unconscious suicide-like motivation" in some other cases.

In a more recent series of papers,[13, 14, 15] Tabachnik has questioned the suicidal and self-destructive hypotheses discussed earlier. Much of this is based on an intensive study of twenty-four serious accident cases, twenty-nine severe suicide attempt cases, and thirty-one post appendectomy cases who were interviewed at considerable length using a psychoanalytic technique. Contrary to the previous opinions and expectations of these authors and of the psychoanalytic raters, they did not uncover any case of suicidal behavior among the accident victims. Both the suicidal and the accident group showed heavy, daily drinking, but none of the hypotheses linking automobile accidents to suicidal and self-destructive trends were confirmed. It should be pointed out that this was a study of attempted—not completed suicide, even though the attempts were serious; furthermore, the serious accident cases were not fatalities either. Tabachnik has stated more recently[16] that more recent analyses of this data have given some support to the idea that some drivers are suicidal; these later findings are not yet published.

SUMMARY OF RESEARCH STUDIES

The author and his associates have conducted two major research projects which are relevant to the topic of self-destruction and the automobile. The first project[17, 18] was a part of a large scale study designed to examine in great detail a series of automobile crashes, investigating the human factors along with vehicular, roadway, engineering, and other factors. The parent study included a complete psychological and personality study, to the extent made possible by the fact that the subjects were dead, of twenty-eight consecutive auto fatalities in Houston, Texas, during the period of 1967 to 1968, in each of which it was judged that the deceased was responsible for the crash. In addition to study of personality and psychological factors, each case was examined and assessed for the role of social factors and health factors, including a complete autopsy and toxicological studies, complete body X-Rays, a detailed study of the vehicle by automotive and engineering specialists, plus a complete review of the crash event by police traffic investigators. We therefore did not only a physical autopsy, but also a "psychological autopsy" and an "automobile autopsy."

For study of the behavioral aspects, we administered five sets of questionnaires and structured interviews covering these areas: (a) social history, (b) driving history, (c) alcohol involvement, (d) psychiatric evaluation, and (e) evaluation of the person being interviewed. Data were obtained from relatives, friends, and employers and other associates. There was specific focus on obtaining information available on any indicators of depressive or suicidal trends, sociopathic, homocidal, impulsive, paranoid, or psychotic tendencies. In addition, the alcohol intake history of each subject was explored in detail. From all of this information, behavioral ratings and judgements were made independently by two psychiatrists. The data from all sources were then integrated in correlation conferences including the entire investigating team of psychiatrists and epidemiologists, a forensic pathologist, a radiologist, a police traffic specialist, an expert auto mechanic, a civil engineer, and an attorney.

The classification of death in this report is based on the psychological autopsy and the decision of the correlation conferences. The psychiatric diagnoses were based on information from informants, relatives, hospital records, autopsy findings, and all other available documentary sources. The ratings of alcohol intoxication were based on history and blood alcohol level.

It was found that twenty-five of these twenty-eight consecutive fatalities were males, and this approximated the usual sex ratio for driver fatalities in our community.

The twenty-eight fatalities were compared with a "control" or comparison group made up of drivers who lived in the same voter precincts as the fatalities and who were matched for sex, age, and income level and quality of housing.

With regard to the apparent mental state during the hours or minutes just before the crash (or just before the interview in case of the control group), it was found that twenty-five of the fatalities were in an abnormal mental state, versus only three in the control group. Among the twenty-eight fatalities, twelve were found to be depressed and four were thought to be clearly suicidal. Eighteen were intoxicated, nine showed impaired judgement and poor impulse control, etc. It was clear, therefore, that the fatality group was made up of intoxicated, depressed, angry and impulsive persons.

An example of a case which we judged to be clearly suicidal is our Case No. 2.[18] This was a seaman who typically got into his car to "speed it off" whenever he got emotionally upset. He had been reared by parents who had discouraged any expression of negative or hostile feelings. His death took place soon after he had asked his wife to buy him a book; she had replied she didn't have time, whereupon he promptly became mute and sullen. He then went to the kitchen and wrote a note stating,

"You'll be sorry when I'm dead!" He then drove his wife downtown, let her off at her destination, roared away, and was dead within two minutes, having struck a tree adjoining the highway. The police accident report said, "It looked like he pointed it into the tree."

Another of our suicide cases had phoned his wife on the day of his death and had told her, "It's up." Later that day, he was found after his car had hit a bridge abutment, traveling at an estimated speed of sixty to seventy miles per hour. At the time of autopsy, it was found he had also made a superficial knife cut on his chest over his heart before the crash.

Since four out of these twenty-eight deaths were judged to be suicides, this means that approximately 15 percent of these fatalities represented suicide. This is close to the percentage of traffic fatalities judged to be suicides in the report by Edland cited earlier. If this percentage should hold true generally, this would have very significant implications with respect to corrective and control measures. We would need to think not only in terms of law enforcement, licensing, and engineering aspects of automobile safety, but would need to think in terms of suicide prevention, crisis intervention, and especially early recognition and treatment of depression, plus early recognition, appropriate management and treatment of alcoholism.

Our second study[19] dealt with the matter of automobile maintenance in relation to personality disorder. Many auto crashes are the result of driver psychopathology which translates itself into dangerous driving behavior, but there may be a further role caused by psychopathology in terms of poor auto maintenance. The National Safety Council has estimated that 11 percent of all crashes are due to defective vehicles, and other estimates are even higher. It has been noted that persons with certain life styles, such as impulsive, irresponsible, and anti-social personalities, exhibit risky driving practices; we hypothesized that these characteristics might also lead to risk-taking in terms of poor vehicle maintenance. The person with significant psychopathology would have thereby doubled his chances of being involved in a crash.

To explore this hypothesis, we conducted an intensive investigation of thirty-four randomly selected automobile crashes from among those involving vehicles at least two years old. This study was done in Houston, Texas, during the years 1969 and 1970. As in the first study, we included an investigation of psychological and personality factors, social factors, health factors, and in cases where the subject had died, a complete autopsy and toxicological study. The thirty-four vehicles involved were also studied in detail by engineers and automotive specialists, with particular focus on vehicular subsystems defects or maladjustments. Crash investigators and engineers did a complete review of the roadway environment and the vehicle crash. Again, the total of thirty-four crashes may seem modest, but such broad and intensive case studies are cumbersome and expensive, and it is simply not feasible to accumulate much larger series.

In each crash, it was necessary to evaluate the extent to which any vehicle defect or malfunction had contributed to a particular crash. We assigned numerical ratings ranging from zero to nine to the relative causality-contribution of: (a) the driver, (b) the vehicle, and (c) the roadway, in each case. Such a rating system allowed us to focus upon each factor separately and also upon their interrelationships. The factor with the highest rating will hereafter be called "causative" and other factors with positive but smaller ratings will be called "contributory."

It was found that twenty-six of the thirty-four study vehicles (76%) had one or more defects which were considered to be causative or contributory to the crash. The most common causative defect was poor brakes, and this was likewise the most common contributory cause. Of the twenty-one automobiles with defective brakes, rated either causative or contributory, nineteen had more than 45,000 miles on the odometer. This immediately raises the point that cars with this much mileage should have specific emphasis on brake inspection.

When we studied the drivers of the cars involved in these crashes, we found that 65 percent of them had abnormal personality functioning. This included 27 percent with passive aggressive personalities and 24 percent with sociopathic personalities. This raised the questions: (1) does the abnormality personality functioning contribute to crashes by influencing vehicle maintenance? or (2) does it lead to faulty driving behavior, irrespective of the mechanical condition of the car?

When we studied these relationships, we found that vehicular subsystems defects do reflect personality disorders. Of the twelve drivers who were diagnosed as psychiatrically normal, only one was driving a vehicle with a subsystems defect which was judged to be causative in the crash. On the other hand, of the twenty-two drivers rated as psychiatrically abnormal, it was found that ten were driving vehicles with subsystems which were defective and which were rated as causative; this is a statistically significant difference. Abnormal personality functioning, therefore, significantly influences the lack of maintenance of a vehicle.

Another way of viewing the findings was that among the twelve drivers who were rated as normal in personality functioning, only two had received tickets for traffic violations in relation to the investigated crash. On the other hand, of the twenty-two drivers rated as abnormal in personality functioning, fifteen received tickets and two more were considered to be at fault but had died in the crash; therefore, seventeen of a total of twenty-two were judged to be at fault. This is again a highly significant difference. We concluded that abnormal personality leads to poor vehicle maintenance and to poor driving. The abnormal personality patterns involved are mainly passive aggressive or sociopathic personalities.

A typical case history is subject I.A.P.[19] This subject received a citation for negligent collision and for driving without a valid operator's license. He was divorced from his wife and had not seen either his wife or his two children for six months prior to being interviewed. He had recently lost his job as a laborer after he had broken his ankle while drunk, and since that time had been unemployed. His vehicle was found to have defective brakes, defective steering, a defective suspension system, and slick tires which resulted in poor friction on the wet pavement, plus inoperative windshield wipers which had helped to obstruct his vision. When he was asked why he had allowed his vehicle to get into such a state, he said, "I thought I could adjust to it."

In summary, this investigation of thirty-four randomly selected vehicles involved in crashes showed that 65 percent of the drivers had significant psychopathology, notably personality disorders. Of those with abnormal personality disorders, significantly more received tickets for traffic violations in connection with the crash and significantly more were found to be driving vehicles with subsystems defects judged to be causative in the crash. We concluded that abnormal personality functioning contributes to auto crashes both through faulty driving and faulty vehicle maintenance. A man not only "drives as he lives" but maintains his car as he lives.

DISCUSSION

The consensus of opinion certainly appears to be that self-destructive trends contribute substantially to automobile crashes and the resulting deaths and injuries. This applies to the extreme case in which the automobile is used as an instrument of suicide. More commonly, however, self-destructive trends are expressed through increased risk-taking behavior, faulty vehicle maintenance, driving while intoxicated, driving while under emotional stress, and so forth.

It appears that if we are to intercede and alter this state of affairs, it will require a combination of several approaches including attention to legal aspects, design and engineering features, educational measures, the correctional system, therapeutic measures, the probation system, etc.

Among all of these approaches, one area in which progress is lagging and which appears to be least well represented across the country is that dealing with the emotional, personality, and psychiatric factors, including DWI.

What should we, therefore, be doing in this area? One can suggest only the beginnings. In the Baylor study[17] of automobile fatalities, it was suggested that identification of the problem was the necessary first step; this is one area in which our present system is markedly deficient. It was also recommended that a trained professional should conduct an evaluation of each drinking driver (and other disturbed drivers) so as to assess the problem and to apply professional judgement, so as to assist the courts and agencies in recommending further management.

It was also recommended that pilot studies be carried out to evaluate the efficacy of known or new treatment methods when applied to the high risk driver.

It was also recommended that priorities be established to increase the "payoff." Some of the personality disorders, such as sociopathic personalities, are notoriously difficult to treat, and the payoff in these areas is likely to be smaller than in treatment of depressive disorders.

It was also recommended that acute high risk drivers, who have usually had a serious recent stress, be given special handling. Another identifiable group on which to focus would be the chronic high risk driver whose problems are apt to be different, although also susceptible to intervention.

It was also recommended that preventive education of the driver and pre-driver levels in school be started, emphasizing the relationships of emotions and drinking to driving dysfunction.

It was also recommended that law enforcement officers and officials in the legal system be conditioned to recognize psychologically vulnerable individuals.

MacDonald[2] advocates prompt psychiatric evaluation and treatment of any person who attempts to take life on the highway; he points out, however, that such persons seldom seek help directly. He urges that police officers and hospital surgeons remain alert to this possibility. Family members, as well as the subjects, may talk more readily to physicians if encouraged to talk about the crash. This suggests one logical point of intervention, i.e. the Hospital Emergency Room. There are other logical entry points into the world of emotionally disturbed drivers, and perhaps our efforts should be concentrated on these.

Finally, it should be stated that the problem is more easily identified than remedied. Some of the groups of individuals and some of the processes mentioned earlier in this chapter will be difficult to change. We therefore need continuing research, innovation, and trials of new approaches in this important area.

From a psychiatric standpoint, the two areas which seem the most promising for intervention are: (1) recognition and appropriate treatment and management of depression, along with suicidal and other self-destructive trends. Effective treatments are available for these conditions if they are recognized and if treatment resources are made available. (2) Early recognition and appropriate treatment and management of alcoholism. This will probably work best if there is a combination of preventive, diagnostic, therapeutic, and rehabilitation measures along with law enforcement and probation approaches.

REFERENCES

1. Moseley, Alfred L.: Research on Fatal Highway Collisions, *Papers* 1062-1963, Cambridge, Harvard, 1963.
2. MacDonald, John M.: Suicide and Homicide by Automobile. *Am J of Psychiatry, 121:* 366-370, Oct. 1964.
3. Selzer, Melvin L., Payne, Charles E., Westervelt, Franklin H., and Quinn, James: Automobile Accidents as an Expression of Psychopathology in an Alcoholic Population. *Q J Stud Alcohol, 28:* 505-516, 1967.
4. Selzer, Melvin L., Rogers, Joseph E., and Kern, Sue: Fatal Accidents: The Role of Psychopathology, Social Stress, and Acute Disturbance. *Am J Psychiat, 124:* 1028-1036, Feb. 1968.
5. Selzer, Melvin L.: Alcoholism, Mental Illness, and Stress in 96 Drivers Causing Fatal Accidents. *Behav Sci, 14:* 1-10, 1969.
6. Edland, John F.: Suicide-By-Car Called Widespread in U. S. *U S Med,* July 15, 1968.
7. Hamburger, Ernest: Vehicular Suicidal Ideation. *Milit Med, 134:* 441-444, June 1969.
8. Siegel, Peter V.: Medical Link seen in Crashes. *U S Med,* Sept. 1, 1968.
9. Schmidt, Chester W., Perlin, Seymour, Townes, Wayne, Fisher, Russell, and Shaffer, John W.: Characteristics of Drivers Involved in Single-Car Accidents. *Arch Gen Psychiatry, 27:* 800-803, Dec. 1972.
10. Huffine, Carol L.: Equivocal Single-Auto Traffic Fatalities. *Life-Threatening Behavior, 1:* 83-95, Summer 1971.
11. Tabachnik, Norman., Litman, Robert E., Osman, Marvin., Jones, Warren L., Cohn, Jay, Kasper, August, and Moffat, John: Comparative Psychiatric Study of Accidental and Suicidal Death. *Arch Gen Psychiatry, 14:* 60-68, Jan. 1966.
12. Tabachnik, Norman, and Litman, Robert E..: Self-Destructiveness in Accident. *Proceedings of the Fourth International Conference for Suicide Prevention,* International Association for Suicide Prevention, Delmar Publishing Company, Los Angeles, 1968.
13. Tabachnik, Norman: Self-Destruction in Automobile Accident: A Psychoanalytic Research Report. *Proceedings of the Sixth International Conference for Suicide Prevention,* Ann Arbor, Edwards Brokers, 1972.
14. Tabachnik, Norman, and Wold, Carl I.: Suicide and Self-Destruction in Automobile Accidents: A Psychoanalytic Study, Research and

Relevance, Vol. XXI of *Science and Psychoanalysis*, Jules H. Masserman, Editor. New York, Grune & Stratton, 1972, pp. 89-100.
15. Wold, Carl I., and Tabachnik, Norman: An Evaluation of Interviewer Bias, Research and Relevance, Vol. XXI of *Science and Psychoanalysis*, Jules H. Masserman, Editor. New York, Grune & Stratton, 1972, pp. 129-135.
16. Tabachnik, Norman: Personal Comunication, 1973.
17. Finch, John R., and Smith, James P.: *Psychiatric and Legal Aspects of Automobile Fatalities.* Springfield, Thomas, 1970.
18. Pokorny, Alex D., Smith, James P., and Finch, John R.: Vehicular Suicides. *Life-Threatening Behavior,* 2: 105-119, Summer 1972.
19. Pokorny, Alex D., Smith, James P., and Finch, John R.: Do Problem People Drive Problem Cars? *Traffic Safety,* 72: 16-17 and 37-39, Sept. 1972.

CHAPTER 6

DRUG ABUSE AS SELF-DESTRUCTIVE BEHAVIOR

WALTER R. CUSKEY AND BONNIE MOREL EDINGTON

WHAT BEHAVIOR IS SELF-DESTRUCTIVE and what is not? Behavior that we may define as self-destructive does not exist in isolation, but is usually part of a complex of behaviors that may have different meanings and significances for the persons who perform them. Few people are so masochistic that they seek pure pain and self-destruction; even masochists, by definition, get *something* positive out of it all.

Drug addiction and drug abuse are not, per se, destructive. They may provide many useful functions for the addict and abuser: identity and a focus to existence for those who have little of either without drugs;[1, 2] solace and retreat for those who live in intolerable situations. Drugs are often a method of coping, whether in the slums, in combat, or in everyday life. They may give meaning and purpose to otherwise directionless lives—even feelings of accomplishment and worth.[3] Combat veterans from Vietnam have stated flatly that heroin and other drugs not only tended to relieve the tedium and fear of combat service, but that they even made effective combat possible by calming the soldier so that he could endure the tension and fear.[4] Brecher describes an art teacher who had been a hospitalized schizophrenic before he took to heroin, and later to methadone, and who declares that he has no intention of doing without them.[5]

In addition, the accumulated evidence indicates quite clearly that the destructive potential of many drugs, particularly marijuana and the opiates, is greatly and perhaps entirely dependent on the legal sanctions and the persecutions that the abusers endure, not the drugs themselves.[6, 10]

Thus, trying to determine what is self-destructive is not a simple matter. The "self" may not perceive the effects as destructive, merely as alleviating pain, or enhancing life, or even a time-killer. Even if he knows that some harm may result, he may think that the benefits outweigh the damage.

Destructive and enhancing forces tend to come together, and sometimes are the same forces, providing both good and ill at the same time. All of us do daily things that harm our healths and futures without being considered reprehensible, or self-destructive. The drug user may have another definition of what life is all about, and consider alleviation of stress or intensification of consciousness more important than physical well-being, and closer to "where it's at."

What appears to be self-destructive behavior in drug abuse may be a form of risk-taking or gambling in which the abuser saw the probability of beneficial effects outweighing the probability of negative effects; or risk-taking as an end in itself—an adventure—with little consideration for the probabilities of good or bad consequences.

The problem of "intent" includes not only the fact that unconscious motivations are extremely difficult to identify, but even conscious intent often cannot be inferred. How many overdose deaths are accidental, how many are disguised suicides, how many represent a form of shooting craps with death in which the addict lost? The impurities in black market drugs complicate this problem; an addict may not know how much of anything he is actually getting. Brecher, in the Consumer's Union report, reaches the conclusion that overdose deaths, as such, hardly occur at all—so-called overdose deaths are actually deaths from allergic reactions to impurities or to combinations of previously taken drugs or alcohol and the impurities.[11] Many people die of alcohol and barbiturates taken together, but in quantities of each that are nonlethal alone.

How often are the OD deaths, or suicides, really disguised murders? Getting rid of troublemakers by giving them nearly pure heroin is not unknown in the jungle world that the Harrison Act created. One addict graphically described to the senior author how distributors had killed his father, a pusher, by holding him down and shooting a heavy dose in him. This death appeared on the police registers as an OD.

How shall we define self-destructive or life-enhancing behavior —by intent or by effect? Since intent and effect interact, sometimes conflicting and sometimes reinforcing both the destructive and life-enhancement aspects of drug abuse, it is possible to plot these four elements on a graph of Cartesian coordinates, in which intent moves along the abscissa from life-enhancement, whether conscious or not, toward life-destroying elements; and effects move from enhancing toward destructive along the ordinate.

Thus, the medically-induced addict whose life is affected adversely by his addiction would be somewhere near point 1. But the user who seeks kicks or social acceptance and subsequently views the effects as more handicapping than facilitating his enjoyment of life would also fall near point 1.

Timothy Leary types—ardent proponents of drug use who see few or no negative effects—would be at point 2.

The already-addicted person whose only goal has come to be the maintenance of nonpain would be at 3. Included here would be the people Dole and Nyswander feel have been metabolically

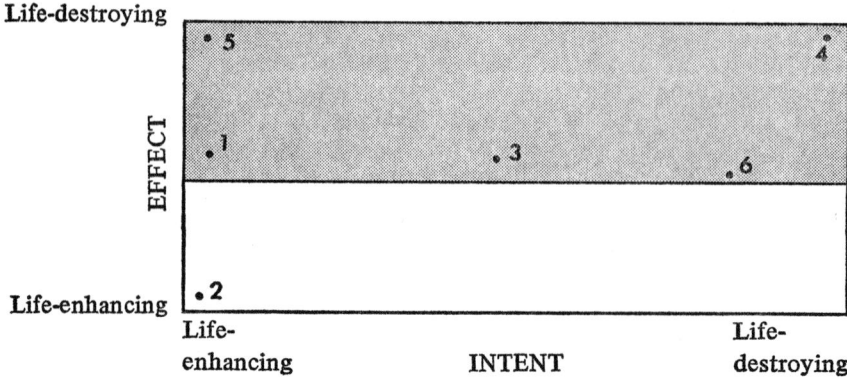

altered to crave opiates,[12] or those with an "artificially induced instinct."

Those who are not really drug abusers but who use drugs as a convenient means of committing suicide would be at 4, as would regular users and abusers who also use this means of suicide.

Proponents who OD, and LSD users who test their indestructability would be at 5.

Six might be those who believe they are using drugs destructively but who are actually able to cope with life only because they use drugs and who, without drugs, might be *really* suicidal.[13] Those who could be classified as using drugs with self-destructive effect would fall in the cross-hatched section of the diagram.

Another taxonomic system based on the same paradigm would be to infer self-destructive drug abuse behavior from three kinds of observable effects: (1) Suicides of drug abusers, whether or not drugs are implicated as a cause of death; (2) excessive risk-taking behavior among drug abusers that cannot be explained by any reasonable expectation of gain commensurate with the risk, with which, in fact, rationality has very little connection; and (3) "accidental" death or injury that can be attributed directly to drug abuse.

In the first case, suicide, the self-destructive *intentions* are presumably obvious; therefore, it is not unreasonable to assume that the drug abuse was part of a self-destructive pattern of behavior. In the second case, intentions are not clearly manifest but the effects are likely to be self-destructive. In the third, the self-destructive *effects* of drug abuse are identifiable, although the intent cannot be inferred.

These areas can be indicated in our "intent-effects" model shown on the following page (dichotomy of suicide into "acute" and "chronic" will be explained subsequently):

These behaviors are effects of—and in turn may be causes of—psychological and cultural conditions.

Depression is perhaps the most ubiquitous component of suicide. Drugs often seem to the abusers as a means of escape from depression and its associated anxieties.[14-16] Depression and alcohol seem to work together in facilitating suicide—in a sense

142   Self-Destructive Behavior

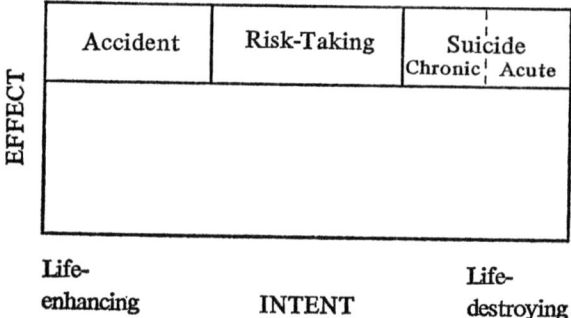

depressives take alcohol for relief and alcohol lowers the barriers to suicide,[17-19] "[Suicide] attempters appear to 'throw caution to the wind' when they are confronted with depressive stimulation."[20]

An enthusiast for opium, Thomas DeQuincey, called the sequel to his "confessions" "Lavana and Our Ladies of Sorrow"—which, translated from poetry to prose means depression. There is little doubt that the interactions between depression and the various drugs, particularly the soporifics, open the path to self-destruction for many people.

Social factors in drug abuse include ready availability of drugs, the frequently promoted thesis that chemicals can solve most problems, and such factors as subcultural values favoring risk-taking. The increasing use of drugs in suicide occurs to some extent for the same reason as does the increasing use of guns, that is, because they are convenient, easily available, and because cultural values give them at least indirect support.

We live in a society in which, in many respects, the environment, values, pressures and trends tend to contribute both to the use of drugs, and to their use in self-destructive behavior.

Perhaps at least partly because of our economic and advertising imperatives, we are a hedonistic, consumer-oriented society. Urbanization, competition, the break-up of the extended family and the fragmentation of community and of tradition, and the rapid changes of the latter half of the twentieth century, have tended to increase isolation, alienation, anomie, depersonalization and loneliness. From the vast reservoir of persons who have been affected negatively by these forces have come many depressed drug abusers.[21-27] The ready availability of drugs of all kinds—including the acceptance for everyday use of drugs that used to be made available only on prescription, and the constant iteration over the media that many good things can be had by ingestion or use of the proper chemical—have all encouraged the belief that many of life's problems can be solved by the needle or the pill. We must include also the promotional efforts of the great drug houses that produce barbiturates and amphetamines, and are not always too scrupulous about who uses them as long as they are sold.[28] One result has been the growing addiction of many people, particularly women, to these "licit" drugs, and the increase of the use of barbiturates for suicide.

Finally, an intensely competitive society that considers success the highest form of virtue as well as the only important way to achieve financial security and prestige, leaves little for the loser but some form of self-destruction.

SUICIDE

Suicide may be dichotomized into "acute suicide," which is the direct taking of one's own life (or attempting to take it) by a single, deliberate self-destructive act; and what Karl Menninger calls "chronic suicide, or chronic self-destruction" that is, a long-term deliberate practice that must inevitably lead to death.[29]

In the case of drug abuse it is sometimes difficult to distinguish the "acute" suicide from the "chronic," in the sense that a single death-inducing drug ingestion may occur among chronic drug abusers whose death wish may have antedated and motivated their drug abuse, as well as those who choose suicide as a means of escape from their drug dependency. For our purposes, however, we will assume that any apparently deliberate death-inducing act is "acute suicide."

It is interesting that the most suicidal among drug abusers are those who use the soporifics—the opiates, the barbiturates and alcohol. Those who use the stimulants like amphetamine, or the psychedelic-hypnotic drugs like LSD, have a high rate of mortality and damage to self, but these are not as easily traceable to deliberate suicidal tendencies. They tend, rather, to be associated with psychotic or delusional episodes of frenzy.[30-32]

Mikawa suggests that suicide should not be regarded as an isolated act, or as behavior characteristic of certain kinds of persons, but as a maladaptive response to stress, the culmination of a series of maladaptive responses.[33] Addiction and abuse often qualify as maladaptive responses leading to a culminating act.

ACUTE SUICIDE

Opiates

Glatt, et al. found the rate of suicide among British narcotic addicts to be 20 to 50 times as great as among the general population.[34] Deaths among opiate users in most western nations have been increasing substantially. A recent study of addict deaths in London revealed that 12 percent were by suicide.[25] Addicts often tend to be much concerned with the subjects of death and suicide, knowing that they are in considerable danger of early death. Glatt, et al. quoted a jazz junkie who describes what might be concerned a representative attitude:

> [T]here is a kind of rotary; as one dies, you know, everyone looks to the next one, you know, a kind of measurement. John's been on a year more than me, then I'm the next one to go since John's died; .... often one can be pointed out in town as ... "this one's the next to go". ...[36]

This jazz junkie himself died in jail of suicide at twenty-six, having been addicted since fifteen, and having given up family, talent, career, and everything else to his habit. He is an illustration of Nils Bejerot's concept of the "artificially induced instinct" that comes to by-pass or dominate other drives when full physical and psychological dependency sets in, and becomes the be-all and end-all of existence.[37]

His career is not unique, and illustrates some of the reasons for suicide. Older addicts often eventually find themselves in an unresolvable bind: they can no longer go on as they have been, and, there is no apparent way out. These are often the "burned out" addicts for whom there may be most hope in such programs as methadone treatment. Some come to these programs as a way to reduce the hassle, to cut the dependency and bring it under control; some, literally, want out, and are willing to make the sacrifice.[38] If they find every exit blocked and their problems insoluble, or think they do, suicide is the obvious solution.

The punitively oriented American and Canadian systems help this process along by the stigma, punishment and generally hopeless future they impose on the addict, forcing him into the junkie life, giving him a prison record and the addict label, making it almost impossible for him to work and live in a reasonable and relatively normal manner.[39, 40] Like Keats, they see as a great attraction "to cease upon the midnight with no pain."

Adding to the bind is, of course, the pain of withdrawal. To some people, death is less painful, and less shameful. The purely physical components of that pain are generally not very severe in the United States because street heroin is so dilute.[41, 42] This may also partially explain the higher rate of suicide in Britain, where the heroin tends to be purer: "No listen, I couldn't [withdraw]. My partner killed himself [by jumping in the river while trying to withdraw]."[43] But the psychological stress, the social pressures and conditioning, tend to fill the gap. The fact is that very few former addicts become drug-free through treatment programs; those who do become drug-free through forced withdrawal, as in prisons, almost invariably revert. The recovery rate in federal hospitals is only a few percentage points.[44] Even the modern, often highly praised, drug-free therapeutic communities seldom produce more than a five percent recovery rate, and that from the most motivated addicts.[45] For most addicts, suicide is an easier, and often more logical, option than withdrawing and remaining drug free.

It should be remembered that suicide is a real option. The suicide chooses his own form and time of death—generally more pleasant and less messy than occurs to most of us naturally. The addicts, almost by definition, are losers. In choosing suicide they express a power of choice absent in most other aspects of their lives.

> What people mainly fear in *death* is . . . a minus-life. It is irreversible failure—a permanent defeat of their most cherished values and directives. . . . Basically, *fear of death* is the dread of not

being able to die one's own death, a fear that corresponds to not being able to live one's own life . . . .

Suicidal acts may, in themselves, also represent life-enhancing behavior by finding, in death, some form of terminal fulfillment.[46]

Howard and Borges, examining the motives of addicts in Haight-Ashbury for behavior that could result in death, report that they spoke of "gratification in self-destruction."[47]

The connection between addict suicides and loneliness and hopelessness may be strikingly illustrated by a study of suicides among 43,215 addicts admitted to Lexington between 1935 and 1967. Thirteen committed suicide for various reasons, mostly related to their inabilities to cope with their life situations either in or out of prison and hospital.[48] This rate, three per 10,000, is considerably less than the suicide rates in other total institutions, though three times as much as in the general population.[49] However, quoting from other studies, they found that 14 percent of a sample of female patients had evidence of suicide attempts before entering Lexington,[50] and studies of post-Lexington patients showed suicides rates of 263 per 10,000 after discharge, and 85 per 10,000 in the first year.[51, 52] Apparently, the problems of coping with addiction alone, outside, are even more severe than in an institution. Cuskey, et al. in a study of three drug treatment centers prepared for the National Commission on Marijuana and Drug Abuse, found that a disproportionately high percentage of abusers lacked affective relationships. Their attitude score also suggested much alienation and anomie. The negative attitudes of those who had been in treatment longer were significantly better than the attitudes of newcomers.[53]

The addiction caused by opiates, and the legal and social sanctions that result from its use, apart from the pharmacological effects, tend to obscure the direct relationship between opiate—mostly heroin—use and suicide.

According to Sundby: "Psychiatrists familiar with young addicts are often struck with the lack of interest in their own lives and future. This attitude . . . also raises the suspicion that underlying suicidal tendencies are operative in many so-called accidental types of death among them."[54] There is little doubt that many so-called accidents are really suicides, labeled as accidents by shamed relatives, or because intent cannot be precisely determined. So-called overdose deaths in many cases certainly fit into this category. The same study that found that 12 percent of the deaths of a sample of narcotic addicts were due to overt suicide, also found that 81 percent were due to "drug misuse" including "overdosage", withdrawal and abstinence effects (treatment) and infection.[55] Damage resulting from extreme carelessness is not really accidental.

Alcohol

Alcoholics as a group are also exceptionally suicidal. Since alcohol is legal and alcoholism tends to be treated in hospitals rather than jails, a study of alcoholics and alcoholism might give clearer insight into the relationship of drugs and suicide relatively unmuddied by the association with crime and the furtive life habits of the junkie.

Data about the relationships between alcoholism, suicide, self-destructive behavior, and the increased susceptibility to suicide under intoxication are plentiful. Alcoholism was not only found to be a form of suicide, in effect, in the line of poisoning, but to have various trigger effects on suicidal impulses.[56-59] (On the opposite side of the scale, however, Menninger and others consider alcoholism often to be a *substitute* for suicide.)[60]

The cause and effect relationships are not always clear. Ringle and Rotter found three groups among intoxicated suicide attempters: a small group in which alcohol reinforced suicidal impulses, a second group of angry abreactors, and a third group in which suicide attempts occurred during the period of grief, remorse and self-hatred (and self-pity) after a long binge.[61] Sundby suggests that the feeling of having deviated from expectations and from group norms, may be the most common motive.[62] This, of course, is not far from Durkheim's classical theses of suicide as related to isolation and anomie.[63, 64]

Addicts and alcoholics often refuse help. Sundby reports on the experience of an Oslo clinic in 1970, that provided medical and social care for alcoholics as an alternative to arrest, and found that "many of them refused to accept the kind of help we could offer them. Quite a few of the 250 males we saw in this clinic died from suicide shortly afterwards. We were not able to prevent this outcome."[65] Sundby uses alcohol and drugs almost interchangeably in most of his arguments, and such interchangeable use may be well founded, since both are influenced or "caused" to some extent by phenomena of modern urban society: increasing concentrations of lonely people, stress, competition, lack of belonging, and the like. Epidemiological studies both of suicide and drug abuse (alcohol, opiates, and the rest) show a high correlation with these factors.[66-68] Murphy and Robins found that non-abuser suicides, who had affective disorders, did not differ significantly from the general population in marital state, a measure of loneliness and alienation, although they were more depressed. Almost half of the alcoholic suicides in that sample had suffered loss of close relationships within a year, the great majority of those within six weeks.[69]

Barbiturates

Barbiturates are very similar in their effects to alcohol; they have, in fact, been called "solid alcohol."[70] There is, however, a significant difference: while alcohol may encourage many more people to commit suicide, barbiturates are becoming a major *means* by which they commit suicide.

Roberts points out that poisoning is the second most common method of committing suicide (the most common among women), and that seven of ten of those who poison themselves with analgesics or soporifics use barbiturates.[71] Evidence is accumulating that barbiturates may be considerably more dangerous than opiates; certainly they directly kill many more people; yet they are legal, widely prescribed by physicians, widely used by people who believe they have insomnia, and widely available in medical chests for others to use. Even when prescriptions are deliberately restricted, patients can, by saving a few from each prescription, quickly build up a lethal dose. Barbiturates in the medicine chest are like loaded guns, waiting for people who have temporary fits of depression. In a study of a year's population of self-poisoners in an Edinburgh clinic, it was found that 55 percent had taken barbiturates. More than one person in every thousand goes to the hospital each year in Edinburgh for self-poisoning.[72]

The use of barbiturates, and other "ethical medicines" for suicide is rapidly increasing. The growth of pharmaceutical products has made highly dangerous drugs readily available, and frequently prescribed. Barbiturate suicide is an almost classic example of the availability of means tending to encourage the commission of the act.

The importance of the factors of availability and increasing social acceptance on the one hand, and addiction and abuse often leading to self-destructive behavior on the other, is well illustrated by statistics over the years. Add fatigue, personal crisis, depression, or psychotic episodes, and the mixture becomes explosive.

Barbiturates are so dangerous that the steady use of them could be called a self-destructive act. This is especially true if alcohol is also being used. The cumulative effect may very well be lethal, even if the amount of each ingested is not.

Intoxication by barbiturates, or the combination, may so confuse the abuser that he may continue to take the drugs until he is poisoned. Lawrence Kubie calls this phenomenon "toxic perseveration," and considers it "accidental suicide," although it may not always be so accidental.[73]

Drug abuse has always been disproportionately common among medical professionals, who have the greatest access, and who are very often overworked and tense. A major reason that Britain has kept drug abuse treatment under medical control is that when it became recognized as a problem, it was largely an internal family problem: physician, heal thyself.[74] Continuing studies of suicides among physicians show that those most apt to commit suicides are psychiatrists with a rate of about 6.1 per 10,000 according to the most recent studies (about six times the national average). Two-thirds had used drugs, and almost 40 percent of the suicides were caught up in drug dependency. Blachly, et al. suggest that society does not regard drug use by physicians as seriously as by other groups (particularly, perhaps, the young).[75] With barbiturates, and other dangerous licit drugs, that acceptance has spread to the housewife.

CHRONIC SUICIDE

Alcohol and Drugs

Alcohol and drugs can be, and often are, methods of slow suicide. In *Man Against Himself*, Karl Menninger popularized the notion of "chronic suicide," and pointed to addiction, both alcoholic and narcotic, as prime examples of such "chronic self-destruction." He considers "the psychology of the man impelled to ruin himself by self-poisoning, in spite of disaster, remorse, and resolutions to abandon it," as a phenomenon that is basically different from drinking or drug-taking for enjoyment—and different only in time and in degree from abrupt suicide.[76]

At that time (1938), he considered drug addiction to be essentially similar, but, since socially disapproved and relatively rare, not nearly as important. Since then, as Sundby puts it, "The recent rapid development of excess mortality in young addicts indicates that [Menninger's] interpretation is as relevant to these new forms of toxicomanias."[77]

Menninger sees such chronic suicide as "a form of self-destruction used to avert a greater self-destruction," a need for punishment arising from guilt about unacceptable aggressive impulses and thwarted sexuality.[78] This is, of course, a classical Freudian explanation. But the idea that long-term self-destruction may be a form of transaction in which the immediate goal seems worth it, or at least seems more immediately real and important, is common enough to fit other explanations. Slow suicide, in effect, need not be total death; it may be temporary surcease, sleep, or relaxed intoxication; or unconsciousness taken to the borderline of death, but over which we may not have to take the final step. (And in time the final step may not seem all that important.)[79-81] A slum addict may find his dreams and a retreat to narcotics a preferable alternative to everyday life. The long term death may seem quite distant, or an acceptable price to pay. In effect, he has already resigned from life.

Greenwald reports that in interviews with twenty "elegant" prostitutes, all had attempted to find relief from anxiety in alcohol, marijuana or other drugs; 15 had attempted suicide. Those who used narcotics said that it helped them forget, at least temporarily, how debased and degraded their lives were.[82]

Less elegant, black slum prostitutes have even greater need. The high price of black market heroin has forced many addicts into prostitution, in a tightening viscious cycle. Chronic suicide does not always seem so bad a means of dealing with a degraded and meaningless life. One final consideration about drug abuse as a form of chronic suicide deals with the concept mentioned earlier, that addiction becomes an "artificial drift," or even an artificial "instinct," so powerful in its demands on the addict that it tends to bypass and supersede normal drives. [83, 84] A confirmed addict has no other career. Sex, shelter, safety and even hunger become secondary needs.[85] Even life can become secondary, and ultimate poisoning, or overdose, can be considered as the logical conclusion to the need to keep taking drugs.

Risk Taking

Risk-taking behavior as it applies to drug abuse it not too different, in many respects, from its application to other areas. There is, for instance, what might be called "essential" risk-taking motivation, in which the thrill of the risk itself, of gambling much of life on the blind throw of the dice or the pressing of a trigger is very important. With addicts, risk-taking involves the injection of a syringe with unknown quantities of mostly unknown substances with mostly unknown effects.[86] Addicts often speak of this aspect.

Interviews by the authors with drug addicts on their motives in taking drugs when they knew at least something of the severe penalties involved, brought varied answers. However, in at least one area there was a continuing theme: they enjoyed the thrill of the risk, of shooting craps with possible disaster, even death.

Courting Death

Risk-taking, in which the chances of gaining anything worth-while (as we interpret it) are very minor compared with the dangers incurred, is often considered to be a mask for self-destructive impulses. Russian roulette it not really a game, but a toying with, and eventual acceptance of, death.

Sundby considers that the excessive use of alcohol and drugs, with their dangers of overdose, is similar to other kinds of deaths by poisoning in that the putative suicide, by taking the poison, is "gambling with death" rather than deliberately seeking it.[87] After all, various things might still happen to save him. In a classical article on suicide, Stengel states flatly that "there is a marked similarity between gambling and most suicidal acts."[88] Numerous studies and authorities have established the fact that there is little or no personal physical damage resulting from even large daily dosages of pure heroin.[89] But there is seldom pure heroin in the bag the addict takes in America.

The junkie life involves hepatitis, a disease that could generally be avoided by a little care with the needles—but few addicts ever take that care. In fact, their deliberate carelessness with needles, often using the same needles that other addicts have recently used, is so common that many authorities consider it a major phenomenological aspect of drug addiction. In a study of needle-sharing in Haight-Ashbury, Howard and Borges found that 92 percent of the subjects were aware of the risks in needle-sharing; yet, by and large, they kept on, inviting disease, rather than give up the "camaraderie."[90]

Much the same might be said about the dangers of other infections, of venereal disease and childbirth disorders among addict prostitutes and the like.

Percy Mason points out that about 1 percent of the total addict population dies each year from "overdose," and wonders "why addicts persist in injecting into themselves a substance of unknown composition and potency . . . . which is known to be potentially lethal." He concludes that such repeated risk-taking must be due to self-destructive drives.[91]

There is the persistent belief among Freudians such as Menninger, that the steady use of drugs, and risk-taking in circumstances in which there is little long-term hope of success, are expressions of the death wish. The stubborn persistence with which many abusers continue to harm and destroy themselves while thoroughly cognizant of the consequences, and despite desperate attempts to save them, would seem to defy any other rational explanation.

Control Over Life

Strange as it may seem to an outsider, the gamble of drug abuse attracts many addicts because it gives or seems to give them some choice, or control, over many otherwise hopeless areas of their lives. Slum addicts may find a meaning and direction to life and an identity which makes the price acceptable. As Preble and Casey point out, this can best be grasped if one understands the desperation and helplessness of life in the slums. Welfare, sub-standard housing, little schooling, violence:

> "In one short block where one of the authors worked, there was an average of one violent death a month over a period of three years—by fire, accident, homicide and suicide....
> The most common legitimate career is a menial job, with no future.
> ... If anyone can be called passive in the slums, it is not the heroin user, but the one who submits to and accepts these conditions."[92]

There is also (though perhaps it is not as important as many think) the hope of winning something—escape, new insight, new life, etc. Many addicts do win new forms of identity as part of a drug subculture in which each person has his role, and some measure of prestige and belonging. There is even a brotherhood of addicts in informal mutual aid societies. This sense of sharing, fraternity, socialization and mutual protection is part of the mystique of needle-sharing and makes the attendant risk "worth it."

Even outside the drug culture, risk-taking is often considered to be an essential element of a full life, giving the risk-taker some ability to control his fate, especially in times when the passive tend to "play it safe." Cradle-to-grave security, or even the "secure job" for thirty years to retirement, really means turning control of your life over to someone else. "Without risk in the pattern of human living, there can be no fulfillment; no distinctively human kind of life."[93]

The free enterprise ethos emphasizes the superiority of the man willing to take risks; deviants are often mirror-images of our approved social roles, using different methods, but applying similar energy and dedication to achieve similar goals, especially money, status and independence. McClelland, and others, have emphasized the necessity of the achievement motive and risk-taking for progress.[94] Carney indicates the negative aspects:

> Those who would find ways to provide satisfaction for their achievement motives must increasingly turn to behaviors which are nonconstructive and have as their major risk element social disapproval and personal danger. This is particularly true at the critical time of physical maturity.[95]

Street addicts refer to their activities as "taking care of business." Except for the brief moments of euphoria under influence of the drug itself, according to Preble and Casey, "they are aggressively pursuing a career that is exacting, challenging, adventurous and rewarding,"[96] and they are willing to pay the price.

Coping

Coping includes the relief from anxiety. Many drugs are taken precisely for that purpose. Opiates, alcohol, and barbiturates tend to give euphoria and to induce relaxation while psychedelics and stimulants give new sensations, distractions, feelings of omnipotence. We have already discussed the testimony of the elegant prostitutes who relieved depression and anxiety with alcohol and drugs. It is perhaps significant that suicide for drug addicts occurs most often after the addict has been withdrawn; early in the course of readdiction or just before, when the illusion is gone and he realizes how hopeless his situation is, and how difficult the world.[97, 98]

Ronald Maris states that the majority of self-destructive women are engaged in forms of ego-defensive risk-taking which could prove fatal but are really intended to be problem-solving coping mechanisms and that much, if not all, of incorrigible suicidality among women comes from society's reactions to what might have started as a relatively harmless deviance. He points out that female suicide attempters behave differently from those who succeed, and that this difference reflects a will to live. He believes that the ultimate suicides of female addicts typically result, not from the addiction, but from the stigmatization and social reaction to the addiction. He concludes that the majority of self-destructive women, including the drug abusers, are actually trying to cope with their problems. "The 'job' is to stay alive through a kind of psychic surgery: cutting themselves off from pathological families . . . evolving a narcissistic personality to fend off labels of 'worthless' and 'inadequate' . . . withdrawing from time to time into a subcommunity of drug users . . . . stigmatizing the female . . . drug abuser, legal authorities, physicians, and therapists can unwittingly contribute to future, more serious public health problems—such as suicide attempts."[99] Self-destructive behavior can become intertwined with, or caused by, stigma resulting from social punitive philosophies that break down self-image and create ever greater anxiety and depression among those already afflicted.

The Fatalistic Ordeal and the Cry for Help

Taking severe risks with life, through drugs or other means, is one way of keeping some control, or at least decision, about life in the hands of the addict. But it may often serve as a way of avoiding ultimate responsibility and throwing it onto something else, perhaps God, or chance: If only I get by this time, perhaps then I am meant to.[100, 101] Stengel speaks of the "ordeal, i.e. a dangerous trial whose outcome is accepted as the will of God or of Providence."[102]

McHugh and Goodell rate the self-destructive intent of patients who attempt to poison themselves with drugs both by the lethality of the amounts they take and the efforts they make to see that they might possibly be found in time. The categories range from *minimal,* in which the amount taken is probably not lethal and in a setting where help is immediately available, to *most severe,* where the amount ingested is potentially lethal and efforts are made to avoid discovery. Of the four grades, three leave much to chance. Even the most severe does allow something to chance, if only through miraculous intervention. At least three-quarters, then, leave a chance for outside intervention to change the decision, and, in effect, take the decision out of the poisoner's hands.[103]

Chein, et al. describe a similar evasion of final responsibility on the side of the addict. "The fact that he is an addict, despite the personal and social implications of opiate addiction in our society, allays the anxiety he would experience if he were to face, express, or act out certain impulses and wishes . . . in effect, he can say: 'Not I, but the drug in me does these things. I am not responsible; it is the monkey on my back!' "[104] Addicts are willing to undergo considerable risk, often until death or ruination of life, to achieve this result.

Suicidologists have long known that suicide, particularly attempted suicide, includes a cry for help or at least for notice.[105] There is in fact, a recognized period before suicide in which the victim clearly signals his intention, and even speaks of it. Much the same is true of drug abuse and addiction. Parents and society have to take notice. Perhaps they will also feel guilty. It is "a dramatic *communiqué* and plea to a public that stigmatized and ostracized them."[106]

For revenge is also part of deliberate personal degradation, risk-taking, drug-taking and even suicides for many people. "The addict may begin to express hostility toward parental figures . . . through theft . . . the spiteful, wasteful or destructive use of parental furnishings, money, decorations or clothing. Even his general delinquency and the use of narcotics itself . . . ."[107] "The career of a heroin user serves a dual purpose . . . it enables him to escape, not from purposeful activity, but from the monotony of a [limited] existence . . . and . . . provides a way for him to gain revenge on society for the injustices and deprivation he has experienced."[108] The final act of revenge is to wipe out the offending world, or to punish the parents, by the death of the addict.

ACCIDENTAL EFFECTS

Although, as we have seen, there may be "unintended" self-destructive effects resulting from the use of other drugs, the stimulants and psychedelic drugs are the most unpredictable and the consequences of their use can more readily be disclaimed by the users.

Amphetamines and LSD are not soporifics; they do not lull. They excite and distort. The amphetamines are stimulants, and high dosages, particularly in injections, will often result in bizarre, erratic, overstimulated and frantic behavior, with a good deal of excessive talk, little sleep, rapid ideation, and finally delusional and paranoid behavior. LSD is a psychedelic drug, and the delusions and distortions of perceptions are usually not harmful in themselves. However, they can be severe enough to cause considerable damage to persons who are anxious, fearful, or borderline psychotic.[109]

Continued use of such substances, with knowledge of the possible consequences, can be considered self-destructive. The danger in amphetamine abuse comes primarily when the speed freak mainlines. Extreme overstimulation and lack of sleep will obviously undermine his health. Eventually he may have psychotic episodes with paranoid delusions.[110] In some ways the speed freak is even more vulnerable to counteraction by the police and society than the heroin addict. The heroin addict lives in a world with defined norms and traditions, and within its limits he knows what he is doing and may even be very competent. The speed freak has no such guidelines. He belongs nowhere, not even in the slums, because he is usually middle class. He is an outcast among outcasts, very visible, very vulnerable.

As noted, those who abuse amphetamines and LSD excessively are often pre-psychotics, or neurotics—precisely the persons who should not. LSD can easily tip an incipient schizophrenic into psychotic episodes. It may very well exaggerate and aggravate pre-existing tendencies, causing them to surface.

Karl Menninger has described what he calls "focal suicide," mostly self-mutilations on specific portions of the body that might have special meanings for the patients.[111] A few papers have recently appeared describing a particular kind of focal suicide that seems to be appearing with increasing frequency among temporarily or permanently psychotic LSD abusers: severe self-induced eye injury. Rosen and Hoffman report on two young men who plucked out their right eyes, quoting from Matthew, "And if thy right eye offend thee; pluck it out . . . ."[112]

A similar incident occurred in a Baltimore jail.[113] Thomas and Fuller describe a man with whom they worked who wanted to carry Matthew to the extent of cutting off his hand as well, but instead enucleated both eyes.[114] In the entire literature, Rosen and Hoffman could find only ten cases of focal eye damage not associated with LSD usage. As the Bible quote indicates, the guilt and the drive to punish and harm the self were there beforehand, though they might not have been released and exaggerated without the drug. Thus, a form of self-destruction is implied.

The danger of LSD, in and of itself, has not been determined. Scare talk has not helped. For instance, the claim of chromosomal damage has little present support.[115] In contrast, Levine and Ludwig claim that a total review of the statistics indicate that the drug is *exceptionally safe* rather than dangerous.[116] Whatever happens in controlled circumstances, with normal patients and proper followup, is one thing. Those are not the settings for most abusers. The drug is so powerful that it can cause serious and sometimes uncontrolled perceptual disorders. Sometimes distortions and upset will result in danger, damage, and psychosis, particularly when used by unstable persons. Reviewing the literature on the complications of LSD, Smart and Bateman,[117] and Schwarz[118] (in separate articles) point to a number of reported suicides that seem to be connected to LSD use or its cessation.

Some LSD-influenced deaths might seem to have no connection with self-destructive intentions, e.g. the person who jumped out the window believing he could fly. Others, however, follow so closely after serious family quarrels or the termination of love affairs that suicidal intent can be reasonably inferred. All authorities seem to agree that uncontrolled use, in private surroundings, by persons who have not been carefully selected, can result in the release of self-destructive behavior. Regardless of how rare such instances are in reality, they are so well publicized in the mass media that those initiating the use of such drugs are aware of the attendant dangers and may even overestimate their probability of occurrence; yet are undeterred in using the drug. This would indicate a propensity for self-destruction or at least a penchant for exposing oneself to it.

SUMMARY

"Self-destructive behavior" is an exceptionally difficult concept to define objectively. Behavior one man feels is necessary or at least innocuous may well be the same behavior another finds inimical to his survival or well-being. In this chapter we have attempted to assume the subjective view of the actor and to label as "self-destructive" only that which he gives us reason to believe *he* feels is self-destructive. Even then we are beset with the problem of distinguishing those effects the drug abuser may admit are destructive but which he sought, consciously or unconsciously, from those effects he admits are destructive but were unintended.

Using a two-dimensional model of intent and effect, each dimension a continuum between life-enhancing and life-destroying polarities in behavior, we have indicated three areas in which self-destructive drug-taking behavior may be inferred: (1) suicide ("acute" and "chronic"), (2) risk-taking, and (3) behavior resulting in "accidental" effects.

REFERENCES

1. Preble, Edward A., and Casey, John J., Jr.: Taking care of business—the heroin user's life on the street. *Int J Addict, 4:* 1, 1969.
2. Chein, Isidor, Gerard, Donald L., Lee, Robert S., and Rosenfeld, Eva: *The Road to H.* New York, Basic Books, 1964.
3. Preble and Casey, 1969.
4. Westin, Av, and Shaffer, Stephanie: *Heroes and Heroin: The Shocking Story of Drug Addiction in the Military.* New York, Pocket Books, 1972.
5. Brecher, Edward M., and the Editors of *Consumer Reports: Licit and Illicit Drugs.* Boston, Little, Brown, 1972.
6. Cuskey, Walter R., Klein, Arnold W., and Krasner, William: *Drug-Trip Abroad: American Drug-Refugees in Amsterdam and London.* Philadelphia, University of Pennsylvania Press, 1972.
7. Cuskey, Walter R., and Krasner, William: The needle and the boot. *Society,* May/June, 1973.
8. Chein, et al., 1964.
9. American Bar Association Special Committee on Crime Prevention and Control: *New Perspectives in Urban Crime.* Washington, American Bar Association, 1972.
10. Schur, Edwin M.: *Crimes Without Victims.* Englewood Cliffs, Prentice-Hall, 1967.

11. Brecher, et al., 1972.
12. *Ibid.*
13. Maris, Ronald W.: Deviance as therapy: The paradox of the self-destructive female. *J Health Soc Behav, 12:* 113, 1971.
14. Chein, et al., 1964.
15. Preble and Casey, 1969.
16. Sundby, P.: Socio-culture studies in specific situations: Drug addicts and alcoholics. In Waldenstrom, Jan, Larsson, Tage, and Ljungstedt, Nils (Eds.): *Suicide and Attempted Suicide.* Stockholm, Nordiska Bokhandelns Forlag, 1972.
17. Mayfield, and Montgomery, Dan: Alcoholism, alcohol intoxication, and suicide attempts. *Arch Gen Psychiatry, 27:* 349, 1972.
18. Whitehead, Paul C.: Notes on the association between alcoholism and suicide. *Int J Addict, 7:* 525, 1972.
19. Menninger, Karl A.: *Man Against Himself.* New York, Harcourt, Brace, 1938.
20. Kochansky, Gerald E.: Risk taking and hedonic mood stimulation in suicide attempters. *Journal of Abnorm Psychol, 81:* 80, 1973, p. 85.
21. Durkheim, Emile: *Suicide,* trans. J. A. Spaulding and G. Simpson. New York, Free Press, 1951.
22. Melman, Seymour: *Our Depleted Society.* New York, Holt, Rinehart and Winston, 1965.
23. Chein, et al., 1964.
24. Cuskey, Walter R., Premkumar, T., and Segal, Lois: Survey of opiate addiction among females in the United States between 1850 and 1970. *Pub Health Rev, 1:* 5, 1972.
25. Cuskey, Walter R., Ipsen, Johannes, and Premkumar, T.: An inquiry into the nature of changes in behavior among drug users in treatment. In National Commission on Marihuana and Drug Abuse Third report, in press, 1973.
26. Cuskey, et al.: *Drug-Trip Abroad,* 1972.
27. Cuskey and Krasner, 1973.
28. Cuskey, Walter, Klein, Arnold William, and Krasner, William: Abroad thoughts from home. *The Pennsylvania Gazette,* 70 (4): 28, 1972.
29. Menninger, 1938.
30. Thomas, R. Buckland, and Fuller, David H.: Self-inflicted ocular injury associated with drug use. *J S Carolina Med Assoc, 68:* 202, 1972.
31. Rosen, David H., and Hoffman, Arthur M.: Focal suicide: Self-enucleation by two young psychotic individuals. *Am J Psychiatry, 128:* 1009, 1972.
32. Smart, Reginald G., and Bateman, Karen: Unfavourable reactions to LSD: A review and analysis of the available case reports. *Can Med Assoc J, 97:* 1214, 1967.

33. Mikawa, James K.: An alternative to current analyses of suicidal behavior. *Psychol Rep, 32:* 323, 1973.
34. Glatt, Max M., Pittman, David J., Gillespie, Duff G., and Hillis, Donald R.: *The Drug Scene in Great Britain.* London, Edward Arnold, 1967.
35. Gardner, R.: Deaths in United Kingdom opioid users 1965-69. *Lancet, 2:* 650, 1970.
36. Glatt, et al., p. 41, 1967.
37. Nahum, Louis H.: Addiction and preaddiction. *Conn Med, 35:* 560, 1971.
38. Cuskey and Krasner, 1973.
39. Cuskey, et al.: *Drug-Trip Abroad,* 1972.
40. Schur, 1967.
41. Brecher, et al., 1972.
42. Chein, et al., 1964.
43. Cuskey, et al.: *Drug-Trip Abroad,* 1972, p. 116.
44. Vaillant, George E.: A twelve-year follow-up of New York narcotic addicts: I. The relation of treatment to outcome. *Am J Psychiatry, 122:* 729, 1965.
45. National Commission on Marihuana and Drug Abuse: *Drug Use in America: Problem in Perspective.* Washington, U. S. Government Printing Office, 1973.
46. Weisman, Avery: Death and self-destructive behavior. In Resnik, H. R. P., and Hathorne, Berkley C. (Eds.): *Suicide Prevention in the 70's.* Washington, U. S. Government Printing Office, 1973, pp. 14-15.
47. Howard, Jan, and Borges, Phillip: Needle-sharing in the Haight: Some social and psychological functions. *J of Psychedel Dr, 4:* 71, 1971.
48. Chambers, Carl D., and Ball, John C.: Suicide among hospitalized opiate addicts. In Ball, John C., and Chambers, Carl D. (Eds): *The Epidemiology of Opiate Addiction in the United States.* Springfield, Thomas, 1970.
49. Mikawa, 1973.
50. Chambers and Ball, 1970.
51. Mason, Percy: Mortality among young narcotic addicts. *J of the Mount Sini Hospital, 34:* 4, 1967.
52. O'Donnell, John A.: *Narcotic Addicts in Kentucky.* Washington, U.S. Government Printing Office, 1967, chap. 2.
53. Cuskey, et al., 1973.
54. Sundby, 1972, p. 206.
55. Sundby, 1972, p. 205.
56. Sundby, 1972.
57. Mayfield and Montgomery, 1972.
58. Whitehead, 1972.
59. Menninger, 1938.

60. Ibid.
61. Ringle, E., and H. Rotter: zum problem does selbstmordversuches in Rousch. *Wein Z Nervenheilk, 13:* 406, 1957.
62. Sundby, 1972, p. 211.
63. Durkheim, 1951.
64. Maris, Ronald W.: *Social Forces in Urban Suicide.* Homewood, Ill.. Dorsey Press, 1967.
65. Sundby, 1972, p. 211.
66. Sundby, 1972.
67. Whitehead, 1972.
68. Rushing, W. A.: Suicide as a possible consequence of alcoholism. In Rushing, W. A. (Ed.): *Deviant Behavior and Social Process.* Chicago, Rand McNally, 1969.
69. Murphy, George E., and Robins, Eli: Social factors in suicide. *J Am Med Assoc, 199:* 303, 1967.
70. Brecher, et al., 1972.
71. Roberts, A. R.: Suicide and suicide prevention: An overview. *Pub Health Rev, 2* (1): 3, 1973.
72. Kessel, Neil: Self-poisoning. In Shneidman, Edwin S. (Ed.): *Essays in Self-Destruction.* New York, Science House, 1967.
73. Kubie, Lawrence S.: Multiple determinants of suicide. In Shneidman, Edwin, S. (Ed.): *Essays in Self-Destruction.* New York, Science House, 1967.
74. Cuskey, et al., *Drug Trip Abroad,* 1972.
75. Blachly, P. H., Disher, William, and Roduner, Gregory: Suicide by physicians. *Bull of Suicidol,* December 1, 1968.
76. Menninger, 1937, p. 161.
77. Sundby, 1972, p. 205.
78. Menninger, 1938, p. 184.
79. Mikawa, 1973.
80. Greenwald, Harold: *The Elegant Prostitute: A Social and Psychoanalytic Study.* New York, Walker, 1970.
81. Maris, 1971.
82. Greenwald, 1970.
83. Nahum, 1971.
84. Sundby, 1972.
85. Cuskey, et al.: *Drug Trip Abroad,* 1972.
86. Kochansky, 1973.
87. Sundby, 1972.
88. Stengel, Erwin: The complexity of motivations to suicide attempts. *Bull of Suicidol,* December 35, 1967, p. 38.
89. Brecher, et al., 1972, Chap. 4.
90. Howard and Borges, 1971.
91. Mason, 1967, p. 7.

92. Preble and Casey, 1969, p. 22.
93. Tomkins, Siloan S.: A theory of risks-taking behavior. In Carney, Richard E. (Ed.): *Risk-Taking Behavior: Concepts, Methods and Applications to Smoking and Drug Abuse.* Springfield, Thomas, 1971, p. 24.
94. McClelland, D. C.: *The Achieving Society.* Princeton, Van Nostrand, 1961.
95. Carney, Richard E., and Carney, Jane R.: Motivational factors in risk-taking. In Carney, Richard E. (Ed): *Risk-Taking Behavior: Concepts, Methods, and Applications to Smoking and Drug Abuse.* Springfield, Thomas, 1971, p. 54.
96. Preble and Casey, 1969, p. 2.
97. Chein, et al., 1964.
98. Mason, 1967.
99. Maris, 1971, p. 123.
100. Kochansky, 1973.
101. Sundby, 1972.
102. Stengel, 1967, p. 38.
103. McHugh, Paul R., and Goodell, Helen: Suicidal behavior. *Arch of Gen Psychiatry, 25:* 456, 1971.
104. Chein, et al., 1964, pp. 223-234.
105. Stengel, 1967.
106. Maris, 1971, p. 123.
107. Chein, et al., 1964, p. 234.
108. Preble and Casey, 1969, p. 22.
109. Brecher, et al., 1972, p. 375.
110. Brecher, et al., 1972, Chap. 37.
111. Menninger, 1938
112. Rosen, David H., and Hoffman, Arthur M.: Focal suicide: Self-enucleation by two young psychotic individuals. *Am J of Psychiatry, 128:* 1009, 1972.
113. *National Observer,* November 6, 1971.
114. Thomas, R. Buckland, and Fuller, David H.: Self-inflicted ocular injury associated with drug use. *J S Carolina Med Assoc, 68:* 202, 1972.
115. Brecher, et al., 1972.
116. Levine, J., and Ludwig, A. M.: The LSD controversy. *Compr Psychiatry, 5:* 314, 1964.
117. Smart and Bateman, 1967.
118. Schwarz, Conrad J.: The complications of LSD: A review of the literature. *J Nerv Ment Dis, 146:* 174, 1968.

CHAPTER 7

ALCOHOLISM AND DESTRUCTIVE BEHAVIOR

MARC HERTZMAN AND EMILE A. BENDIT

AN ACCUMULATING BODY OF EVIDENCE strongly implicates the role of alcohol in various types of self-destructive violent behavior. Theoretical controversy surrounds the exact nature of these relationships. Of the available models, Deviance Theory as propounded by Rushing appears to provide the best sociological fit with the data. From the psychiatric standpoint, Menninger's work has remained the most critical formulation on self-destructive behavior for three decades.

International comparisons of death rates from cirrhosis and four categories of violent death rates are correlated. The highest correlation is between suicide and cirrhosis, and this increases monotonically with age. Homicide rates are correlated at the younger ages, and the accident categories peak between homicide and suicide.

These data suggest a theoretical connection between the principal sociological and psychiatric models. By analogy to depression, the rage of alcoholic people is directed outward at first and with age is turned inward. From this review some programmatic implications are clear.

---

* Points of view or opinions stated in this chapter are those of the authors and do not necessarily represent the official position of the National Institute on Alcohol Abuse and Alcoholism (NIAAA).

Fascination for the subject of suicide is practically instinctual to the psychologically-minded. Each generation of social historians, philosophers, psychologists, and sociologists produces new explanations of why people commit violent acts, particularly to themselves. Perhaps this is but a measure of our continued puzzlement. The study of violence is both alluring and repelling, and it is precisely this approach-avoid-approach ambivalence that makes the understanding of this form of behavior so elusive. "Do not be too quick to understand me," Andre Gide implored. Despite the reams written upon the subject of self-destructive violence, we have continued to ignore the forest— the few threads of clear continuity—for the complications of the paths through the trees.

Our purpose is to draw attention to a few aspects of self-destructive behavior that stand out for themselves, and still demand explanation. The remarks that follow focus upon alcoholism mainly because the relationships of alcohol and especially self-destructive violent behavior are paradigmatic of both the difficulties and pitfalls of academic discussions of violence. They illustrate that approaches can be taken to relieve a problem even when there is little consensus about what the problems are, the magnitude of the problems is not easily measured and the causes are not understood.

DEFINITIONS

Since it is often difficult to get consensus about the meaning of words in this field, we wish to begin with some definitions. They will be assumed henceforth in this chapter.

—ALCOHOLISM is "a chronic behavioral disorder manifested by repeated drinking of alcoholic beverages in excess of the dietary and social uses of the community and to an extent that interferes with the drinker's health or his social or economic functioning."[1]

—ACUTE ALCOHOLISM is alcoholism in which the drinking person has been without intoxication for a period of at least three months before the current episode, and in which the current episode is of two months duration or less.

—CHRONIC ALCHOLISM is all alcoholism that is not acute.
—SUICIDE is killing oneself as intended by self.
—VIOLENT BEHAVIOR (for purpose of this study only) is death by suicide, homicide, war or accident.

ALCOHOLISM: ITS RELATION TO VIOLENT BEHAVIOR

National and international suicide rates have been a subject of investigation at least since the time of Durkheim's first sociological formulation on *Suicide*. The collection of statistical data and conclusions drawn from them have been subjected to searching, often justified, criticisms. Nevertheless, it cannot be ignored that alcohol is present in the social circumstances of a significant proportion of violent behavior. This includes suicides in a host of studies,[2,3,4,5] homicides in others.[6,7]

For example, in a recent confirmatory autopsy study, blood-alcohol levels (BAL) of .01 mg. percent or higher were present in as many as 71.4 percent of homicide victims in a given urban police precinct; BALs of .01 or higher in as many as 48.7 percent of homicide victims. In 50.8 percent of all traffic accident fatalities victims had a BAL of .01 or greater; in 42.2 percent of all accidental, nonvehicular deaths, the BAL was .01 or greater. For suicides, a measureable BAL was found 40 percent of the time, 23.8 percent of these greater than .10 BALs.[8]

In a careful retrospective analysis of suicides in which diagnosis could be made Murphy and Robins conclude that 25 percent of all the diagnoses were of alcoholism, and 50 percent of affective disorder (depression).[9] However, since the depressives largely resembled the general population, at least another 5 to 10 percent of the affective disorder group were possibly alcoholic people. Moreover, the alcoholic group was the only distinguishable group of any size which did significantly differ from the general population on a variety of demographic variables.

This type of statement, of course, does not say anything about cause and effect. Do people commit suicide because alcohol somehow impels them, as by releasing pent up suicidal impulses? Or do people drink to make themselves brave enough to do violent acts? Is alcohol present incidentally in a number of cases, e.g. since drinking is normative in the population,[10] may it not simply be a concomitant of types of social situations, in which the likelihood of suicide is increased? Currently there are no certain answers to these questions, but future research must clarify what the relations are.

ALCOHOLISM IN RELATION TO SELF-DESTRUCTION

We shall examine below some of the prominent hypotheses of suicide, and try to assess how well the data on alcoholism and its correlations with self-destructive behavior fit these proposals.

The relationship between alcoholism and theories of suicide depends at least in part upon demographic variables. In the case of alcoholism, there is emerging evidence of dual age peaks of incidence, one in the twenties and one in the forties.[11] Although this is not inconsistent with any of the theories, none of them has the dimensions that would have predicted such a bimodal curve. Therefore, this dimension of demographic variable presents a peculiar problem for the theories to take into account.

(We might note in passing that it poses more of a problem for theories of the genesis of alcoholism than for theories of suicide [although, as we are trying to demonstrate, they are inextricably tangled]. For, if either early childhood events or genetics are involved, one must still postulate two separate groups of events or genes in order to account for the phenomenon. This is contrary to current evidence on the elusive "alcoholic personality."[12] There is no reason to believe that such an identifiable group of people exists, let alone two such groups—but see also below.)

Sex

In terms of sex differences in the United States, both alcoholism and suicide show a significant preponderance of males. Although the ratios are much higher for the former, it is difficult to make much of a case from this, because the figures for female alcoholism are almost certainly underestimated.[13] In addition, numbers of suicides are also almost certainly in error. Males are implicated substantially more frequently than females in traffic accidents. If we were to count some proportion of traffic fatalities as being suicides, which seems likely, the male-female ratio for suicides might very well increase substantially. (See Pokorny's chapter.) Probably the most that can be said about this variable, therefore, is that there may be some correlation between the sex ratios for alcoholism and suicide.

Duration of Stress

Several lines of evidence are suggestive of intriguing parallels between acute suicidal attempts and bouts of alcoholism. The first is the well-known elevated mortality rate among widows from suicide and other forms of death in the year immediately following the death of a spouse.[14] The discovery of this risk factor has led a number of suicide centers to engage in programmatic activities directly intervening among widows during the period at risk. Murphy and Robins made a similar, though perhaps less well-known discovery; in a group of suicides, the distinguishing feature of the large alcoholic group of suicides was the loss of a loved object or other significant loss in the *six weeks* prior to presentation as a suicide.[9] In a similar vein, Smith has recently shown, based on work with a "Critical Life-Events" scale, that "Five markers occurred more frequently ($P<0.01$) in the patient group (as opposed to "normals") within one year prior to contact: (1) being in trouble with the police; (2) development of problem drinking; (3) divorce/separation; (4) loss of employment; and (5) having a member of the immediate family develop a problem with alcoholism . . ."[15] Although not all these events are necessarily of the same type, they certainly do suggest that loss and alcoholism both seem to occur together and that these may be a prelude to increased risk of suicide.

Religion and Ethnicity

Although much comparative work has been done in both the alcoholism and suicide fields on the influence of religion and ethnicity, there are, to our knowledge, no systematic attempts to deal with crossovers between them. This is an area that may shed light on both phenomena and clarify their relationships.

For example, it has become a commonplace observation in

American society that transplanted Irish are characterized by a high rate of alcoholism, and that this has its roots in customs brought with them in immigration.[16] Yet, whether native Irish in Ireland are prone to alcoholism is at least controversial.[17] The changing patterns in what is now at least the third substantial generation of Irish-Americans would tell much about the disruptive effects of migration and whether suicide and alcoholism are simply both the results of an antecedent variable. In like manner, it has been suggested[18] that the strength of religious ties in America is not weakening, and may be playing a stronger role in some areas such as politics with each passing generation. If this is so, we might predict certain groups with strong prohibitions against both suicide and alcoholism, notably Jews and Italian Catholics, to show decreasing rates of both over time. However, the patterns almost surely will turn out to be much more complicated than we have stated them here.

Rural-Urban and Socioeconomic Comparisons

As with religion and ethnicity, these phenomena do not correlate simply with suicide,[19] varying from place to place. Similarly, alcoholism rates were shown to be significantly different in urban and rural settings, but it was later shown by Pearl, et al.[20] that *intra*urban differences, even within the same community, at least partially accounted for by socioeconomic differences, were sufficient to vitiate some of the simplicity of the earlier data.

Socioeconomic comparisons are no less complex. For instance, for many years it had been repeatedly demonstrated in this country that rates of alcoholism based on cirrhosis rates seemed to vary inversely with socioeconomic status. However, this is certainly not universal. In Great Britain, exactly the reverse is true, and alcoholism seems to be a function of the relative availability of alcohol as an intoxicant.[21] It is difficult to know what implications this has for suicidal potential in people prone to use alcohol, if there are such people.

The examples we have given above illustrate the relative poverty of what Merton has termed "Theories of the Middle

Range" that might bring some order to interesting confusion. It seems most unlikely that any of the theories currently in use, with the possible exception of the Theory of Deviance (see below), can be characterized by sufficient comprehensiveness and systematization to explain the bulk of the observations. In the next section we briefly review the merits of some of these theories, and propose a starting point for new frameworks based upon previous work on the nature of depression.

SOME THEORIES OF SUICIDE AND THEIR RELATIONS TO CHRONIC ALCOHOLISM

Durkheim's *Suicide* is, of course, the prototype of sociological theories of suicide. While his data were by his own admission rather crude, his theory has been exhaustively reviewed and rebutted by each subsequent generation of sociologists. Nevertheless, it continues to resurface, as in the recent version of the theory of "Status Integration" of Gibbs and Martin.[22] We do not propose to review any of these in detail, since this has been done in recent works.[23]

However, we mention Durkheim's theory of *anomie* and its elaborations because the basic notion of alienation is quite consistent with sociological explanations of the origin of alcoholism. The problem from the point of view of the present discussion is that the theory can explain both alcoholism and suicide, but is not nearly sufficient to explain either in entirety. In other words, it is an old problem of prediction: there is no particular reason for a given person to pick one outcome over another. In fact, one might even say that it is a function of the opportunities available at the time of some critical event in the person's life, akin to Cloward and Ohlin's theory of the origin of delinquency as being a function of the opportunities available.[24]

Theories of suicide dependent upon economics may be exemplified by that of Henry and Short.[25] They propose that economic gains or losses respectively decrease or increase frustration. The *expression* of frustration, however, or the type of outlet for aggression, is characteristic of the restraints imposed by social class. Lower class people are considered more impulsive and given to aggression directed outwards.

This vastly oversimplified version of their theory can be tested by means of the international comparison data (see below). Compared to rich nations, poor nations had significantly greater positive *rho* values for *both* suicide and homicide. Henry and Short's postulates would presumably predict that the high suicide-alcoholism correlation should be among the rich nations instead. Morever, the result is consonant with the growing evidence that alcoholism may be a prominent factor in a number of types of violence.

There are a number of difficulties with trying to fit alcoholism into this type of schema. First of all, economic factors probably can account for only a limited part of the variance in suicide rates. In addition, as we have seen, both suicide and alcoholism appear to be complex in relation to SES. There is very little comparable data about the correlations of alcoholism and SES over time. However, there is an accumulating body of evidence that cost factors and the availability of absolute alcohol may be most critically related to the complications of alcoholism, including fatalities from cirrhosis and other causes.[26] Since government regulation and taxation can control the bulk of the liquor supply in most nations, there is little reason to believe that cost or the availability of alcohol could have much effect upon suicidal rates, except perhaps in the most indirect ways (e.g. suicide might rise because alcoholic people were deprived of a life-sustaining drug).

A number of other theories have been examined exhaustively by Douglas.[23] Of interest to note in regard to most of them—including Douglas's own—is that they generally begin historically with sociological parameters and move progressively, through revisions by later critiques of their own work, towards the position that no such models can be complete without some integration of psychological factors, especially individual attitudes and meaning. The sociology of alcoholism, however, does not seem to have reached this point. Whether this is a difference in historical development is unclear. Nevertheless, it seems to us that the two types of explanation are inextricably linked, and must somehow be taken into account by both schools of professional thought, psychological and sociological.

We have intimated above that the "Deviance" theory of suicide attempts to do just this, to integrate sociological and psychological data. In a series of recent articles, Rushing has elaborated this point of view between alcoholism and suicide. Figure 7-1 is a diagram of the "Deviance" theory in systems terms.

Rushing has described the propositions in simplified form as follows:

"*Proposition 1.* Suicide is directly related to loss in social interaction.
Proposition 2. Suicide is directly related to deviance.
Proposition 3. Deviance is directly related to loss in social interaction.
Hypothesis Suicide and deviance are related because loss in social interaction is a consequence of deviance and an antecedent of suicide." [5]

However, as Figure 7-1 demonstrates, a number of implied relationships are omitted from this formulation. For example, social rejection is certainly a multi-dimensional item, as we have suggested above. Does one type of loss lead to a particular form of deviance? The theory would suggest not. But clearly in cer-

DEVIANCE THEORY — FIGURE 7-1

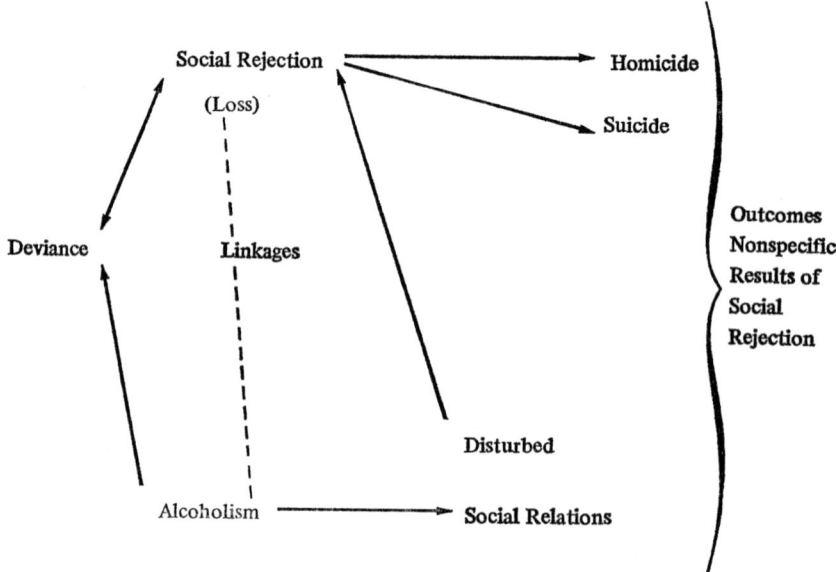

tain subcultures homicide or suicide is a form of loss, and results in a chain of either homicides (feuds) or suicides (the obligations of spouses).

Moreover, in at least one instance, Rushing's evidence would appear to be on shaky grounds. This relates to the fact that homicides tend to precede suicides, and in 96 percent of cases in one study,[27] "The homicide victim was either a relative or a paramour of the offender." But this may be a simple function of greater exposure to those immediately around them. In other words, the statistic is meaningful only if one knows the relative likelihood of exposure, and this would be extraordinarily difficult to measure. Nevertheless, his general point does seem valid, and the theory lends much structure to the subject. This is particularly true of his discussion of the alcoholism-suicide relationship, in which he points out that mediating links have yet to be described, but that his theory is basically consistent with Menninger's earlier psychological "depth" theory formulation (see below).

PSYCHOLOGICAL THEORIES

From a psychological perspective much has been written concerning why people become chronically alcoholic, why people attempt suicide and other forms of self-destructive behavior, and why the coincidence of both occurs in a larger than expected segment of the population. In this section we will review the psychological models developed to understand alcoholism, the diagnostic categories that are used clinically, and the explanations offered for the significant association that occurs between alcoholism and the various forms of self-destructive behavior. As will be seen, the work that has been done to date represents only a most basic attempt to understand this problem and while some clarity has been achieved, the most important benefit to be gained from these efforts is direction for further investigation.

In the study of alcoholic people, theories have developed around at least two basic notions. One school of thought is that this illness is a symptom of an underlying emotional or personality disorder, while the other maintains that alcoholism, like other behavior, is learned behavior and follows the laws developed in various theoretical models of learning. The first approach represents psychodynamic thinking, which as we shall see shortly is not of one mind, while the second approach represents behaviorism and learning theory. Each framework provides a different perspective that is informative but in and of itself incomplete. Perhaps most important, though, is that guidelines that might be drawn from a proper theoretical understanding of this illness to aid in formulating treatment programs have not been as successful as might be desired.

PSYCHODYNAMIC FORMULATIONS

The intrapsychic approach was first explored by Freud (1897) in his comments on addictions.[28] He along with Abraham, Ferenczi and Knight emphasized the release from inhibition afforded by alcohol, allowing expression of repressed urges.[29, 30] The repressed tendencies of prime importance to this school of thought are oral dependency and latent homosexuality. They suggested that in chronic alcoholic people specific oral functions in childhood were created because of difficult family constellations. Consequently, oral fixations developed from these frustrations precluding the learning of self-confidence and necessitating continuing oral gratification. In boys, these frustrations also result in a turning away from the frustrating mother to the father, setting the stage for (more or less) repressed homosexual tendencies. Fenichel points out that latent homosexuals, seduced by social frustrations, are particularly fond of alcohol rather than that alcohol through its toxic effectiveness is particularly conducive to homosexuality.[31] Alcohol is seen in this context, then, as banishing care, making obstacles smaller and wish fulfillments nearer. It allows for the escape from external frustrations through pleasurable fantasies or from internal inhibitions through the reduction of caring.

Menninger in his landmark book, *Man Against Himself*, presents the self-destructive tendency as having prime importance.[32] He proposes that a person resorts to alcoholism to avert a greater self-destruction. While he notes the frustration of early childhood oral gratification needs as being preliminary, he draws attention to the consequence of this; the child becomes angry towards his parents and guilt subsequently develops from the anger. Drinking behavior arises from this guilt and thus may serve three purposes: oral gratification, self-punishment for anger towards his parents, and symbolic revenge against his parents.

Key to much of this thinking is a lack of self-respect or some defect in self-esteem. This is similar to the determinants of depression. A model of this syndrome which seems to us to be particularly relevant is the work of Bibring.[33] He adopts the viewpoint that depression represents a basic reaction to situations of narcissistic frustration which the ego appears powerless to prevent. Thus an individual who is dependent on external "supplies" for the maintenance of his own self-esteem is prone to narcissistic injuries and oral recovery mechanisms (alcohol).

Behavioral Approaches

Miller and Barlow[34] in their recent paper summarize social learning formulations related to alcohol use as a socially acquired, habitual behavior pattern maintained by reinforcement contingencies. The most important of these reinforcing conditions seems to be the reduction of anxiety. The alcoholic person is able to avoid or escape from unpleasantness by excessive drinking. He is able to exhibit more varied, spontaneous social behavior, gain increased social reinforcement (either positive or negative) from relatives and friends, or avoid withdrawal symptoms associated with cessation of drinking. That aversive consequences such as hangover, nausea, physical disorders, loss of family or employment, and arrests seem to have such as apparent lack of influence appears to be related to the long delay between actual drinking behavior and occurrence of these events. In addition, studies of alcohol abuse from an approach-avoidance viewpoint reveal that low doses of alcohol reduce anxiety and concern about punishment.[35]

The behavioral point of view makes no mention of a self-destructive component in alcohol abuse. Rather it seems to say that alcohol abuse serves a protective function. While the behavioral model in some ways is similar to much of psychoanalytic thinking, it differs significantly from Menninger's proposition, which clearly posits a self-destructive component.

Other Models

Efforts have been expended to develop a definition of an alcoholic personality. The hope is to define those common characteristics which might be found in the pre-alcoholic stage and would thus correlate with a predisposition to alcoholism. Blane has identified the following characteristics which he suggests also have relevance for treatment and rehabilitation: low frustration tolerance, sociability, feelings of inferiority combined with attitudes of superiority, fearfulness, and dependency.[36] Lisansky[37] lists the following: an intensely strong need for dependency, a weak and inadequate defense mechanism against this excessive need, which leads, under certain conditions, to an intense dependence-independence conflict with a low degree of tolerance for frustration or tension, and unresolved love-hate ambivalences.

We have seen that the psychological models proposed come in almost every shape and design conceivable. This might be expected when a complex process such as alcoholism comes under scrutiny. Research support for any of these has been minimal and far from conclusive. The differences between alcoholic individuals are far greater than what they share in common. The characteristics that have been identified to describe alcoholic people are, of course, not unique to them but are found among many persons, especially those with psychological difficulties. This is pointed out not to make light of a psychological approach to understanding this illness but rather to highlight that our current knowledge exists on a most elementary level.

CLINICAL RELATION OF ALCOHOLISM AND SUICIDE

In our overview of the theoretical models of alcoholism there were only two which mentioned self-destructive behavior explicitly, Menninger's and Rushing's. Menninger used the term "chronic suicide" in describing alcoholism. Other researchers have been interested in the relationship between alcoholism and suicide. We shall now present some of the alternative interpretations that have been proposed.

As Rushing[5] notes (see above), the possibility exists that both alcoholism and suicide are expressions of a common underlying variable, such as urbanization, social disorganization, the death instinct, or oral personality type. A second alternative is that social rejection is an intervening variable in the alcoholism-suicide relationship. It is this proposition which Rushing feels is supported by the data he has examined. By this he means that alcoholism contributes to suicide partly because it creates disruptions in the alcoholic person's social relations. By his excessive consumption of alcohol, the alcoholic person may shirk economic and social roles, and engage in various forms of public deviance that are embarrassing, threatening and repugnant to relatives, friends, and others. Disruptions in social relations are frequent antecedents of suicide.

Whitehead[4] reviews these approaches and concludes from his own work that both alcoholism and a breakdown of interpersonal relationships occur prior to the onset of suicidal thoughts. He is wary of the explanations that the alcoholism-suicide relationship is an effect of the same cause or that alcoholism is a form of suicide. His data supports the following order of occurrence for the events involved: alcoholism occurs first, followed by breakdown in interpersonal relations and this is followed by the suicidal thoughts.

Ringle and Rotter describe three groups among intoxicated suicide attempters: a small group in whom intoxication seems to facilitate a suicidal impulse, a second group in whom intoxication induces an angry abreaction, and the largest group consisting of chronic alcoholic people who make their attempts during periods of "grief and remorse" at the end of prolonged drinking episodes.[38] Others have noticed this depressive phenomenon.[39, 40] Mayfield and Montgomery postulate two mechanisms underlying drunken suicide: an abreactive mechanism and a depressive mechanism secondary to chronic drunkenness.[3] Their thought is that the abreactive suicide attempts should occur at the onset of drinking or at a time of rapid increase in the level of intoxication. Alcohol-induced depression leading to suicide attempts clinically results from a prolonged period of drinking lasting at least two weeks. Behaviorally the two types differ markedly with the former showing explosive, aggressive, motorically hyperactive behavior while the latter is alone and quiet at the time of his attempts.

We would like to suggest a model of self-destructive behavior which involves alcohol, and attempts to take into account both psychological and sociological explanations (Fig. 7-2). The major difference between this theory and that of Rushing is the concept of a continuum of aggressively self-destructive behavior that stems, in part, from the data to be presented on international comparisons of violent behavior and cirrhosis (alcoholism). It appears that one plausible explanation of our data is that there is a gradual change in behavior with age. In the earlier age groups, aggression is directed toward others. This is manifested by the peak of homicide-cirrhosis rates in the lower adult age groups. At the other end of the age spectrum, the available object of violence is the self. In between is the peak of accidents—traffic accidents and cirrhosis, where it is often uncertain whether the behavior is directed at others, the self, or both.

Outcome, then, is not accidental. It may well be age-specific, as Lester has also observed.[41] Furthermore, "social rejection,"

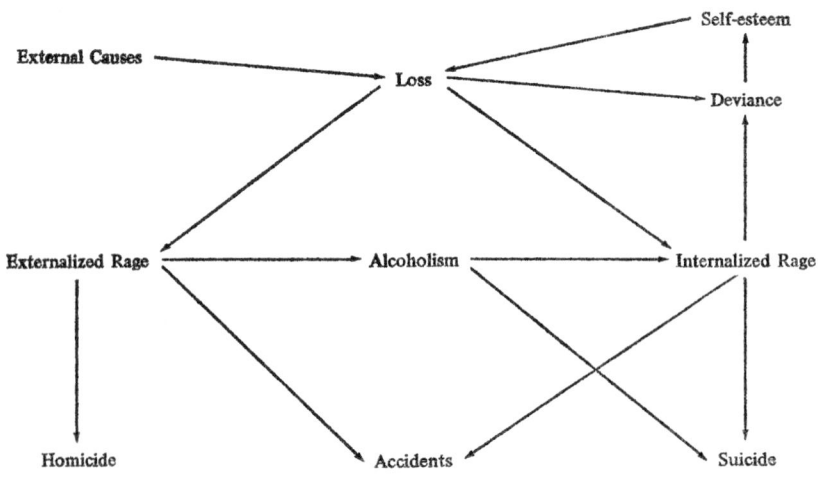

DEPRESSION EQUIVALENCE THEORY — FIGURE 7-2

would appear to be but one (external) dimension of a broader variable which we have labelled "loss." Loss can be either external or internal, and probably most frequently consists of both. This explanation is consistent with the clinical occurrence of both reactive depressions in which alcoholism may be a component, and depressive illness in which external losses appear to have little or no relationship to the presence of symptomatic depression. Menninger's concepts seem to be most operative at the older ages, whereas Rushing's apply most accurately to the younger to middle ages of adulthood. We believe that our formulation combines them into a single framework.

INTERNATIONAL DATA ON ALCOHOLISM AND VIOLENCE

In order to test some epidemiological relationships transnationally, recent World Health Organization (WHO)[42] statistics on cirrhosis and alcoholism rates were correlated with rates for four categories of violent behavior: suicide, homicide and casualties of war, traffic accidents, and other accidents which resulted in fatalities.[43]

These comparisons, for all countries available in the 1955 to 1960 period, are subject to the many limitations of such data.[44] Indeed, they are less reliable than in more microscopic comparison studies because in most cases we do not know the limitations on the collection methods for a given nation. However, they do have one advantage. It is highly unlikely that the statistics in the violence categories were collected with either alcoholism or cirrhosis rates in mind.

The principal findings are as follows:

1. Preliminary analysis showed that there was a high correlation between death from alcoholism and death from cirrhosis of the liver (RHO=.94). Therefore, the complete analysis was done for cirrhosis rates only, to simplify the evaluation.
2. There was a significant correlation for each of the years under study between suicide rates and rates of death from cirrhosis of the liver. These rates were calculated on a country-by-country basis, so that for any one given year the range of N=14-26.

3. The relationship between suicide and alcoholism was true when the sex variable was controlled.
4. In the other three categories of violent behavior, only the category of "Other Than Traffic Accidents" was significantly correlated with cirrhosis death rates overall in several years under study. However, the overall correlations in all four categories were positive in all five years, and this was true when sex differences were controlled. Taken together, these findings are significant.
5. In the years 1956 to 1959 for which data from at least twenty-three countries were available, there was a rise in the correlation between suicide and alcoholism rates with age, true for both males and females, though more so for males. As a result, most of the overall correlation is accounted for by the relatively high correlations at later ages (specifically, 65 years and older).
6. There was a tendency for homicide rates and cirrhosis rates to be correlated only at the lower adult age groups. Furthermore, the RHO values for homicide versus cirrhosis consistently declined with age. In other words, they are significant only up to age 45.
7. The two categories Traffic Accidents and Other Than Traffic Accidents show a tendency for the RHO values to form a U-shape curve with age, with the peak of incidence at a slightly older age than for the homicide-cirrhosis versus age curve and slightly younger age than for the suicide-cirrhosis versus age curve (Fig. 7-3).

Implications for Prevention and Therapy

While the field abounds with attempts at unraveling this fascinating and complex issue we are left with a situation that demands attention. That a correlation between alcohol and suicide exists is beyond question. That alcohol is involved in other forms of self-destructive behavior, accidents—whether auto, home, boating, airplane, or industrial—is also beyond question. The chronic alcoholic person undergoes severe emotional torment and physical deterioration, and the families of alcoholic people, spouse and children, suffer immeasureably.

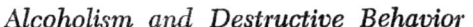

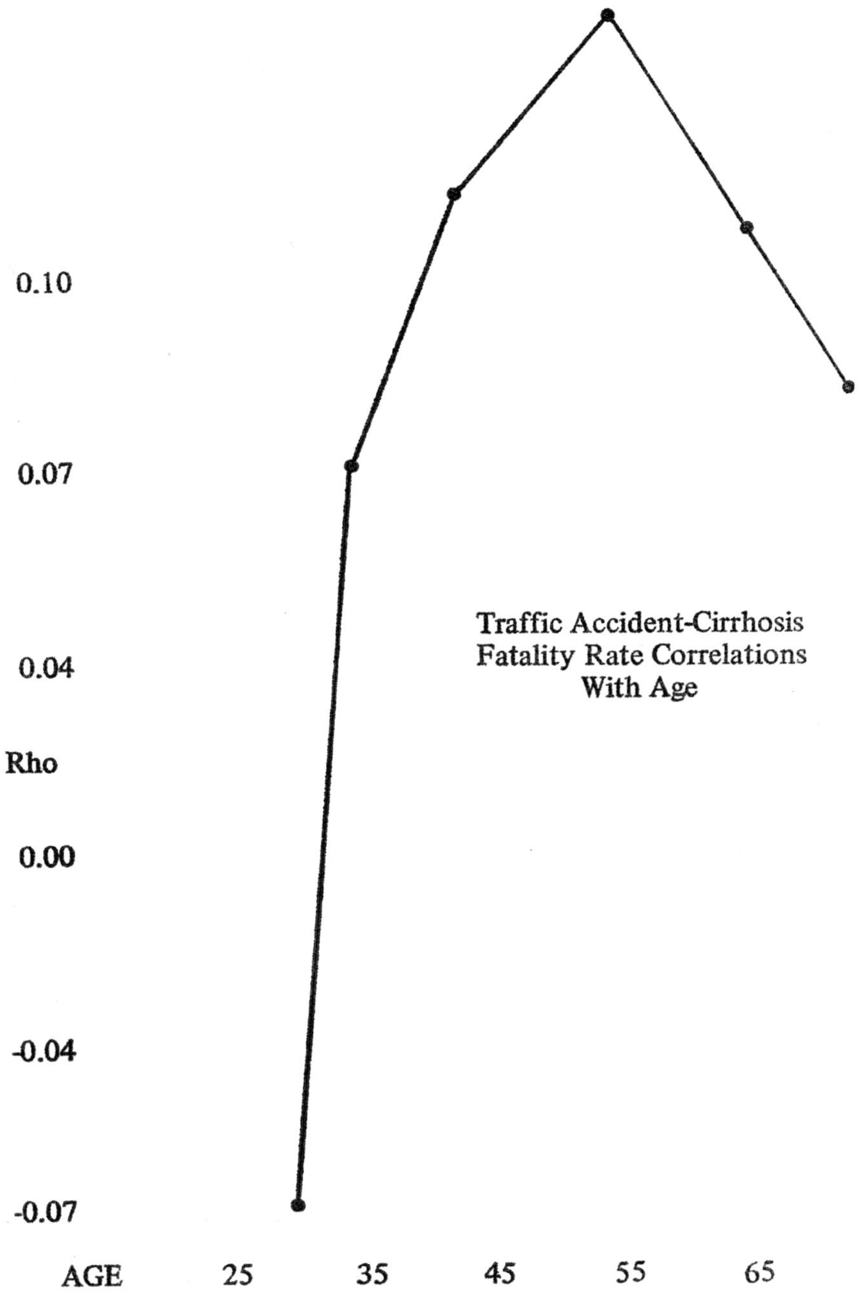
0.10
0.07
0.04
Rho
0.00
-0.04
-0.07
AGE
25
35
45
55
65
Traffic Accident-Cirrhosis
Fatality Rate Correlations
With Age

FIGURE 7-3

What can be done? What does our present state of knowledge, albeit incomplete, allow us to propose as fruitful avenues to deal responsibly and realistically with this preventable problem?

Suicide Prevention

This draws attention to the period of increased risk of suicide for the alcoholic person immediately following the loss of an external object. At the time such a situation arises, it behooves the caregiver to offer additional support through this time, *at least for six weeks,* and to use hospitalization if this seems appropriate. In fact, an ongoing register of such people at risk should be developed by treatment centers, and active outreach to the alcoholic people vigorously pursued.

In addition other mechanisms are available. Ritson reports that suicide may occur in alcoholic people relatively soon after discharge from the hospital.[2] It is important to recognize that successive attempts at suicide may occur within a relatively short, critical period of time. There is a highly significant tendency for the suicide group to have attempted suicide previously. Adequate active support during the post-discharge period is critical.

There is a need to devise systematic procedures for awareness in emergency rooms, clinics, and suicide centers. Incipient and chronic alcoholic people often present with a variety of masked complaints. These may range from an upset stomach secondary to alcoholic gastritis to seemingly improbable accidents that are explicable only if the history of alcohol is given by the patient. This may happen only if the caregiver inquires about drinking habits in detail. Silent collusion between patient and caregiver often prevents adequate care from being rendered. An index of loss available to and utilized by caregivers could serve as an alerting mechanism.

Early casefinding of the individual who is beginning his career of using alcohol dysfunctionally might portend a significant reduction in fatal outcomes. Arresting the process prior to the destruction of interpersonal relations and interference in meeting social and occupational responsibilities augurs for more rapid recovery as well. Alcohol safety action programs, for individuals arrested while driving under the influence of alcohol, and industrial programs geared to identify individuals who, although still working, are showing signs of decreased job performance are examples of what is beginning to gain acceptance for the early identification of the alcoholic person.

TREATMENT AND REHABILITATION

With this in mind a whole range of approaches are available. These include inpatient detoxification, quarter and halfway houses, the use of Antabuse (a pill which if taken regularly causes a severe reaction if alcohol is then consumed), Alcoholics Anonymous (AA) groups, group therapy, individual therapy, family therapy, psychodrama, and any of the other psychological and social methods of support and rehabilitation known. Special attention must be paid to maintain physical health as chronic alcoholic people notoriously have poor nutrition and are consequently more susceptible that the average person to infection and other forms of physical illness.

A complete treatment program will undoubtedly involve the simultaneous utilization of a number of techniques. Which specific ones to use will be solely based on the individual involved and his specific constellation of problems. For a very large number of people AA has been singularly appropriate and effective while for others it would have been counterproductive. Getting the right people into the right programs is critical to the overall success of treatment.

It is an old adage that an alcoholic person will not get help until she or he is ready to do so. All too often this becomes the basis for the caregiver's rejection. It puts the burden of waiting out the client squarely upon him. By waiting we mean an active process of willingness to listen and understand the cries for help, which often come in the most muffled forms and at the most (for the caregiver) inopportune times. Getting the individual interested in changing his behavior patterns is a major challenge. This can be done, and it will succeed to the degree that it is developed around the client's current self-perception of his needs.

Specialization is the bane of successful treatment of alcoholism. The modalities of treatment are variegate, and sometimes quite offbeat and colorful, and cover the entire range of therapies from individual psychotherapy to physical treatments like Antabuse. Programs must be flexible enough not to mold clients to fit the treatments that their professionals know how to perform. Rather, the treaters must learn new methods, and make use of all the resources in their own communities. Getting the right people matched to the right program is a minimal critical step in achieving success in treatment by whatever measures one chooses to employ. An appropriate contract must be negotiated with the client at the beginning of treatment for what is to be expected of both treater and client, and this contract should be adhered to insofar as possible. To be sure, this must be consistent with the caregiver's need to be flexible about the treatments rendered. However, the client is ultimately the consumer, not the professional.

The contract provides the focus for the work of therapy. The patient will continue to test the contract. Indeed, if he does not, that may be cause for concern. By the behavioral outcomes of these tests, the treatment will either progress or wither. It is our impression that the caregiver's own attitudes towards alcoholism may be a major determinant of this process. The treatment of alcoholic people provides one of the most graphic instances of the necessity for self-examination of counter-transferences. Properly employed, they can work to everyone's essential advantage.

PREVENTION — A NATIONAL ISSUE

One thing that should be obvious from what has been said above is that irresponsible use of alcohol levies a severe toll. The damage is not limited to the individual casualties but also includes their families, places of employment and the community at large. The number of casualties is great, and they deserve and can benefit from treatment. But as long as the available resources are directed primarily towards the treatment and rehabilitation of those already suffering nothing will happen to prevent new casualties.

Clearly the issue of prevention is important if we ever hope to have a significant impact on alcoholism. The time has come to give some priority to trying to influence people before their use of alcohol becomes uncontrolled or even before they start to use alcohol at all.

Our data suggest that the focus on various target groups should emphasize different features of drinking alcohol. Perhaps the most striking is the national neglect of the aged drinker. It was found in Maryland that the State mental hospitals are populated with a substantial number of people with drinking problems who had never had them before age 65.[45] The rise in suicide-cirrhosis correlations with age may simply be an expression of our societal attitude towards the elderly, or it may be partially a reflection of the despair and helplessness that accompanies institutionalization. Whatever the explanation, the group at risk is readily identifiable and the solutions are relatively simple programmatically.

The point is that critical decisions about national priorities must be made, and whether the prevention and treatment of alcoholism is to be one of them merits public discussion. Certainly, if crime and violence are issues of major concern, and if, as we have suggested, suicide is a colossal waste of human beings, then alcoholism requires fresh examination in light of the emerging evidence on its interrelationships with self-destructive violent behavior.

REFERENCES

1. Keller, M.: Alcoholism: nature and extent of the problem. *Am Acad Pol Soc Sci, 215:* 1-11, 1958.
2. Ritson, E. B.: Suicide among alcoholics. *Br J Med Psychol 41:* 235-42, 1968.
3. Mayfield, D. G., and Montgomery, D.: Alcoholism, alcohol intoxication, and suicide attempts. *Arch Gen Psychiat, 27:* 349-53, 1972.
4. Whitehead, P. C.: Notes on the association between alcoholism and suicide. *Int J Addiction, 7:* 525-32, 1972.
5. Rushing, W. A.: Deviance, interpersonal relations and suicide. *Human Rel, 22:* 61-76, 1969.
6. Derrick, E. H.: A survey of the mortality caused by alcohol. *Med J Aust, 2:* 914-19, 1967.
7. Wolfgang, M. E.: A sociological analysis of criminal homicide. In *Crime in America: Perspectives on Criminal & Delinquent Behavior.* Cohen, B.J. (Ed.): Peacock Pubs., Itasca, Illinois, 1970.
8. Deasy, S., Rupper, G., and Nordmos, D.: Alcohol-related violent deaths.

Unpublished study, Wayne County (Michigan) Inter-Agency Council on Alcoholism, May 8, 1973.
9. Murphy, G. E., and Robins, E.: Social factors in suicide. *J A M A, 199:* 81-6, 1967.
10. Cahalan, D., Cisin, I. H., and Crossley, H. M.: *American Drinking Practices: A National Study of Drinking Behavior and Attitudes.* Rutgers Center of Alcohol Studies, New Brunswick, 1969.
11. Cahalan, D.: *Problem Drinkers: A National Survey.* San Francisco, Jossey-Bass, 1970.
12. Blane, H. T.: *The Personality of the Alcoholic.* N.Y., Harper & Row, 1968.
13. Compare Ullman, A. D.: First drinking experience as related to age and sex. In *Society, Culture, and Drinking Patterns,* Pittman, D. J., and Snyder, C. R. (Eds.): N.Y., John Wiley & Sons, 1962, 259-66, with Cahalan, D., op. cit.
14. MacMahon, B., and Pugh, T. F.: Suicide in the widowed. *Am J Epidem, 81:* 23-31, 1965.
15. Smith, W. G.: Critical life-events and prevention strategies in mental health. *Arch Gen Psychiat, 25:* 103-09, 1971.
16. Bales, R. F.: Attitudes toward drinking in the Irish culture. In *Society, Culture, and Drinking Patterns,* Pittman, D. J., and Snyder, C. R. (Eds.): N.Y., John Wiley & Sons, 1962, 157-87.
17. Bales, R. F.: Cultural differences in rates of alcoholism. *Quart J Stud Alc, 6:* 480-99, 1946.
18. Lenski, G. E.: *The Religious Factor: A Sociological Study of Religious Impact on Politics, Economics and Family Life.* Garden City, Doubleday, 1961.
19. Dublin, L. I.: *Suicide: A Sociological and Statistical Study.* N.Y., Ronald Press, 1963.
20. Pearl, A., Buechley, R., and Lipscomb, W. R.: Cirrhosis mortality in three large cities: implications for alcoholism and intercity comparsions. In *Society, Culture, and Drinking Patterns,* Pittman, D. C., and Snyder, C. R. (Eds.): N.Y., John Wiley & Sons, 1962, 345-52.
21. Terris, M.: Epidemiology of cirrhosis of the liver: National mortality data. *Am J Public Health, 57:* 2076-88, 1967.
22. Gibbs, J. P., and Martin, W. T.: *Status Integration and Suicide: A Sociological Study.* University of Oregon Books, Eugene, Oregon, 1964.
23. Douglas, J. D.: *The Social Meanings of Suicide.* Princeton, Princeton University Press, 1970.
24. Cloward, R. A., and Ohlin, L. E.: *Delinquency and Opportunity: A Theory of Delinquent Gangs.* Glencoe, Free Press, 1960.
25. Henry, A. F., and Short, L. F.: *Suicide and Homicide: Some economic, sociological, and psychological aspects of aggression.* Glencoe, Free Press, 1954.

26. Popham, R. E. (Ed.): *Alcohol and Alcoholism,* Toronto, University of Toronto Press, 1970.
27. Wolfgang, M.: An analysis of homicide-suicide. *J Clin Exper Psychopath, 19:* 208-18, 1958.
28. Freud, S.: *Standard Edition of the Complete Psychological Works of Sigmund Freud,* James Strachey, (Ed.): London, Hogarth Press, Vol 1, p. 272, 1949.
29. McCord, W., and McCord, J.: *Origins of Alcoholism.* Stanford, Stanford University Press, 1960.
30. Knight, R. P.: The psychodynamics of chronic alcoholism. *J Nerv Ment Dis, 86:* 538-548, 1937.
31. Fenichel, O.: *The Psychoanalytic Theory of Neurosis.* N.Y., W. W. Norton and Co., 1945.
32. Menninger, K. A.: *Man Against Himself.* N.Y., Harcourt, Brace, 1938.
33. Bibring, E.: The Mechanism of Depression, in *Affective Disorders: Psychoanalytic Contributions to Their Study,* P. Greenacre, (Ed.). N.Y., International University Press, 1961.
34. Miller, P. M., and Barlow, D. H.: Behavioral Approaches to the Treatment of Alcoholism. *J Nerv Ment Dis, 157:* 10-20, 1973.
35. Vogel, S., and Banks, R. R.: The effect of delayed punishment on an immediately rewarded response in alcoholics and nonalcoholics. *Behav Res Ther, 3:* 69-73, 1965.
36. Blane, H. T.: The personality of the alcoholic. In *Frontiers of Alcoholism,* Chafetz, M. E., Blane, H. T., and Hill, M. J.. (Eds.): N.Y., Science House, 1970.
37. Lisansky, E. S.: The Etiology of Alcoholism: The role of psychological predisposition. *Q J Stud Alco, 21:* 314-343, 1960.
38. Ringle, E., and Rotter, H.: Zum Problem des selbstmordversuches. In Rousch Wein Z. *Nerven Heilk, 13:* 406-416, 1957.
39. Litman, R. A.: Suicide as acting out. In Shneidman, E. S., Farberow, N. L., and Litman, R. A. (Eds.): *The Psychology of Suicide.* N.Y., Science House, 1970.
40. Bleuler, E. P.: *Textbook of Psychiatry.* A. A. Brill (tran-ed). New York, Dover Pub., 1951.
41. Lester, D.: Suicide, homicide, and age dependency ratios. *Hum Dev, 4:* 127-32, 1973.
42. *W.H.O. Statistical Reports, 21:* 629, 1968.
43. Hertzman, M., and Bendit, E.: submitted for publication, 1973.
44. Stengel, E., and Farberow, N. L.: Certification of suicide around the world. In Proceedings *Fourth International Conference for Suicide Prevention.* Los Angeles, Delmar Publishing, 1968.
45. Wiseman, M.: Moderating speech by M. Chafetz, Taylor Manor Hospital, Maryland, 1973.

CHAPTER 8

OBESITY AND SELF-DESTRUCTIVE BEHAVIOR

SAMUEL H. WAXLER AND EDWARD S. LISKA

CLICHES ARE CONSTANTLY BEING COINED to admonish people for excessive indulgences. Thus the adage "each cigarette a coffin nail" for the excessive smoker, "drinking yourself to death" for the chronic alcoholic, and "digging one's grave with a spoon" for the obese. In all such cases society becomes concerned with the individual who smokes, drinks, or eats beyond some local socially accepted standard. The afflicted may assume a feeling of guilt and stigmatize himself with such stereotypic terms as "compulsive eater," "problem drinker," or "chain smoker." We can state categorically that neither the concern of society nor the awareness of the involved person adds much to the resolution of the specific problem. Although a few investigators have lumped all of these troubled individuals into one category for description and treatment, this generalization is of little help in clarifying the problem. Since the subject of obesity is of such magnitude and complexity we will confine ourselves to it without any attempt to associate it with the other social excesses. We shall dwell briefly on some of the facts and conjectures of the obesity syndrome, before trying to relate it to the problem of self destructive behavior. Subsequently we shall discuss the concept of self destructive behavior and differentiate it from self destruction.

What is obesity? Who are the obese? As it is generally understood, the term obesity refers to a condition characterized by an excessive, generalized deposition and storage of body fat. Clinically obesity has been defined as weight per height increase above the average of desirable weight. The tables published by the Metropolitan Life Insurance Company in 1959 set forth such weights for men and women over the age of twenty-five of small, medium, and large frames.[1] Although based on data which are somewhat controversial, they have come into general acceptance. Some few studies rigidly define obesity as an increase of 10 percent or more above a prescribed weight, but most investigators reject this standard and set as a criterion a figure of 20 to 25 percent above the so-called ideal weight. We regard the latter figures as reasonable and arbitrarily consider all other persons with increased poundage but below this value as *overweight*. A diagnosis of obesity based on height and weight alone, without consideration of the total configuration of an individual, is not valid. Another method used to establish the diagnosis of obesity is somatotyping.[2] This is essentially body measuration, using sketches and photogrammetry.[3]

In our opinion, the use of Ponderal Index would give a more definitive value, in that weight-height categories would be transformed into a definitive number (height in inches over the cube root of the weight). The Ponderal Index would represent the measure of body volume, and the volume would increase according to the cube of the linear weight. We feel that the Ponderal Index is especially useful in children and adolescents, since their linear spurts do not occur at the same ages in all individuals and the number of combinations produced by the variables of weight and height within the same age groups are infinite.[4] After the early twenties any significant increase in body weight in healthy adults represents primarily an increase in adiposity and thus the use of standardized weight tables can be justified.

Obesity is widespread in both sexes and in all age groups. Let us consider infancy. The first real question of course is whether or not obesity and/or overweight exists at birth. The pediatric literature reveals no overall difference at the 50th percentile of the birth weight of children born now in comparison with those born forty years ago, although it has been the general impression that the infant of today is somewhat heavier.[5] Some investigators believe that obese adults are generally heavier at birth than those who do not become obese. However, most competent observers find no difference in the birth weights between subsequently obese and non-obese subjects.[6]

People interested in the natural history of obesity have tried to correlate the rapidity of weight gain subsequent to birth with the initial birth weight. They have concluded that the rate of gain may be a better presager for developing obesity than the birth weight. There are at least two peaks which have been noted in the growing child. The first can occur between the ages of 0 to 4 and the second between seven and eleven.[7] Some people describe a third period or peak which occurs in adolescence.

Some researchers have questioned the consequences of obesity on growth or maturation. What may appear to be excessive growth during childhood in the obese may be only acceleration of maturation.[8] Obese children are tall for their age, but since epiphyseal closure takes place earlier than normal, they are ultimately only as tall or rarely slightly taller than normal. The accelerated maturation occurs despite the low growth hormone secretion and elevated insulin levels found in obese children. Bruch and others have observed that early pubertal development is not uncommon in such obese boys and girls.

Numerous studies, from different sections of the United States, have reported on the incidence of overweight children. The data comes primarily from elementary and high schools and the degree of obesity varies markedly from study to study and from area to area. Without going into a myriad of statistics, one can conclude that a significant number of children, particularly adolescents, are overweight and in all probability obese.[9]

Most parents are content that their children are growing and appear healthy. Childhood obesity is not recognized as a problem and by the time attention is directed to it, the obesity has become excessive. A recent paper reported on 364 obese boys and girls, ages seven to fourteen. In only 8 percent of the cases had parents asked for a medical examination of a child because of obesity. The remainder had been referred by school doctors and nurses.

Most studies indicate that juvenile obesity persisting into adult life tends to be more severe and more difficult to treat than adult-onset obesity. One specific study was done by Hasse and Hosenfeld on 335 overweight children first examined between 1936 and 1940. On re-examination, when the majority of these patients were between the ages of 20 and 36, more than 80 percent of them were more than 80 percent overweight. Other studies tend to confirm this observation, though the results are generally not as extreme. In juvenile obesity the prognosis tends to be worse for girls than for boys. Obviously, children do not outgrow their obesity but in fact maintain it and remain obese as adults.

It is difficult to document the estimates of the incidence of obesity in this country and in other countries of the Western World.[10] Statistics which have been gathered from various sources indicate that at least 20 to 30 percent of the adult population of the United States can now be considered obese.[11] At the turn of the century only about 15 percent of the population was considered heavy enough to fall into this category. British investigators indicate that probably 25 percent of the women in England over the age of 30 are obese, and that the incidence of obesity in females is greater than that of males.[12] The same figures prevail within our experience. A week-long survey of all persons (visitors or patients), entering the Clinic of the University of California Hospital, indicated that there was an overwhelmingly larger percentage of obese females than obese males.

Parents are slow to recognize the obesity of their children; they are also loath to recognize it in themselves.[13] It is well known that obese people are extremely reluctant to present themselves to their physicians with this singular complaint. Mullins observed 200 patients between the ages of 20 and 60.[14] He considered 9 percent of the men and 20 percent of the women to be obese, yet only 3 out of these 58 individuals asked for treatment of their obesity. In a similar study Hopkins adjudged

20 out of 115 consecutive patients to be obese, yet only two of these complained to him of their obesity.[15]

The etiology of obesity is an intricate, unsettled problem, a source of perplexity, distress, and frustration. There are now very few physicians that accept the simplistic explanation of the cause of obesity: an excess of food intake beyond that required for energy expenditure. The great majority appreciate the fact that the mechanisms that regulate food intake and utilization are complex and only partially understood. Although they are aware that the clinical problem of obesity also has physiological, metabolic, genetic, and sociological implications, they place most of their emphasis on the psychological features.

Obesity can be thought of as a physiological variation of the mechanisms which regulate appetite and satiety and of related psychological disturbances. We may postulate that genetic and physiological mechanisms produce a desire to eat and that whether this desire is or is not fulfilled may be altered by psychological processes. There have been many attempts to discover the fundamental etiology of obesity and the subsequent maintenance of the obese state. This always introduces the controversy concerning the relative importance of genetic and environmental factors.

The genetic approach to the regulation of eating presents several interesting aspects. Genes per se do not specifically program eating behavior but they do influence development so that the same environment leads to a quite different response.[16] In this interplay, it is interesting and important to know to what degree heredity plays a significant role. As psychological, sociological, and physiological factors operate on this basic genetic structure, the number of variables which are produced is infinite. As we observe the wide range of variations, we arbitrarily decide what we wish to consider as basic normal limits within a specific milieu.

Selective breeding experiments with domestic and laboratory animals can produce striking changes in body weight and accumulation of body fat. Successful selection for these factors is evidence for the inheritability of body configuration. We can appreciate this even though we have no detailed knowledge of the manner in which genes exert their influence. It is difficult to relate to humans conclusions drawn from experiments on other animals. This is particularly true in dealing with genetic patterns because humans are subjected from birth to social and psychological stimuli not present in well-controlled animal experiments.

Statistical studies of identical twins do show that there is a correlation in weight despite environmental differences and this is evidence of a strong hereditary factor.[17] Though the sample is not large, monozygotic twins brought up apart were closer in body weight than dizygotic twins raised together.[18] Gurney and others support the genetic hypothesis, noting that weight patterns of children tend to correlate with those of their parents and that there are marked differences between siblings brought up in ostensibly the same environment.[19] Adopted children do not necessarily follow the weight patterns of the adoptive parents,[20] nor do foster children tend to resemble their custodians. It has also been recognized that there is resemblance in the fat distribution and the androgynic appearance of obese mothers and their daughters.

Man has an opportunity to regulate his own diet from a great variety of foods. He develops patterns and preferences which are influenced to an important degree by ethnic and social forces. Food acts as a stimulus by way of the gustatory, olfactory, and visual senses. The eating response is not dependent on sensory stimulation alone but is associated with activity of the appetite center and to an even greater degree with the satiety center.

The regulation of food intake is commonly assigned to two discrete hypothalamic centers. Brobeck demonstrated in his animal studies that one center regulated feeding and the other regulated satiety.[21] Anatomically and behaviorally the medial hypothalamus is concerned with satiety, whereas the lateral areas are responsible for appetite. Although the regulation of food intake is commonly assigned to hypothalamic centers, it has been recognized that many extra-hypothalamic factors contribute to it. Belagura believes that no single stimulus acts as a cue for hunger or satiety.[22] He believes that these states are induced by a combination of various stimuli acting upon the brain and involve various complex hormonal and neurochemical mechanisms. At any given moment the eating behavior may be responsive to either the appetite or satiety centers or to both, directly or by extra-hypothalamic factors.

In 1949 Brecher and Waxler first reported the experimental production of obesity in mice induced by a single intraperitoneal injection of gold thioglucose.[23] Mice so treated developed varying degrees of marked obesity which autopsies and chemical analyses showed to be an increase in adipose tissue.[24] They noted that animals made obese could be starved to the pre-treatment level and maintained at normal weight by paired-feeding against normal mice. Subsequent ad libitum consumption of food allowed the mice to return to the obese state. They also demonstrated that mice injected with gold could be prevented from becoming obese by pair-feeding. Although the hypothalamic "lesion factor" induced by this chemical was permanent, the potential obesity could be manipulated by feeding patterns. Localization of the lesion hypothalamus was not delineated at that time. However, later studies noted the lesions in the hypothalamus and emphasized the presence of both an appetite and a satiety center or centers.[25] Subsequent research indicated that the lessened response to satiety cues was probably more important than the basic hunger drive or appetite. This concept has also been proposed for human beings. If there is any validity in this theory, it is reasonable to suspect the existence of genetic variations in eating behavior in man.

There is evidence that excessive ingestion of food alone can produce permanent metabolic changes related to adipose tissue. Hirsch and his group showed that in rats that were overfed in the first three weeks of life there was a permanent increase in the size of the fat cells without any increase in number.[26] Overfeeding of adult rats produced only an increase in the size of the fat cells without any increase in number. Biopsy studies of human adipose tissues showed that a similar situation prevails. Persons with adult-onset obesity have in general the same number of fat cells as normal individuals but that their fat cells are larger and contain more lipid per cell. In contrast, the adult with childhood-onset obesity showed a hyperplasia of fat cells as well as an anticipated increase of lipid within the cells. On this basis some people have designated two types of obesity: hyperplastic and hypertrophic. During the course of weight loss there is no decrease in number of fat cells in either type; only a decrease in the amount of overall fat. Of note is the fact that marked obesity produced in adult rats by hypothalamic lesions is achieved primarily by increase of cell size with no increase in the number of adipose tissue cells.

It is apparent that factors other than genetic or physiological are involved in the question of obesity. Social factors such as race, religion, national and ethnic origin, eating habits, customs, educational level, and social status have long been known to play a role. The Midtown Manhattan Study in 1965 examined the weight patterns of a large sample of New Yorkers drawn from nine ethnic groups.[27] It presented data to show that only 5 percent of the women in the upper class were obese, compared with 30 percent of lower class women. Other information obtained from this study showed that the incidence of obesity lessened in those that moved upward in status, whereas obesity increased in those who had a decline in socioeconomic class. The incidence of obesity was also related to the length of time the person had been in America. It was higher in first generation women than those of the fourth generation.

In Great Britain a comparable study showed similar trends: an inverse relationship between social class and obesity.[28] However the differences were not as great as in the Manhattan Study. In both countries these trends were much less apparent in men than in women. There are no comparable studies of similar scope and analysis from countries with static populations, little mobility, and a minimum of immigration. It would be interesting to know if such a study would show similar trends and relationships between obesity and the various social and economic parameters.

In children the effect of social factors on the incidence of obesity is of even greater importance. In one study Kahn found that childhood obesity was four times more frequent in that group which had a history of separation from the mother than in a controlled nonobese group.[29] Absence of the mother from the home for part of the day produced no significant difference in either group. The pathogenesis of obesity associated with mother-child separation is uncertain and many explanations have been presented.

Everyone talks about obesity; everyone seems to be dieting. Most people do not consider obesity a disease and much of the medical profession would rather not concern itself with it. Recently the University of California at San Francisco closed its obesity clinic which had been operative for over twenty years. Facilities for the management of exogenous obesity are available only to those obese patients who have an associated metabolic disturbance.

It can be stated unequivocally that the end results of management of the obese person in the outpatient clinic, hospital, private medical practice, and in social organizations have been uniformly poor. We choose the term "management" since there is no definitive treatment for obesity other than the reduction of food intake. All studies conducted over an extended period of time demonstrate that the great majority of obese people show no substantial loss of weight from the pre-treatment level. Some individuals not only fail to lose but eventually gain while under medical or social management. If significant weight losses are achieved they are rarely sustained for any appreciable length of time. If management were successful, 486 articles would not have been published between 1960 and 1967 under the heading "Treatment and Control of Obesity." The large numbers of additional papers published over the past five years are mainly modifications and recapitulations of previous ideas.

The almost total lack of success in handling the problem of obesity is extremely exasperating to those persons involved in its management. Physicians of all specialties become frustrated with attempts to *cure* obesity, forgetting how very few cures they achieve with other diseases. It is not unusual for physicians to characterize obese patients as uncooperative, weak-willed, compulsive eaters unwilling or unable to follow a therapeutic regime.

Physicians are not alone in their failure to induce the obese to control their weight. Reports from insurance companies, government agencies, medical societies, and health departments indicate that a large proportion of our population weighs more than is considered desirable for optimum health, that obesity occurs in one third of the adult population over thirty years of age. They emphasize that the mortality rate is definitely higher among individuals who are 25 percent or more overweight than among individuals who are not overweight. Insurance statistics show that the general mortality among obese men and women increases with each 10 percent of ideal weight. *When the level of 30 percent above ideal weight is reached in the 40 to 70 age groups, the mortality in men increases to 42 percent above average and in women to 36 percent above average. They note the greater incidence of cardiovascular disease, hypertension, diabetes mellitus, gout and cholecystitis among the overweight persons.* In addition, obesity is known to increase certain surgical risks, to be a hazard in pregnancy, and to interfere with ambulation in arthritis. Some endocrine and metabolic changes have been described in the obese individual. The doctrine that obesity, per se, carries a risk of coronary heart disease has recently been questioned in part by Keyes. However, *there is no doubt that extra weight places undue demands on the cardiac and pulmonary system with an eventual impairment in performance in both.*

This frequent recounting of medical danger and health problems associated with obesity has seemingly little effect. Millions of dollars are spent on radio, television, magazine, and newspaper advertising to exhort the population to lose weight by means of sugarless candies, drinks, low calorie foods, cosmetics, exercises, and non-proprietary drugs. Such advertising emphasizes the problem graphically and in a format easily appreciated by the public. Presumably a demonstration of the immediate benefits to the individual of improved appearance, better social acceptance, greater physical fitness, should be a more effective stimulus towards weight reduction than the promise of lessened morbidity and mortality. Neither seems to be of much aid in the resolution of this problem. With all of this emphasis on weight loss, the adult and adolescent population in the United States is growing heavier rather than lighter.

And lastly the patient. We wish to be explicit about this individual. He is not simply obese. More importantly, this is the obese individual who presents himself because he is troubled by or about his obesity and wants relief. In many instances, especially with children, some other individuals, be they parents, teachers or pediatricians, initiate the help-seeking process. The obesity may be a primary concern or it may derive from anxieties linking the obesity with other aspects of his total well being and considered as undesirable. He consciously wants to be relieved of the burden of extreme weight. Virtually all of these individuals have tried various and ingenious diets, they have read extensively and have gone to control centers. Some have experienced significant weight loss but few have sustained such achievements for any length of time. If you ask what they think about themselves, their responses are invariably deprecatory. If you ask what they feel about their obesity, they hate it and don't like what they see. In most instances there is an underlying poorly concealed depressive mood. Most of them hope for immediate relief. They cannot face the prospect of an extended management regimen. The failure to achieve quick and spectacular weight loss contributes to their depressive mood. For many, the loss of weight is equated with far-reaching personality changes and improvement in their interpersonal relationships. This equation, when its condition is met, is rarely followed by the hoped-for alterations. It is such patients about whom we wish to make our speculations. What is there about these individuals—a deficit? a defect? an interference?—making their basic conscious efforts to achieve their explicitly-stated goals so unrewarding. This is the problem of special interest to us. It is linked with the title suggested by this chapter "Obesity As Self-Destructive Behavior." We underscore "self" and shall proceed to examine its meaning by way of quotations from various texts, paraphrases of some authors, as well as personal musings.

Webster offers this definition of the self: "man viewed by his own cognition, as the subject of all his mental phenomena, the agent of his activities, the subject of his feelings, the possessor of capacities and character."[30] The term "self" has been used by many authors[31] in a variety of hyphenated combinations. There are Sullivan's "self-system;"[32] Mead's "self-concept;"[33] the "self-experiences"[34] described by Schilder, Federn[35] and others; Hartman's "self-representation;"[36] Freud's[37] ego and "self-esteem;" Fromm's[38] "true self;" Horney's "actual self." Any discussion of the "self" inevitably requires attention to the concept of the ego.

Erikson[39] says that "in order to clarify and even quantify man's attitude toward himself, philosophers and psychologists have created such nouns as 'I' or the 'self,' making imaginary entities out of a manner of speaking." In psychoanalytic psychology, the ego is conceived as being that part of the psychic apparatus which is the mediator between the person and reality. Its primary function is the perception of reality and adaptation to it. Subsumed under this primary function are such tasks as perception (to include inner processes as well as external events), thinking, experiencing affects and motor control. It is considered as performing a general synthetic function in assimilating internal and external elements, reconciling conflicting ideas, uniting contrasts and activating mental activity. Its functions develop gradually. Their emergence depends upon unfolding physical maturation and concurrent experimental factors. The ego is considered to be the executive organ of the reality principle.[40] For Sullivan,[32] the term "self-system" denotes the final formation of the self, sifted out of a greater number of potentialities through parental influence on the developing personality of the child. For him, humans are concerned with two goals essentially. One is the pursuit of satisfaction, dealing chiefly with biological needs. The second is the pursuit of security. This latter deals with cultural pressures. To maintain security, to avoid anxiety, the child develops and strengthens that side of his nature which is pleasing or acceptable to the significant adult. Those actions or attributes of the child which meet with disapproval tend to be blocked out of awareness and become disassociated. Attainment of satisfactions and the maintenance of security is necessary for the preservation of a sense of personal worth. Sullivan's system stresses what goes on between people in the dynamic interaction between individuals. For some, Sullivan is seen as being preoccupied with the interpersonal and having a cultural-dynamic orientation. For others Freud is seen as mechanistic and biological, concerned primarily with the intrapsychic. In the world of "reality" it appears that both points of view must be included to make possible an acceptable hypothesis.

Jung discriminated between the ego and self.[41] For him the ego is not identical with the totality of the psyche. He says the ego is the subject of consciousness—"the centrum of my field of consciousness"—while the self is the subject of his totality.

Horney uses the term "actual self."[42] For her this conveys the meaning of the whole person in its somatic and psychic aspects, including its conscious and unconscious elements, as the person exists at any point in time. The "real" self is the person's potential for further growth and development.

Fromm's term, the "true self,"[38] is used to connote the sum total of a person's potentiality which might be developed under the most favorable social and cultural conditions. Real self respect is seen as essential to genuine love and respect for others. For him, the purpose of therapy is to develop a sense of integrity and respect for the true self.

Menninger reminds us that the genesis of the ego has been a subject of much speculation and research and that opinions are divided as to whether it is the product of differentiation of instincts, an epiphenomenon of drive-dynamics, or whether it was always there, at least in embryonic form, with its own potential structure, its autonomy and its primal reality.[43] It has often been described as an emergent entity, the product of conflict and yet at the same time it is assumed by many theorists to antecede conflict, being present in embryonic form, as it were, prior to birth as a biopsychological Anlage. Whatever else may be said about it, there is general agreement that it significantly relates and is applicable to the bulk of processes used in the self-regulation of human behavior.

For Becker, the ego grows by discovering what makes the organism anxious and then defending itself against the anxiety.[44] The ego creates an action world which excludes what it has learned to abhor. He sees the child as being primarily driven to the maternal object rather than to coerce the environment to fulfill his own purportedly biological and inflexible needs. In this sense Becker's view is more in keeping with Sullivan's mentioned above.[45]

In this context it is useful to mention the concept of body image or body identity. This is the conceptualization of one's body structure and its functions that grows out of the awareness of the self and one's body in interrelated actions. The body concept includes perceptions, thoughts, feelings, and actions which the ego has in reference to its own body.

Mead[33] has traced the development of this conscious self awareness by postulating that in the beginning of the infant's awareness, both he and the objects around him appear as things. Since the organism is acting in the environment, he exerts an effort to meet and manipulate the objects e.g. the succoring mother. All objects may be visualized as having both an outside and an inside but, according to Mead, dawning consciousness in the infant cannot yet know this. The infant may know its own insides by direct experience but it can come to know its outside boundaries only in relation to outside objects. The infant can come to know the outside of his mother's breast by vision, touch, taste and smell but has no way of getting a notion that the mother has an inside.

Mead concludes that the only way we can give outsides to ourselves and confer insides upon others, is by "taking the attitude" of other persons toward ourselves. This primitive identification, as the basis for human growth, has been well understood by psychoanalysis. The infant identifies with the object, and so gains an awareness of his own feelings, then of the object's feelings. The fact that the infant has to identify first and then dedifferentiate himself means that his very first identity is a social product. It is created by union with a prior object. This earliest of identifications is the basis for self-objectification and as Becker puts it, "Man is the only animal—in the universe for all we know—who sees himself as an object."

Many workers have examined the child-rearing practices of widely divergent cultures. There is a consensus that a specific and definite relationship exists between childhood training practices and the child's personality.* The basic personality structure is composed of certain basic attitudes toward the self and towards objects which remain part of the individual's world. Biological and psychological needs of infants are customarily met by parents or parent surrogates. There is utter dependence of the child on the parenting person. But this dependency undergoes attenuation through time. At some early stage developmentally the infant begins to differentiate between self and nonself, me and not me, I and they. Worth or lack of worth become reflections of the affectional climate between the developing infant and the nurturant parent. From a postulated, undifferentiated state, there emerges a conscious self, increasingly adept at using its developing skills to master, to cope, to be free, to depend on the nurturant and protective person as need be. The identity of the child is built on a growing sense of mastery and the executive control of one's power of action becomes a source of one's sense of self worth as increasing autonomy permits the successful execution of these activities. And growth toward autonomy essentially involves the acquisition of newer, more sophisticated modes of maintaining mastery. An integrated ego allows the individual to handle present anxiety, having dealt successfully with past anxieties, and to quietly anticipate the successful mastery of future ones. Concurrently, society's major cultural task is to provide the individual with the conviction that he and his actions have primary value in a world wherein action is meaningful and purposive. When childhood training and the adult world of action do not mesh, the child grows up to find himself unprepared and unable to feel warm about himself by doing things in that adult world.

Self esteem, then, is seen as an aspect of self awareness. It is a feeling of self warmth, that all is right with one's self in one's world. "I like me" appears to be the core of human adaptation. Coopersmith's book on self esteem concerns itself with the antecedents, precursors, or determinants of self esteem.[46]

---

* For a comprehensive review of the literature on child rearing practices and personality development see Albert R. Roberts (Ed.): *Childhood Deprivation* (Springfield, Charles C Thomas, Publisher), 1974.

But by whomever viewed, whether they be anthropologists, psychologists, psychiatrists, philosophers or other behavior scientists, all seem to emphasize, in concert, how extraordinarily significant is the nature and quality of the interdependent relationship between the infant and the parenting other person. Aside from meeting biological needs, this relationship provides the matrix within which mental and emotional development can proceed. It can serve as an unequalled opportunity for optimum growth. Conversely, it may result in an infinite variety of impaired levels of growth and achievement depending on the quality and quantity of the distortions existing in the ongoing relationship.

Generally stated, Coopersmith finds these to be the antecedents of self esteem: that there is nearly total acceptance of the child by his parents; that there are clearly defined and enforced limits; and that there is respect and latitude for individual action within these defined limits. For him the relationship between parental self esteem and the child's self esteem indicates that there are unconscious identifications and conscious modelling underlying the self-evaluations of individuals. Specific, determinable variables of self esteem may be subsumed under the concepts of success, values, aspirations and defenses. The degree of self esteem expressed by the individual reflects to what extent that individual's success approached aspirations that were truly valued with his defenses acting to define and interpret what is valued and what is regarded as successful. Subjectively, self esteem is frequently affected by parental treatment and their personal attitudes. He found that consequences of parental treatment as they influence those individuals with high self esteem, provide the following kinds of observation. That such individuals are personally effective, poised, competent, capable of independent and creative actions; that their prevailing anxiety level appears to be low; that their ability to deal with anxiety appears to be better than that of other persons; that they are socially skilled and able to deal with external situations and demands in a direct and incisive way; that they are relatively unaffected or distracted by personal difficulties; that they gravitate to functions of influence and authority; that they appear more likely to expect success in social and academic endeavors. Concurrently, parents of high esteem children expect their children to strive and comply with standards they have established. Their expectations represent a belief in their child and a conviction that he has the ability to perform and succeed. Their convictions are supportive and encourage the child. To the child, these convictions are clear indications of what is desired and attainable. Implicit in the parental expectations and in the child's expectations of himself is the conviction that one's personal behavior will indeed affect what happens with a corresponding feeling that one can control one's destiny. Within high esteem families there is a high level of activity. These are strong-minded parents with independent and assertive children. There is stricter enforcement of rules, more stringent demands for performance and greater possibility for open dissent and disagreement. There are firm convictions and frequent strong exchanges. Such children have a good experience dealing with adults who help them achieve their own self definition. High esteem children however, are likely to be a source of travail to parents, teachers and others in authority because they manifest independence, they assert their rights, they are outspoken. They engage in exploratory behavior, are aware of other persons' views but are inclined to pay greater attention to their personal feelings and convictions.

The parental self and social expectations of families with low self esteem are marked by lack of faith, expectations of failure, anticipation of rejection. They believe they cannot learn, are not important, have no power or privileges. They believe this is their due and they expect similar treatment from others. Such anticipation can lead to withdrawal and passivity and feelings that they cannot improve their lot. There is anticipation of failure, poor motivation, reduced personal vigor, leaving little hope or courage for dealing with people and problems. And now to some observations about self destruction and self-destructive behavior.

The generally accepted psychodynamic formulations about self destruction and self-destructive behavior concern themselves with individual, idiosyncratic ways of handling aggression. The aggression may be directed outwardly towards thing-objects or person-objects; thus a toy is smashed or a homicide committed.

Or it may be turned against one's self or the self's object possessions. The self or the self's objects become the objects of attack. The latter may include a broad spectrum of behavior such as self-inflicted, non-fatal injuries; recourse to excesses of physical emotional or chemical kind; all known to have deleterious consequences to the individual and culminating in the ultimate action of self-destruction, i.e. suicide. Whether these various acts are consciously or unconsciously determined remains a continuing field for dispute. A safe position, and perhaps more inclusive, would be to consider both as operative. However to consider that a successful, self-destructive act, consciously and deliberately planned, as non-pathological, is not acceptable to large segments of our society. Others assert that no one in his "right mind" would willfully seek to end his life. Implicit in this assumption is the notion that life, no matter what its quality or prospects, should and must be lived. To choose otherwise is prima facie evidence of a diseased, disturbed mind. Here we see graphically demonstrated what the consequences of one's given belief system may be. It is not enough to reconcile cultural differences on the grounds that one sanctioning self-destruction or immolation is "sick," and one opposing it is "healthy." All that can be said is that differences exist and without necessarily taking recourse in levity, "vive la différence."

Some reference should be made to *volition*. This is not a favorite topic in American psychiatry or psychology. Usually, the concept is considered in opposition to scientific determinism and relegated to philosophy. Arieti says that volition requires that several conditions be met: the ability to evaluate alternatives, the choice of one alternative, planning of the chosen alternative, will or determination to carry out the chosen and planned alternative, the execution of the chosen alternative.[47] The last presupposes another condition, i.e. in order to will the individual must be able to inhibit the nonwilled forms of behavior. These steps overlap and blend into one another. The first three of these steps are viewed as cognitive processes. With step four conation is added to permit willed behavior. He observes that physiological knowledge of willed behavior is very meagre. He tends to feel that volition is partially a psychological process mediated by the nervous system. Volition, like awareness, is a characteristic making it impossible to approach man as if he were a complicated physical-chemical machine.

One may ask, at this point, what the relevance of these observations is to the subject of our chapter. It is of little value to discuss obesity without recognizing there are many obesities. We find it useful to think of two general categories of obesity based on their appearance in time—those appearing in infancy and persisting despite heroic efforts into adulthood—and those appearing most commonly in latency, adolescence, the middle years, especially in women and coincident with successive pregnancies, and adulthood.

In the first of these broad categories, having given appropriate consideration to genetic and constitutional factors, the most significant contributory elements in its appearance derive from cultural factors. Parental attitudes about the role and function of food become incorporated in the child's mind and contribute to his body image and concurrent self-esteem. The parent espouses the view that it is good to be obese. The child eats to please the parenting person. This is in keeping with Becker's and Coopersmith's observations in which the purpose of the child's behavior is to please the parent rather than satisfying a basic biological need. There exist cultures and sub-cultures where obesity is valued because of certain beliefs about its esthetic implications. So long as these supporting cultural attitudes obtain, the child is not in conflict. But inevitably most such children are exposed to opposing attitudes about obesity. Conflict eventually develops and as with all psychological conflict, failure to resolve it eventually leads to symptom formation. When this occurs, this obesity subtly merges into and becomes indistinguishable from the other obesities. Now they may all be seen as having a common denominator—excessive ingestion of food—with or without accompanying energy expenditures produces a weight surplus.

Motivation for excessive eating comes from a defensive use of eating to allay anxiety, whatever the nature or source of this anxiety may be. Anxiety is seen as a response by the individual to a felt threat to his integrity whether real or imagined. To date, the nature of those neuro-physiological mechanisms which translate the subjectively felt anxiety to affect the hypothalamically-located satiety and appetite center is unknown. As with all other psycho-physiological disease states, no acceptable explanations exist to account for the emergence of a given symptom in a given organ or organ system as a reaction to stress. A genetically determined organ inferiority or a susceptibility peculiar to the individual in question has been postulated. Experience suggests that individuals respond to stress with symptoms arising from an organ or organ system regularly. Too, some individuals will develop symptoms in more than one organ or organ system. What determines variations remains a mystery.

Earlier we mentioned some attributes found in the obese patient. Consistently and with no exceptions, all have been troubled about their obesity and all have had a deprecatory attitude toward themselves. We see obesity as a psycho-physiological disease state, almost always chronic in nature, developing at all ages. From its physiological aspects, there exists a genetically determined vulnerability of the hypothalamic satiety and appetite centers which, when subjected to anxiety arising from whatever source, causes dysfunction or malfunction of one or both of these centers leading to excessive ingestion of food and consequent obesity. Psychologically we believe these individuals suffer an ego deficit, specifically a diminished self esteem, making their efforts at weight reduction ineffectual. We do not believe their failures are the expression of self-destructive tendencies and find Eisenberg's statement[48] appealing "Would it not be far more parsimonious to begin with the assumption that men are by nature neither aggressive nor peaceful, but rather are fashioned into one or another as the result of a complex interaction between a widely, but not infinitely, modifiable set of biological givens and the shaping influences of the biological environment, the cultural envelope, and individual experience?"

We consider the following to be significant considerations in the management of obesity.[49] Aside from prescribing a simple, understandable diet, we emphasize especially the psychological aspects. The physician's own feelings about obesity and the obese patient cannot mirror those of the patient. To feel so reinforces the very psychological process and defeats any chance for change. Realistic expectations need to be emphasized, small gains are to be approved and encouraged. Acceptance of the patient, a readiness to listen, and regular visits over long periods of time are necessary. The chronicity of the process must be constantly emphasized and a long standing effort on the part of the patient is expected. We cannot really expect "cure" and must be satisfied with containment or moderate melioration.

REFERENCES

1. Metropolitan Life Insurance Company, Statistical Bulletin, 40: 2-3, 1959.
2. Craig, L. S., and Bayer, L. M.: Androgynic phenotypes in obese women. Am J Anthrop, 26: 23, 1967.
3. Sheldon, W. H.: An Atlas of Man. New York, Harper, 1954.
4. Falkner, F.: Some physical growth standards for white North American children. Pediatrics, 29: 467, 1962.
5. Waxler, S. H., and Leef, M.: Obesity, Doctors' dilemma. Geriatrics, 24: 98, 1969.
6. Heald, F. P.: Natural history and physiological basis of adolescent obesity. Fed Proc, 25: No. 1, 1966.
7. Wolff, O. H.: Obesity in childhood and its effects. Postgrad Med J, 38: 629, 1962.
8. Lloyd, J. K., and Wolff, O. H.: Childhood obesity. Br Med J, 5245: 145, 1961.
9. Hathaway, M. L., and Sargent, D. W.: Overweight in children. J Am Diet Assoc, 40: 511, 1962.
10. Build and Blood Pressure Study, Society of Actuaries, Chicago, Vols. 1 & 2, 1959.
11. Weight by Height and Age of Adults, Public Health Service Pub. No. 1000, U.S. Govt. Printing Office, May 1966.
12. Silverstone, J. T., and Solomon, T.: Psychiatric and somatic factors in the treatment of obesity. J Psychosom Res, 9: 249, 1965.
13. Wyden, P.: The Overweight Society. New York, Morrow, 1965.
14. Mullins, A. G.: Medical supervision in treatment of obesity. Lancet, 1: 146, 1958.
15. Hopkins, P.: Obesity in general practice. Proc R Soc Med, 58: 197, 1965.
16. Fuller, J. L.: Genetic aspects of regulation of food intake. Adv Psychoson Med. Basel, Karger, 1972.
17. Newman, H. V., Freeman, F. N., and Holzinger, J. J.: Twins, A study of Heredity and Environment. Chicago, U of Chicago Press, 1937.

18. Shields, J.: *Monozygotic Twins Brought up Apart and Brought Together*. London, Oxford University Press, 1962.
19. Gurney, R.: The hereditary factor in obesity. *Arch Intern Med*, 57: 557, 1936.
20. Withers, R. F. J.: Problems in the genetics of human obesity. *Eugenics Review*, 56: 81, 1964.
21. Brobeck, J. R.: Mechanism of the development of obesity in animals with hypothalamic lesions. *Physiol Rev*, 26: 541, 1946.
22. Balagura, S.: Neurophysiologic aspects. *Adv Psychosom Med*, Vol. 7, Basel, Karger, 1972.
23. Brecher, G., and Waxler, S. H.: Obesity in albino mice due to single injections of gold thioglucose. *Proc Soc Exp Biol and Med*, 70: 498, 1949.
24. Waxler, S. H., and Brecher, G.: Obesity and food requirement in albino mice following administration of gold thioglucose. *Am J Physiol*, 162: 428, 1950.
25. Mayer, J.: Genetic, traumatic and environmental factors in the etiology of obesity. *Phsiol Rev*, 33: 472, 1953.
26. Hirsch, J., Knittle, J. L., and Salans, L. B.: Cell lipid content and cell number in obese and non obese adipose tissue. *J Clin Invest*, 45: 1023, 1966.
27. Goldblatt, P. B., Moore, M. E., and Stunkard, A. J.: Social factors in obesity. *J A M A*, 192: 1039, 1965.
28. Silverstone, J. T.: Psychosocial aspects of obesity. *Proc R Soc Med*, 61: 371, 1968.
29. Kahn, E. J.: Obesity in children. *J Pediatr*, 77: 771, 1970.
30. *Webster's New International Dictionary*, 2nd ed. Springfield, G. & C. Merriam, 1955.
31. Hinsie, L. E., and Campbell, R. S.: *Psychiatric Dictionary*, 4th ed. London, Oxford University Press, 1970.
32. Sullivan, H. S.: *The Interpersonal Theory of Psychiatry*. New York, W. W. Norton, 1953.
33. Mead, G. H.: *Mind, Self and Society*. Chicago, U of Chicago Press, 1934.
34. Schilder, P.: *The Image and Appearance of the Human Body*. New York, International Universities Press, 1951.
35. Federn, P.: *Ego Psychology and the Psychoses*. New York, Basic Books, 1952.
36. Hartman, H.: *Ego Psychology and the Problem of Adaptation*. New York, International Universities Press, 1958.
37. Freud, Sigmund: *Complete Psychological Works*, Vol XIX. London, Hogarth Press.
38. Fromm, E.: *Escape from Freedom*. New York, Holt, Rinehart & Winston, 1960.

39. Erikson, E. H.: *Childhood and Society*, 2nd ed. New York, W. W. Norton, 1963.
40. Erikson, E. H.: *Identity, Youth and Crisis*. New York, W. W. Norton, 1968.
41. Jung, C.: Reference No. 31.
42. Horney, K.: Reference No. 31.
43. Menninger, K.: *The Vital Balance*. New York, Viking Press, 1963.
44. Becker, E.: *Birth and Death of Meaning*. New York, Free Press of Glencoe, 1962.
45. Becker, E.: *Structure of Evil*. New York, George Brazilier, 1968.
46. Coopersmith, S.: *The Antecedents of Self Esteem*. San Francisco, W. H. Freeman, 1967.
47. Arieti, S.: *The Intrapsychic Self*. Basic Books, 1967.
48. Eisenberg, L. Science, 176: 1972.
49. Waxler, S. H.: *Current Therapy*, Edit by H. F. Conn, Philadelphia, W. B. Saunders, 1971.

INDEX

A

Abelson, P. B., xii
Adam, K., 102, 116
Addiction, *see* Alcoholism, and Drug-related deaths
Age differentials and suicide, 99-100
  see also Statistics on suicide
Aged and suicide, 8, 9-10, 13, 18, 24, 35-36, 85-88
Alcoholics Anonymous, 183
Alcoholism, xi, 83, 112, 113, 123, 125, 129-131, 136, 147-148, 150-151, 165-187, 188
American Indian and suicide, 33
Anderson, William F., 95
Antabuse, 183-184
Arieti, S., 205, 210
Automobile fatalities, xi, 7, 123-137, 179

B

Ball, John C., 161
Barlow, D. H., 175, 187
Bateman, Karen, 158, 160, 163
Becker, E., 200-201, 206, 210
Bejerot, Nils, 144
Belagura, S., 193, 209
Bell, W., 88, 95
Bender, L., 73
Bendit, Emile A., ix, 164-187
Berman, Alan L., ix, xiii, 5-20
Bertalanffy, Ludwig, 84, 95
Bibring, E., 175, 187
Blanchly, P. H., 149, 162
Blood-alcohol levels (BAL), 5, 166-167
Borges, Phillip, 146, 152, 161, 162
Boswell, John W., 35, 74, 94
Brecher, Edward M., 139, 159, 160, 161, 162, 163, 194
Brobeck, J. R., 193, 209
Bruhn, J. G., 102, 105, 116
Buglass, D., 116
Butler, R. N., 19

C

Cahalan, D., 116, 186
Cain, Albert C., 47-48, 76
Cameron, P., 19
Cannon, W. B., 18
Caplan, G., 116
Carney, Jane R., 154, 163
Carney, Richard E., 154, 163
Casey, John J., Jr., 153, 154, 159, 160, 163
Castanos, J. N., 45, 76, 118
Cavan, Ruth S., 19, 75
Center for Studies of Suicide Prevention, 67-68, 70, 77
Certification of death, 5-6, 10-11
Chambers, Carl D., 161
Chatham, L. R., xiii
Chein, Isidor, 155, 159, 160, 161, 163
Child rearing practices and personality development, 201-207
Childhood deprivation, 202
Children and suicide, 46-49, 86
Cisin, I. H., 116, 186
Citizens for Mental Health, Buffalo, 60, 66
Cloward, R. A., 170, 186
College students as suicide victims, 12
Community Mental Health Center, Washington, D.C., 66, 69
Compulsive eating, *see* Obesity
Contra Costa County Suicide Prevention Center, 60, 66, 69
Cooley, Charles H., 37
Coopersmith, S., 202-203, 206, 210
Cooperstock, R., 107, 117
Corpulence, *see* Obesity
Cost of suicide, 10-11, 24
Cousineau, D. F., 117
Crisis Clinic, Seattle, 66, 68
Crisis intervention services, 50-72, 155-156
Cuskey, Walter R., ix, xiii, 138-163
Cutter, Fred, 72

D

Danto, Bruce, 45, 76
Davidson, K., 119
DeLint, J. E., 117
Demographic trends, 16-17, 22-23, 31-37, 101-104, 144-145
Diagnostic tools, 37-40, 48, 155-156
Dohrenwend, B. S., 117
Dorpat, Theodore L., ix, 35, 74, 78-96
Douglas, Jack D., 21, 28, 73, 171, 186
Drug addiction, xi-xii, 8, 15, 109-110, 113-114, 138-163
Drug-related deaths, xi-xiii, 8, 15, 109-110
Dublin, Louis I., 22, 28, 38, 75, 186
Durkheim, Emile, 21, 26-28, 72, 73, 77, 117, 147, 160, 162, 166, 170

E

Eau Claire Suicide Prevention Service, 60, 69
Edington, Bonnie M., ix, xiii, 138-163
Edland, John F., 125-126, 136
Edwards, J. E., 35, 74, 117
Eisenberg, L., 207, 210
Ellis, G. G., 117
Emergency Mental Health Service of Phoenix, 60, 68-69
Erikson, E. H., 199, 210
Esterson, A., 95
Evans, J. G., 117

F

Farber, Maurice L., 24, 72, 95
Farberow, Norman L., 13, 19, 22, 35, 38-39, 40, 41, 42, 43, 74, 75, 117, 187
Farrar, C., 72
Fast, Irene, 47-48, 76
Federn, P., 199, 209
Felix, Robert H., 25, 72
Fenichel, O., 174, 187
Ferrence, Roberta G., ix, 19, 97-119
Finch, John R., 137
Fisher, Sheila, 70, 77
Flinn, D. E., 19
Flint, Jerry M., 72
Frederick, C. J., xii
Freeman, J. W., 117

Frenay, Adolph, 74
French, Thomas M., 88, 95
Freud, Sigmund, 21, 30, 73, 94, 174, 187, 199, 200
Friends Organization, Miami, 60, 62
Fromm, Erick, 199, 200, 209
Fuller, David H., 157, 160, 163
Fulton-DeKalb Suicide Prevention Center, 60, 69

G

Gardner, R., 161
Gate keeper, 50
Gibbs, Jack P., 21, 27-28, 73, 74, 170, 186
Glatt, Max M., 144, 161
Gold, N., 117
Goodell, Helen, 155, 163
Grau, Joseph J., vii, 77
Greene, C., 118
Greene, W. A., 7, 18
Greenwald, Harold, 150, 162
Grinker, Roy R., 78, 94

H

Hamburger, Ernest, 126, 136
Harvey, C., 119
Haughton, Anson, 77
Hendin, Herbert, 21, 31, 73, 74, 82, 91, 94, 95
Henry, Andrew F., 21, 29, 73, 170, 186
Hertzman, Marc, ix, 164-187
Hill, Oscar W., 48, 76
Hirsch, J., 194, 209
Hoffman, Arthur M., 157, 158, 160
Hoffmann-LaRoche Inc., 67
Homicide, xi, 5, 8, 124, 129-131, 165, 172, 179,
    Attempted homicide, 124
Horney, Karen, 200, 210
Hospital suicides, 42-44, 115, 135, 182
Howard, Jan, 146, 152, 161, 162
Huffine, Carol L., 127-128, 136

I

Ipsen, Johannes, 160
Ireland, Ralph, vii

J

Jackson, Don D., 31, 73
Jackson, Joan K., 95
Jacobson, Edith, 82, 94
Jacobson, S., 117
Jaffee, W. G., 95
Jarvis, George K., ix, 97-119
Johnson, F. Gordon, ix, 19, 97-119
Jones, Kingsley, 43, 75
Jung, C., 200, 210

K

Kahne, Merton J., 75
Kastenbaum, R., 13, 18
Kessel, Neil, 117, 118, 162
Klein, Arnold W., 159, 160
Kochansky, Gerald E., 160, 163
Koller, K. M., 45, 76, 118
Krasner, William, 159, 160, 161
Krieger, George, 93, 96
Krupinski, J., 118
Kubie, Lawrence, 149, 162

L

LaForest, L., 119
Laing, Ronald D., 91, 95
Larson, William R., 95
Lawson, A. A. H., 118
Lee, E., 118
Leef, M., 208
Leonard, C. V., 19, 42
Lester, D., 19, 178, 187
Lester, G., 19
Levine, J., 158, 163
Lidz, Theodore, 91, 95
Linehan, M. M., 118
Lisansky, E. S., 176, 187
Liska, Edward S., ix, 188-210
Litman, Robert E., 19, 22, 40, 49, 72, 75, 84, 93, 94, 128, 136, 187
Los Angeles Suicide Prevention Center, 60, 62, 64, 67, 68, 128
Ludwig, A. M., 158, 163

M

MacDonald, John M., 124, 135, 136
McClelland, D. C., 153, 163
McConaghy, N., 118
McCord, J., 187
McCord, W., 187
McCulloch, N., 118
McHugh, Paul R., 155, 163
Maris, Ronald W., 15, 20, 90, 95, 154, 160, 162, 163
Marital status and suicide rates, *see* Statistics on suicide
Martin, W. T., 170, 186
Martindale, Don, 75
Mason, Percy, 152, 161, 162, 163
Maxmen, J. S., 20
Mayfield, D. G., 160, 161, 177, 185
Mead, George H., 199, 201, 209
Meerlo, Joast A. M., 7, 18, 31, 73, 78, 94
Meier, D. L., 88, 95
Melman, Seymour, 160
Meltzer, Newton E., 67
Mendelson, J. H., 93, 96
Menninger, Karl A., 8, 18, 21, 30-31, 73, 143, 150, 152, 157, 160, 161, 162, 163, 174-175, 176, 179, 187, 200, 210
Merton, Robert K., 169
Metropolitan Life Insurance Company, xii, 189, 197
Middleton, G. D., 118
Mikawa, James K., 161, 162
Miller, P. M., 175, 187
Mintz, Ronald S., 14, 15, 19, 41-42, 75
Mishara, B. L., 13, 18, 118
Mitchell, I., 118
Modan, B., 118
Mode of suicide, 17-18, 32-33
Modell, Arnold H., 81, 82, 94
Montgomery, Dan, 160, 161, 177, 185
Moore, M., 93, 95
Mortality, 5-6, 7-9, 82-83, 140-142, 145-146, 179-180
Moseley, Alfred L., 123, 136
Motto, J. A., 118
Murder, *see* Homicide
Murphy, George E., 148, 162, 168, 186

N

Nahum, Louis H., 161
National Center for Health Statistics, 15-16, 19, 20
National Save-a-Life League, 52, 53, 63

O

Obesity, 188-210
O'Donnell, John A., 161
Ogden, M., 74
Ohlin, L. E., 170, 186
Oliven, J. F., 19
Oliver, R. G., 118
Ovenstone, I. M. K., 118

P

Palmer, D. M., 73
Palola, Ernest G., 88, 93, 95
Parkin, D., 118
Payne, C. E., 96
Pearl, A., 169, 186
Petrovsky, C. C., 43, 76
Philip, A. E., 118
Pokorny, Alex D., ix, 72, 123-137, 168
Powell, Elwin H., 74
Preble, Edward A., 153, 154, 159, 160, 163
Premkumar, T., 160
Prevention, 50-72, 112-116, 135-136, 155-156, 180-183, 207-208
Price, M. P., 118
Prison suicides, 44-46, 107, 113, 157-158

R

Race and suicide rates, 91, see also Statistics on suicide
Rescue, Inc., Boston, 58, 64-65
Resnick, H. L. P., xii, 9, 19
Retka, R., xiii
Rieger, W., 45, 76
Ringle, E., 162, 177, 187
Ripley, Herbert S., 86, 94, 95
Ritson, E. B., 182, 185
Roberts, Albert R., ix, 21-77, 148, 162, 202
Robins, Ely, 83, 94, 148, 168, 186

Ropschitz, D. H., 118
Rosen, David H., 157, 158, 160
Rosenbaum, Milton, 49
Ross, Mathew, 39-40
Rotter, H., 147, 162, 177, 187
Rubenfine, David L., 89, 95
Rushing, William A., 95, 172-173, 176-177, 179, 185

S

Sainsbury, Peter, 28, 73
Samaritans, 50
Sandler, Joseph, 95
San Francisco Suicide Prevention Center, 60, 69
Santa Clara County Suicide Prevention Center, 60
Schapira, K., 119
Schilder, P., 73, 199, 209
Schmale, Arnold H., 89, 95
Schmid, C. F., 118
Schmidt, Chester W., 126-127, 136
Schmidt, W., 117
Schur, Edwin M., 159, 161
Schwarz, Conrad J., 158, 163
Segal, Lois, 160
Self-injurious behavior, 13-14, 25-26, 81-83, 97-119, 205, 207-208
Sells, S. B., xiii
Selzer, Melvin L., 96, 124-125, 136
Sex and suicide rates, 99-100, see also Statistics on suicide
Shaffer, Stephanie, 159
Shapiro, David, 83, 94
Shein, Harvey M., 44, 76
Shneidman, Edwin S., 7, 13, 14, 18, 19, 22, 31, 35, 38-39, 40, 41, 42, 72, 74, 75, 117
Short, James F., Jr., 21, 29, 73, 170, 186
Siegel, Peter V., 136
Sims, M., 119
Smith, A. J., 119
Smith, J. S., 119
Smith, James P., 137
Smith, W. G., 168, 186
Smart, Reginald G., 119, 158, 160, 163

Social integration, 26-29, 90-91, 100-101, 177-178
Statistics on suicide, 6, 13, 14-18, 22-24, 31-37, 98-100, 167-168, 179-180, 197
Stengel, Erwin, 28, 40, 75, 118, 152, 162, 163, 187
Stone, Alan A., 44, 76
Sub-intentioned death, 7-10, 25-26
Suicide, xi, 5-96, 139-152, 166, 170-173, 176-179, 204-207
Suicide attempts, 40-42, 124, 125, 151-152
Suicide prevention, 50-72, 112-116, 135-136, 155-156
Suicide Prevention Center, Dade County, 68
Suicide Prevention Center, Denver, 60, 65-66
Suicide Prevention Center, Kansas City, 66
Suicide Prevention Council at Ancora State Hospital, 63
Suicide Prevention Inc. of St. Louis, 60, 63, 68
Suicide Prevention of Tarrant County, 60, 63, 66
Suicide Prevention Service of Dayton, 63
Suicide Prevention Service of Pasadena, 60
Suicidology, 6-10, 50-72, 156, *see also* Suicide
Sullivan, H. S., 199-200, 209
Sundby, P., 146, 147, 148, 151-152, 160, 161, 162, 163
Suttee, 27

T

Tabachnick, Norman, 7, 18, 72, 84, 93, 94, 128, 136, 137
Tamerin, J. S., 93, 96
Termansen, P. E., 119
Thomas, R. Buckland, 157, 160, 163
Tribe, P., 117
Tucker, G. J., 20
Tuckman, J., 119

V

Vaillant, George E., 161
Van Arsdol, Maurice D., Jr., 118
Veevers, I. E., 117
Vetter, Joseph A., 66
Victim-precipitated homicide, *see* Homicide
Vobecky, J., 119

W

Warren, Harry M., Jr., 52
Waxler, Samuel H., ix, 188-210
We Care, Inc., Orlando, 56, 60, 64
Weisman, Avery, 161
Weissman, M. M., 119
Welu, T. C., 119
Westin, Av, 159
Whitehead, Paul C., ix, 13, 18, 19, 97-119, 160, 161, 162, 185
Whitlock, F. A., 35, 74
Wilkens, James, 69, 77
Wittlin, B., xii
Wold, Carl I., 136, 137
Wolfgang, Marvin E., 18, 185, 186
Wyandotte County Guidance Center, 60

Y

Yolles, Stanley F., 49

Z

Zilboorg, Gregory, 21, 30, 31, 73

616.85 R54   101040

ROBERTS

SELF-DESTRUCTIVE BEHAVIOR

College Misericordia Library
Dallas, Pennsylvania 18612